101+ Careers in Gerontology

Second Edition

C. JOANNE GRABINSKI, MA, MA, ABD, FAGHE

WITH CONTRIBUTIONS FROM

KELLY NILES-YOKUM, MPA, PhD

SPRINGER PUBLISHING COMPANY

NEW YORK

Springer Publishing Company, LLC
11 West 42nd Street
New York, NY 10036
www.springerpub.com

Acquisitions Editor: Sheri W. Sussman
Composition: Amnet Systems

ISBN: 978-0-8261-2008-3
e-book ISBN: 978-0-8261-2009-0

14 15 16 17 / 5 4 3 2 1

Library of Congress Cataloging-in-Publication Data

Grabinski, C. Joanne, 1941–
[101 careers in gerontology]
101+ careers in gerontology / C. Joanne Grabinski, MA, MA, ABD, FACHE, with contributions of Kelly Niles-Yokum, MPA, PhD. — Second edition.
pages cm
Revised edition of the author's 101 Careers in Gerontology published in 2007.
ISBN 978-0-8261-2008-3 (print : alk. paper) — ISBN 978-0-8261-2009-0 (e-book) 1. Gerontology—Vocational guidance—United States. 2. Older people—Services for—United States. I. Title. II. Title: One hundred one plus careers in gerontology.
HQ1064.U5G66 2015
305.2602373—dc23

2014017700

Printed in the United States of America by Gasch Printing.

Find Your Career
With
Springer Publishing Company

101+ Careers in Gerontology

C. Joanne Grabinski, MA, MA, ABD, FAGHE, was president/educator and consultant for AgeEd (1991–2010) and lecturer, Gerontology Program at Eastern Michigan University (1992–2010). While at Eastern Michigan University, she designed and taught the first Introduction to Careers in Gerontology course in the United States. She also served as the continuing education representative for the Gerontology Program and for the Graduate Certificate Program for two cohorts of students at the Northwestern Michigan College University Center (1993–1997), and served as university liaison for ELDERWISE (Institute for Learning in Retirement) for 18 months. Previously, she was assistant professor and the first director of the Interdisciplinary Gerontology Program (1984–1991) at Central Michigan University, where she also served as director, Alzheimer's Disease and Related Conditions Caregiver Training Grant Project (1985–1991, 12-county region). Other academic appointments included visiting summer scholar (1998) and visiting adjunct professor, human development: gerontology, at Saint Joseph College in West Hartford, Connecticut (1998–2009) and two 3-year board-approved appointments as adjunct professor, gerontology, at Western Michigan University.

Grabinski earned a BS and did graduate-level coursework in home economics education at Oregon State University, earned MA degrees in educational administration: community leadership and in family relations from Central Michigan University, and completed doctoral work (ABD) in family ecology: adult development and aging, with cognates in gerontology and sociology, at Michigan State University. She has been actively involved in the Gerontological Society of America (GSA) and the Association for Gerontology in Higher Education (AGHE), serving on committees for both and as an elected member of the AGHE Executive Committee, and she was a long-standing member of the American Society on Aging (ASA). Grabinski is the recipient of four AGHE honors: Distinguished Teacher (1997), AGHE Fellow in Gerontology and Geriatrics Education (FAGHE, 1999), Part-Time Faculty Certificate of Recognition (2004), and Mildred M. Seltzer Distinguished Service Recognition (2010). She is the author of several book chapters and articles (including book and audiovisual reviews) for professional journals and newsletters. She also coauthored the latest version of AGHE's *Brief Bibliography on Audiovisuals on Aging.*

To my husband, Roger, and my son, Larry,
with love through the bumps and
the joys of our journey together.

CONTENTS

PREFACE

In 2007, I was honored with the launch of the first edition of this book at the annual meeting of the Gerontological Society of America (GSA) in San Francisco. Now, 7 years later and approximately 2,812 miles away, I will experience the launch of this new second edition at the GSA annual meeting in Washington, DC. While you will find some aspects of the two editions to be similar, this new edition is different in several ways because of the input across those 7 years from gerontology education colleagues, students, and other readers/users of the first edition. Special appreciation goes to Kelly Niles-Yokum and some of her students at York University, who offered very helpful revision ideas, especially about revision and expansion of the interview questionnaire.

So, what is new or different about this second edition of *101+ Careers in Gerontology*? Having spent a good portion of the last 7 months sitting in front of computers on behalf of this book, I'm ready to get up and get moving, so let's take a quick stroll together to find the answers to that question.

In refreshing the Introduction, two new segments were added. The first of these is a brief listing and discussion of some factors that influence the availability of career positions in the field of aging. The second is a brief description of three types of credentials—licensure, certification, and accreditation—commonly found among the career paths that are part of the field of aging, and I am able to share with you some news about the preparation for accreditation currently being undertaken by the Association for Gerontology in Higher Education (AGHE), the educational unit of the GSA.

As with the first edition, most of the pages of this edition explore an array of possible career positions and interviews with professionals in some of those positions. I've chosen to designate five gerontology-related fields—entrepreneurial gerontology, gerontechnology, global aging, journalism and aging, and urban gerontology—as "emerging fields" with increasing professional visibility, although they are still being defined. Insights into these emerging fields are offered through interviews with one of the first MetLife Foundation Journalists in Aging Fellows, a doctoral candidate in human computer interactions (a gerontechnology-related degree program), two entrepreneurial gerontologists, and the director of operations for a foundation, a person whose career allows him to practice concurrently in two of these fields—global aging and urban gerontology.

Of the 25 interviews in this edition, 12 offer updates on interviewees from the earlier edition, and 13 are with individuals in career positions that were not represented among the first-edition interviews. These new interviewees include a certified geriatric and consulting pharmacist, a geriatrician, a horticultural therapist, a health system specialist, both a gerontology educator and an educational gerontologist, a traveling occupational therapist, and a music therapist who is the new president-elect of the American Music Therapy Association. All interviews are completely new for this edition, so you will have an opportunity to learn about the career trajectories of those who were interviewed in the first edition and some interesting changes that have occurred.

In the ". . . and More" section, potential positions in 22 different fields add 128 possible career positions for persons with gerontology backgrounds or career interests. All field entries have been updated, and the newest field added is emergency medical services.

"Gerontology and Geriatrics Professional Organizations" is a brand-new section in this edition that includes information about two international organizations, the four key national-level societies/associations (including information about student and new professional member sections), Sigma Phi Omega (national honor society), two regional (multistate) organizations, and state-level associations, societies, and councils that are currently active in 20 states.

The Glossary of Acronyms, both the gerontology-specific and gerontology-related sections, has been updated for accuracy and expanded by many new entries.

Thanks for joining me on the stroll through this new edition, and enjoy using it to explore possibilities and, I hope, to find just the right niche for yourself in this constantly growing and changing professional world in the field of aging.

ACKNOWLEDGMENTS

With thanks, appreciation, and gratitude to:

- Sheri W. Sussman, my editor at Springer Publishing Company, who again wisely guided me through the publication process for this book with your characteristic direct approach, patience, understanding, care, and concern through the bumps along the way. It has been such an unexpected gift to have this second time to work with you.
- Kelly Niles-Yokum for joining me through part of this journey and for helping, directly and indirectly, to make this edition even better for those who will use it, and to your students who offered valuable feedback on the Interview Questionnaire.
- Interviewees, I am honored that you so willingly agreed to share your stories and advice, and I am grateful for your patience as we honed your interviews to allow our readers important glimpses into your various professional worlds.
- Margaret Neal, Tracey Gendron, Ayn Welleford, Julie Brown, Alan De La Torre, and Janet Frank for your assistance in finding excellent interviewees, help in developing some career position profiles, and updating me on the status of AGHE accreditation.
- Colleagues and "bosses" who opened doors for my career as a gerontology educator and program administrator for your confidence in and support of me. Special thanks to Loren Bensley and Bill Theunissen (Central Michigan University), Elizabeth Schuster (Eastern Michigan University), Ellen Page-Robin (Western Michigan University), and Mary Alice Wolf (Saint Joseph College in West Hartford, CT).
- My "three musketeers"—Laurie, Grete, and Dawn—who have been there for me through the challenges that threatened to derail this project and reminded me to keep my "nose to the grindstone" so that I could hurry up and get back to our shared passion for needlepoint. Thank you for the blessing of your friendship.

1 ■ INTRODUCTION

> *Wanted:* gerontology workers, gerontological specialists, and gerontologists for careers now and into the future. Work with, for, and on behalf of the growing population of elders, including centenarians and baby boomers, in a wide variety of settings. *Required:* training/education in appropriate field and at appropriate level for specific position; specialization in aging studies/gerontology is highly desirable. Ability to rethink one's concept of old and deconstruct myths about old people and the processes of aging is mandatory. *Compensation:* income varies by specific type of position held; geographic location of employing agency, facility, or organization; education and experience background of applicant; and willingness to get involved with old people [try it—you might like it!]. *Benefits:* learn to grow old well yourself as you help to improve the quality of life for others who are aging.

Although this want ad will rarely appear among newspaper classified ads for employment or online career centers/job postings, it does speak to the growing number of career paths available now and in the future for persons interested in working with, for, and on behalf of the fastest growing age segment of the U.S. population. Through the profiles of possible career positions, interviews with professionals in some of these career positions and the ". . . and More" section, this book offers you a taste of the wide variety of career paths in the field of aging and identifies relevant sources to help you explore further those you find intriguing.

WHAT IS GERONTOLOGY?

From an academic perspective, *gerontology* is the study of the biological, psychological, and sociological aspects of aging. Some recognize gerontology as a discipline or multidisciplinary field of study that draws upon expertise from many disciplines. Others view gerontology as an interdisciplinary field in which two or more disciplines are intertwined to offer more complex insights and understandings about the processes of aging and the elderly population than can be gained through work in just one discipline. Regardless of one's perspective, the three base disciplines for the field are biology, psychology, and sociology, as is reflected in the design of gerontology education programs in higher education. Also, the first gerontological researchers emerged out of these disciplines. Over time, more disciplines (e.g., history, anthropology, religion, political science, philosophy) have become involved in gerontology education and research. More recent disciplines to step into the gerontology arena are from the humanities and arts (e.g., literature, language arts, communication, visual arts), as represented by activities of the Gerontological Society of America (GSA) Humanities and the Arts Committee, including documentary films on aging and discussion with the filmmaker at each annual meeting; the Bo Diddley program track—presentation by and conversation with an elderly blues musician and an evening at a local blues club—at both GSA and American Society on Aging (ASA) annual meetings; and for four volumes (2007 to 2010), publication of the *Journal of Aging, Humanities & the Arts*.

From a professional perspective, medicine, nursing, clinical psychology, and social work were among the first professions to develop aging-specific education and practice orientations to meet the needs of their growing numbers of older adult clients. Today, many other professions—law; occupational, physical, art, and music therapy; home economics/human ecology; nutrition and dietetics; interior design and architecture; business; education; technology and engineering; health administration; and public administration—are entering this realm of research, education, and practice. With this growing interest in aging and the aging/elderly population, gerontology has become the overarching "umbrella" for an ever-expanding number of subfields, including geriatric medicine and dentistry, gerontological social work, gerontological nursing, and professional geropsychology/geriatric psychiatry. Among the newer specializations are educational gerontology, policy and aging, elder law, financial gerontology, geriatric pharmacy, family gerontology, intergenerational studies, and spiritual gerontology. Recently, engineering, technology, and gerontology have merged to create the new field of gerontechnology.

WHAT CREATED THE INTEREST IN GERONTOLOGY AS A FIELD OF STUDY AND AS A PROFESSION?

Why this increasing interest in aging research? What has influenced so many disciplinary and professional fields of study to incorporate gerontology as part of their education/training programs? What is behind the growth and diversity of career paths related to aging? It appears that four factors have been of prime importance:

- Enactment of aging-specific federal legislation, beginning with the Social Security Act in 1935 and, more significantly, the Older Americans Act (OAA) in 1965 that established what is known as the "formal aging network"—a hierarchical system that includes the Administration on Aging (AoA) at the federal level, state units on aging (such as an Office of Services to the Aging or a Department of Aging), Area Agencies on Aging (AAAs) at the regional level within states, and direct service agencies (such as county commissions, departments and bureaus on aging) at the county level. With each OAA reauthorization, new types of programs and services are added to meet newly assessed needs of older adults.
- Growth in the actual numbers of persons who are 65 years of age and older and in the proportion of the total U.S. population that consists of older adults.
- Development of gerontology and geriatrics education programs at institutions of higher education. In 2007, more than 500 institutions of higher education (community colleges, colleges, universities, professional schools) offered degree components (concentrations, specializations, minors, cognates, certificates) or majors and degrees in gerontology (Stepp, 2007).[1] Gerontology educators developed the Association for Gerontology in Higher Education (AGHE) curriculum standards and guidelines for gerontology programs at each academic level and for each type of credential. These standards and guidelines are voluntary and intentionally flexible to allow administrators and faculty on each campus to tailor their programs to fit the uniqueness of their institution's academic programs, students, culture, and environment. Programs that fulfill the standards (14 so far) are eligible to apply for "Program of Merit" status (AGHE's stamp of approval). Core courses in the biology, psychology, and sociology of aging and a practicum or field experience are commonly required in formal gerontology education programs. Students also may select gerontology elective courses (e.g., on policy, family relationships, nutrition, religion/spirituality, gender, economics, sexuality, recreation, interior design, humanities and the arts, death and dying) that fit their professional and personal interests.

---

[1]This information was based on programs listed in the 8th edition of the AGHE *Directory of Educational Programs in Gerontology and Geriatrics*, but because the update and conversion to interactive online access are still underway for the 9th edition, current comparable information is not yet available.

- Creation of national-level gerontology professional organizations, including the GSA, American Geriatrics Society (AGS), AGHE, ASA, and National Council on Aging (NCOA). Additionally, several other professional organizations have member sections specific to aging (e.g., the American Psychological Association's Division 20 on Adult Development and Aging or the American Sociological Association's Aging and the Life Course section). Two regional and 19 state gerontology organizations are currently active; Texas has three regional-in-state organizations (see later section, "Gerontology and Geriatrics Professional Organizations").

FACTORS THAT INFLUENCE AVAILABILITY OF CAREER POSITIONS IN THE FIELD OF AGING

As with any field, careers in aging experience fluctuation in the types of career positions that are available at any given time. Factors that influence position availability include:

- Location: Although research findings indicate a greater density of older adults in rural and inner-city neighborhoods, for example, there are fewer programs and services for older adults in those locations and fewer professional staff members available. In this situation, professional staff members may need to wear multiple professional hats, have a heavier client load, and receive lesser pay and fewer benefits, although some report a higher job satisfaction because they feel they are making a real difference in the lives of their clients.
- Shifting priorities in legislation: This is most obvious in each reauthorization of the OAA. The current reauthorization, which expired in September 2011, is still an open process, partially due to the shifting politics of getting it done. As new initiatives emerge and are prioritized, some existing programs and services are restructured, downsized, or disappear. Some survive, however, by being moved to other governmental departments or integrated into "umbrella" programs that are not aging specific. Although it is not yet clear what the priorities will be when the OAA finally gets reauthorized, some programs and services seem to be emerging as priorities: adult protective services, including elder abuse prevention and consumer protection; mental health care; improving the long-term care ombudsman program; women and retirement; lesbian, gay, bisexual, and transgender (LGBT) aging; and new

demonstration projects related to modernizing senior centers, developing new models of care coordination, and creating a national resource center on family caregiving. While some of these initiatives may not end up in the reauthorized Act, they offer clues as to where there might be new or expanded career opportunities, including entrepreneurial niches, for professionals with aging expertise and experience.

- Greater demand in particular sectors: Health care is definitely a hot career field at this time. There is an increased demand for health care professionals (e.g., geriatricians, gerontological nurses, social workers, physical and occupational therapists, audiologists, ophthalmologists, consulting and geriatric pharmacists, geropsychologists, and geriatric psychiatrists) to respond to the health care needs of older adults, and experts agree that this demand will continue for some time into the future. This increased focus also should expand to other health care career paths and allied health professions that respond to physical and mental health concerns for older adults (e.g., emergency medical services, including paramedics and emergency medical technicians; certified nursing assistants; wellness and fitness educators and trainers; community public and mental health service providers; and occupational, physical, and other types of therapies, such as art, music, and dance).
- The economy: The economy affects both the availability of programs and services for older adults and their ability to utilize the programs and services that are offered. Older adults are more likely to be living on fixed incomes. In a good economy, they are more likely to avail themselves of not only basic needs services but also other programs that support a higher quality of life (e.g., travel, hospitality, entertainment, educational opportunities), and this concurrently creates more opportunities for gerontology specialists and gerontology workers.
- Funding: Certainly, for those who work in government-based organizations, funding of legislated programs and services is critical in relation to job availability and stability at all levels of government, although the impact may be more obvious and more challenging at the local (city or county) level. Full funding of a mandated service can lead, for example, to the hiring of more staff members, lower client loads, and a more positive work environment. Limited funding may mean layoffs, each staff member taking on more job roles/ tasks, longer work hours, and increased stress levels. Another way that funding affects career path visibility and support relates to

funding that comes from foundations and other nongovernmental sources. Several foundations, sometimes in collaboration with higher education institutions or professional organizations, support fellowship and other programs that increase the level of accurate aging knowledge for professionals in fields where gerontology most likely was not included in degree programs (e.g., MetLife Foundation's collaboration with GSA to create the Journalists in Aging Fellows program is increasing the number of journalists/ multimedia journalists and documentary filmmakers who focus on aging and GSA's joint sponsorship with the John A. Hartford Foundation to support the Journalism in Aging & Health Fellows program). This Hartford Foundation also funds several initiatives to increase the size of gerontology- and geriatric-specific workforces in nursing and social work. The Atlantic Philanthropies support a broad and quite diverse array of initiatives specific to aging, including the Lifelong Access Libraries Summer Institute Fellows program and the recently announced Health and Aging Policy Fellows Program. With the increased visibility of aging at the center of grant and fellowship programs funded by foundations, it is likely that there will be some positive spillover to enhance career path opportunities for individuals interested in working with, for, and on behalf of older adults.

- Size of the elderly population: Both the real and the projected growth in the size of the elderly population here and around the world imply a comparable growth in the number and type of aging-related career positions and paths. This newly enlarged population, however, is also a very diverse population and "one size fits all" will no longer suffice, which means there may be a need for creation or replication of programs for specific subgroups (e.g., centenarians, boomers, active agers, frail elders), with one end result being more aging-related jobs.
- Globalization of aging: Working with international organizations and corporations to address the needs and interests of older adults worldwide is among the newest career paths in the field of aging. AGHE's Global Aging Committee (GAC) is intent on shaping new opportunities for faculty members and students to expand their cross-cultural knowledge base and to be involved in gerontology/geriatrics education and research projects in many other countries. More colleges and universities now offer international courses and service-learning opportunities specific to aging. These efforts potentially will help to create some new global aging career path options.
- Entrepreneurship: With downsizing and funding cuts in many traditional career fields, it appears that the field of aging is especially

intriguing to individuals seeking mid-career changes that will allow them more control over the work they do and a better balance between work and other aspects of their lives. Younger and newer students are being exposed earlier in their degree programs to gerontology as a field of study, especially through volunteer, service-learning, and internship or practicum experiences that allow them to try out one or more possible professional path(s). Don't forget the many retirees, regardless of age, who are not ready to disengage and settle into a more sedate retirement; they are seeking out what is often labeled "encore careers" that allow them to continue working in their lifelong fields but in a different way, or they are doing something entirely different. Mix in expanding attention to "the entrepreneurial spirit" and encouragement to find or create a unique niche. The field of aging is ripe with potential for those who find this an appealing idea.

WHAT IS A GERONTOLOGIST?

Until recently that has been a difficult question to answer. Now, a proposed schema makes it possible to organize those who work with or on behalf of elders into three categories:

- ***Gerontology workers*** have no formal gerontology education or training even though they work directly with or on behalf of elderly clients or in an aging-specific organization or facility. They may work in paraprofessional roles (such as certified nurse assistants in a nursing home or a receptionist for a county commission on aging) or as professionals who are fully credentialed in fields other than gerontology (such as social workers who are discharge planners in a hospital or a family practice physician whose practice in a rural medical clinic includes many elderly patients).
- ***Gerontological specialists*** have completed at least one degree in a discipline or professional field that is not gerontology-specific but includes a formal gerontology degree component (e.g., minor, certificate, cognate, or specialization in gerontology), or they obtained specialized postgraduate gerontology training (perhaps through a freestanding credit or noncredit certificate program in gerontology; a profession-specific certification or registration process; continuing education coursework, workshops, or other training programs; or a postdoctoral fellowship) that complements or enhances the field of study in which they received their degree(s). For example, an interior designer–gerontological specialist holds

a degree with a major in interior design and a minor or cognate in gerontology; a director of an older adult library program has a degree in library science to which gerontology expertise has been added through participation in a summer institute on lifelong libraries or completion of an online certificate in gerontology; and a recreational, occupational, or physical therapist obtains gerontology/geriatric certification according to standards set by relevant professional organizations or their accrediting bodies.

- ***Gerontologists*** have earned degrees for which gerontology, aging studies, or geriatrics was the primary, not secondary, field of study. This relatively new category of gerontology professionals is the result of an increasing number of degree programs in gerontology, aging studies, or a similarly titled degree label. By 2005, approximately 126 gerontology-specific degree programs were in existence (18 associate, 41 bachelor's, 58 master's, and 9 doctoral).[2]

Currently, it appears that the majority of gerontology-specific and -related paraprofessional and professional positions are held by persons who are either gerontology workers or gerontology specialists. This is changing as more persons complete formal gerontology education, so for the purposes of this book, the career position profiles and interviews focus on professionals who are gerontological specialists or gerontologists. While this delineation of three types of career positions in gerontology is helpful in thinking about where you might fit in this growing professional field, please keep in mind that this schema is not yet commonly used by either educators or employers.

WHAT TYPES OF JOBS ARE AVAILABLE IN GERONTOLOGY?

According to Peterson, Douglass, and Lobenstine Whittington (2004), seven types of job roles exist for gerontological specialists, and this role delineation also works well for gerontologists:

- Advocate
- Direct service provider
- Educator/trainer
- Manager/administrator
- Marketer and product developer

[2]According to information provided by Derek Stepp, who was AGHE's executive director in 2007. Updated information will be available in the 9th edition of AGHE's *Directory of Educational Programs in Gerontology and Geriatrics.*

- Program planner and evaluator
- Researcher

Each of these roles is represented among the career position profiles and interviews in this book. Although this listing is not intended to be hierarchical, you may find it useful in prioritizing the type of job roles that do or do not interest you. Keep in mind also that many professionals carry out two or more of these roles, with equal or equitable attention to each, as they fulfill their job responsibilities. Some job roles, such as recruiter and counselor/advisor, are not visible in this listing, so it should not be seen as exhaustive of all job roles that exist or are possible. Finally, in some professional sectors, such as health care, there is a need for professionals with aging expertise and skills specific to each of these job roles.

WHERE DO GERONTOLOGICAL SPECIALISTS AND GERONTOLOGISTS WORK?

The array of specific places where gerontological specialists and gerontologists are employed is too extensive to list here, although it is possible to suggest some of the most common types of work settings:

- Educational settings (public and private): community and junior colleges, 4-year colleges, universities, technical/vocational and professional schools, seminaries; community and professional organizations, programs, and foundations that focus on aging and provide educational programs and services for older adults; adult education and older learner programs; libraries and information centers; employee training/education divisions in industry and corporate settings; patient education services in medical centers/clinics; and community-based agencies related to physical and mental health
- Organizations: professional organization conference management and training programs; chronic disease/disorders organizations, associations, and foundations; race/ethnicity-specific councils on aging; gender-specific organizations and initiatives; membership organizations for older persons
- Medical care, rehabilitation and residential settings: adult day programs, long-term care and assisted living centers; hospitals/medical centers; mental health facilities; Veterans Affairs hospitals; rehabilitation centers; in-home care agencies and services; private practice

- Residential communities and facilities: retirement communities, including continuing care retirement centers (CCRCs) and other types of senior living residences; kinship care housing centers; corrections facilities; cohousing for elders; age-friendly neighborhoods, communities, and cities
- Religious and spiritual settings: churches, synagogues, mosques; religious retreat centers; interfaith/interdenominational organizations; faith-based outreach programs
- Governmental agencies: county commissions, divisions, or bureaus on aging; AAAs; state aging services offices and departments; federal Administration on Aging; Social Security Administration offices; Medicare and Medicaid service centers and assistance programs; prescription assistance and counseling programs; public health departments; National Institutes of Health, including National Institute on Aging
- Corporate, industry, and business settings: banks, financial planning firms and services; investment firms and brokerages; law firms and legal assistance services; insurance industry; retail stores and chains; restaurant and hotel chains; trade associations and unions; manufacturing firms
- Self-employment, including freelance work and entrepreneurial ventures

As with the listing of job roles, the preceding listing is not exhaustive.

CREDENTIALING OF GERONTOLOGY PROFESSIONALS

Credentialing of workers in any field implies that the workers have met certain standards of quality in their preparation to work in the field and offers some sense of safety and security to employers and to those who receive services from the worker. Currently, no credentials are mandated for gerontology workers, specialists, or gerontologists because of the gerontological/geriatric nature of their professional roles. For those who wish to practice under the umbrella of another profession, however, some do need to meet standards and regulations governing those other professions. Three types of credentials are most relevant:

- ***Licensure*** is most frequently issued by the state government in the state in which the professional or paraprofessional worker wishes to practice and, for some professions and in some states, there is a state board specific to a profession (e.g., audiology, nursing, clinical psychology) that is the license-granting body. The professions that require licensing are primarily those in which workers will provide direct service to clients. Some national-level professional organizations also grant licensure to qualified members of their profession.

- ***Certification*** of professionals with an educational background or professional practice orientation to aging and work with older adults is most commonly granted in two ways. The first way is based on completion of a set course of study (e.g., an undergraduate minor in gerontology that is equivalent to certification when it is formally entered on a college transcript or a graduate certificate in gerontology, similarly noted on a transcript but also often accompanied by award of a certificate of achievement). The second way is through successfully passing a certification examination that is administered by a national professional organization once individuals have completed relevant degree work, more often at graduate level. For example, the Certification Board for Music Therapists administers the Board Certification Examination for Music Therapists and grants Music Therapist–Board Certified (MT-BC) credentials to those who pass it.
- ***Accreditation*** is designed to ensure that an educational program offered by an institution of higher education meets certain standards of quality. It is different from licensure and certification in that it is granted to an institution rather than an individual. While some geriatric medicine programs, including those for geriatric psychiatry, are accredited through the Association Council for Graduate Medical Education (ACGME), no comparable accreditation is available currently for gerontology education programs. AGHE's Program of Merit (POM) is an effort to indicate a level of quality and professionalism of the gerontology programs that earn this designation, but it is neither an accreditation process nor a formal step on the path toward accreditation. In 2011, AGHE leaders actively started exploring accreditation. As the educational unit of GSA, approval at each step of the accreditation process must come from both the AGHE Executive Committee and the GSA Council. AGHE's Accreditation Task Force has proposed establishment of the Accreditation for Gerontological Education Council (AGEC) as its accreditation body and prepared a set of gerontology program competencies and standards that are congruent with accreditation processes. In November 2013, the GSA Council approved a

motion in support of AGHE's development of a programmatic accreditation process for gerontology education programs, with the contingency that AGHE must secure external funding to support the multiyear process necessary to establish the accreditation. As of late March 2014, the competencies and standards were out for review by and input from both AGHE and GSA members. These are early steps in a long and complex process that requires reviews and approvals at many steps along the way, so it is likely to be several years before accreditation for at least some gerontology degree programs (and, perhaps, some certificate programs) is in place.

LET YOUR SEARCH BEGIN

With this information to help you better understand what you find along the way as you explore potential career paths in the field of aging, let your search to find your niche within the field begin. Best wishes and welcome to the exciting, dynamic, and ever-expanding professional world of gerontology!

REFERENCES

Peterson, D. A., Douglass, E. B., & Lobenstine Whittington, J. (2004). *Careers in aging: Opportunities and options*. Washington, DC: Association for Gerontology in Higher Education.

Stepp, D. D. (2007). *Directory of educational programs in gerontology and geriatrics* (8th ed.). Washington, DC: Association for Gerontology in Higher Education.

2 ■ CAREERS IN GERONTOLOGY

ACTUARY

BASIC DESCRIPTION

An actuary is all about "risk"—the possibility that something undesirable will occur. Actuaries assess the likelihood that risk will occur in the future, design strategies to avoid or prevent risk, measure incidents of and factors related to the occurrence of undesirable events, attempt to reduce the potential for risk, and work to reduce the impact of the undesirable events that do occur. Actuaries are key players in the design of programs and products that control and manage risk through their work in one of the four major actuarial areas: life insurance, property and casualty insurance, pensions, and health. Actuaries continue to be at or near the top of "best careers" listings, including those issued by *U.S. News and World Report*.

EDUCATION AND EXPERIENCE REQUIREMENTS

A bachelor's degree in business, math, finance, actuarial science, economics, liberal arts, or related fields and a strong math background are essential. Required coursework should include finance, micro- and macro-economics, calculus, linear algebra, computer sciences, business courses (e.g., marketing), and communications (e.g., business and technical writing, speech). Courses in literature, history, art, political science, the humanities, and other liberal arts or social sciences are recommended.

CERTIFICATION, LICENSURE, AND CONTINUING EDUCATION REQUIREMENTS

Beyond the bachelor's degree, certification through either the Society of Actuaries (SOA) or the Casualty Actuarial Society (CAS) is recommended. Licensure (acceptance into the Joint Board for the Enrollment of Actuaries, which is maintained by the U.S. Departments of Treasury and Labor), is required for some (e.g., pension actuaries), but not all, actuaries. Both SOA and CAS require continuing education for recertification. Government pension actuaries must be recertified every 3 years.

CORE COMPETENCIES AND SKILLS NEEDED

- Specialized math knowledge (calculus, linear algebra, statistics, probability) and excellent quantitative skills
- Ability to model and quantify risk
- Effective analytical and critical thinking ability
- Effective project-management and problem-solving skills
- Good business sense regarding finance, accounting, marketing, and economics
- Solid oral and written communication skills
- Strong computer skills, including word-processing programs, spreadsheets, statistical analysis programs, database manipulation, and programming languages
- Ambition, self-motivation
- Creativity
- Curiosity and a joy of learning
- Interested in a variety of historical, social, legislative, and political issues

COMPENSATION

This varies by one's status in the national examination system, designation level, licensure, type of professional specialty, and nature of the employment setting. According to Be An Actuary, the average salary is $88,000, and salaries can be up to $150,000 to 250,000 or higher.

WORKPLACE(S)

These include the financial services sector (such as insurance companies, commercial banks, investment banks and firms, retirement fund companies), corporations, state and federal government agencies (e.g., Social Security, Department of Labor, Medicare), colleges and universities, public accounting firms, labor unions, rating bureaus, fraternal organizations, consulting firms, and self-employed private practice.

EMPLOYMENT OUTLOOK

Excellent; the U.S. Department of Labor, Bureau of Labor Statistics, predicts a faster-than-average increase in employment opportunities for actuaries.

RELATED PROFESSIONAL ORGANIZATIONS AND WEBSITES

- Be An Actuary: www.beanactuary.org
- Actuarial Standards Board (ASB): www.actuarialstandardsboard.org

- American Academy of Actuaries (AAA): www.actuary.org
- American Society of Pension Actuaries (ASPA): www.aspa.org
- Casualty Actuarial Society (CAS): www.casact.org
- Conference of Consulting Actuaries (CCA): www.ccactuaries.org
- Society of Actuaries (SOA): www.soa.org

ADULT DAY SERVICES COORDINATOR

BASIC DESCRIPTION

Adult day services offer a coordinated, supervised program of professional and compassionate services in a community-based group setting that is interactive, safe, and secure. Most programs offer a mix of social and some health care services, including social activities, transportation, meals and snacks, personal care, and therapeutic activities. Indirectly, adult day services offer a few hours of respite to caregivers of those who attend. According to the National Adult Day Services Association (NADSA), adult day services are now recognized as an emerging provider of transitional care and short-term rehabilitation following hospital discharge and as the preferred platform for daily management of chronic disorders (e.g., dementia, physical disability, mental health disorders, developmental disability, cardiovascular disease, diabetes). Adult day services coordinators plan and supervise activities that are appropriate to the age, physical health, and mental health status of program attendees. They conduct home visits to assess the needs of clients and caregivers, develop follow-up plans for caregivers, and facilitate educational programs and support groups. As coordinators, they schedule and supervise daycare staff. They also recruit, train, and schedule program volunteers and student trainees, then coordinate and supervise volunteer and trainee interaction with program clients.

EDUCATION AND EXPERIENCE REQUIREMENTS

A bachelor's or master's degree in social work, clinical psychology, occupational therapy, or therapeutic recreation is required; gerontology (either as coursework or a degree component) is strongly recommended. In most settings, prior experience (at least a year or more) as an adult day services worker at a lower level is required for advancement to a coordinator position.

CERTIFICATION, LICENSURE, AND CONTINUING EDUCATION REQUIREMENTS

These vary by place of employment, state licensing requirements, and professional field.

CORE COMPETENCIES AND SKILLS NEEDED

- Good written and oral communication skills
- Attentive observer and listener
- Ability to design activity plans for clients with varying levels of cognitive functioning
- Creativity in planning activities for persons with memory loss and/or dementia
- Ability to quickly mediate problems that occur with day program clients
- Good organizational skills
- Good staff/volunteer coordination and supervision skills
- Patience and a sense of humor

COMPENSATION

This varies by education, experience, nature of employment setting, level of responsibility, and geographical location.

WORKPLACE(S)

These include health care systems, medical centers, long-term care and skilled nursing facilities, community mental health agencies, multi-service organizations serving older adults, and freestanding daycare facilities funded by community or faith-based organizations.

EMPLOYMENT OUTLOOK

Moderate to high, especially with expanded use of adult day services.

RELATED PROFESSIONAL ORGANIZATIONS AND WEBSITES

- National Adult Day Services Association (NADSA): www.nadsa.org

ADVOCATE

BASIC DESCRIPTION

Advocates inform target audiences, including elders, about relevant issues of concern. They also work actively with and/or on behalf of elders to raise awareness about needs, identify appropriate responses to those needs, and then participate directly or indirectly in the enactment of relevant public and/or private policy. In some cases, advocates represent their older adult constituency; in others, they assist and support older adults to speak and act for themselves. They fulfill their job responsibilities through a variety of roles, such as educator, facilitator, spokesperson, policy watcher, policy analyst, policy developer, and policy opponent or proponent.

EDUCATION AND EXPERIENCE REQUIREMENTS

A bachelor's degree or higher in public administration, sociology, applied sociology, or social work, or a graduate degree in public policy, law, or policy and aging is preferred. Gerontology coursework or a degree component is strongly recommended.

CERTIFICATION, LICENSURE, AND CONTINUING EDUCATION REQUIREMENTS

Advocates must meet requirements related to practice in a specific professional field, state, or governmental jurisdiction or employing agency. Continuing education may be more a by-product of the advocate's daily work than a separate requirement.

CORE COMPETENCIES AND SKILLS NEEDED

- Policy analysis and policy development skills
- Working knowledge of grassroots organizational processes and techniques
- Working knowledge of coalition-building and collaborative processes and techniques
- Advocacy skills
- Competence at building and maintaining networks; mediation and conflict-resolution training is encouraged
- Diplomacy; willingness and ability to work successfully within governmental and agency protocol
- Public speaking skills
- Excellent written and oral communication skills
- Ability to multitask

COMPENSATION

This varies by one's education, experience, the nature of the employing organization/agency, and the type or level of the position within the organizational hierarchy.

WORKPLACE(S)

These include national and international advocacy organizations; federal, state, or local-level grassroots organizations; lobbying groups; and an independent or consulting practice as an advocate, organizer, or lobbyist.

EMPLOYMENT OUTLOOK

Good, especially with the anticipated growth of the older adult population over the next few decades and the politicization of aging.

RELATED PROFESSIONAL ORGANIZATIONS AND WEBSITES

- Center for Medicare Advocacy: www.medicareadvocacy.org
- National Senior Citizens Law Center (NSCLC): www.nsclc.org
- National Committee to Preserve Social Security and Medicare (NCPSSM): www.ncpssm.org
- Alliance for Retired Americans: www.retiredamericans.org
- Services & Advocacy for GLBT Elders (SAGE): www.sageusa.org
- National Council on Aging (NCOA): www.ncoa.org
- AARP: www.aarp.org

ALZHEIMER'S ASSOCIATION STATE CHAPTER EXECUTIVE DIRECTOR

BASIC DESCRIPTION

The executive director is the primary liaison between the Alzheimer's Association, chapter volunteers, and the local communities served by the chapter. The director recruits and mobilizes volunteer, community, and corporate support to reach the specific mission and goals set out in the current multiyear strategic plan and into the future. As outlined by the national Alzheimer's Association, essential job functions of this position are to:

- Identify, recruit, train, and manage high-impact volunteers who will assist the organization in increasing concern and awareness and also growing revenue.
- Serve as community liaison by participating in community events, serving as a local spokesperson, and collaborating with other organizations to achieve strategic goals.
- Plan and execute Walk to End Alzheimer's, including recruitment and recognition of team captains and walkers, recruitment and management of a volunteer committee, and identification of media opportunities.
- Work with staff to plan and execute all other chapter special events, donor cultivation, and stewardship programs.
- Oversee advocacy efforts through recruitment of advocates and ambassadors; serve as local point of contact for public policy issues and questions.

- Manage and coach staff to achieve set goals and strategic outcomes.
- Create and manage chapter budget, maintain financial records, oversee everyday office functions, prepare reports, and provide information as requested and required.

EDUCATION AND EXPERIENCE REQUIREMENTS

A bachelor's degree is required; 7 to 10+ years of work-related experience is preferred in marketing, fundraising, nonprofit management, or a related field.

CERTIFICATION, LICENSURE, AND CONTINUING EDUCATION REQUIREMENTS

None is required by the Alzheimer's Association; however, compliance with state certification and/or licensure requirements is essential.

CORE COMPETENCIES AND SKILLS NEEDED

In addition to those noted in the preceding:

- Excellent computer skills, especially Microsoft Office
- Outstanding verbal and written communication skills
- Sales, marketing, volunteer management, and development experience
- Detail oriented, adaptable, organized, and able to successfully manage multiple projects and tasks
- Ability to work evenings and weekends as needed
- Able to travel to offsite meetings and events within the chapter's territory, and occasional out-of-state travel may be required
- If the chapter does not employ a development and fundraising officer, the executive director must have proven success in identifying, cultivating, and securing major gifts from individual, corporate, and/or other major donors

COMPENSATION

This depends on one's education and experience and may vary by factors specific to the chapter.

WORKPLACE(S)

Primarily at chapter headquarters office, although some chapters have sub-chapters and/or multiple offices.

EMPLOYMENT OUTLOOK

Very good; also the Alzheimer's Association website regularly lists a variety of types of job postings available at the national, regional, state, and local levels.

RELATED PROFESSIONAL ORGANIZATIONS AND WEBSITES

- Alzheimer's Association: www.alz.org
- Alzheimer's Association Job Openings: www.alz.org/apps/jobs

APPLIED SOCIOLOGIST

CLINICAL SOCIOLOGIST

BASIC DESCRIPTION

Sociology is concerned with the understanding of groups or populations, such as the older adult population or its subgroups (e.g., boomers, centenarians). A survey of graduate program directors in 2011 showed that close to 50% of master's level programs in sociology are terminal degrees with applied, professional, or clinical labels. These are intentionally designed to help graduates obtain jobs in nonprofit, for-profit, or government organizations where they can use their analytical skills and research experience. *Applied sociologists* use sociological knowledge to understand current problems or issues and their solutions for populations. When the population of interest is the elderly population, applied sociologists use their knowledge in their work at networks, agencies, organizations, and corporations at the community, state, federal, and international levels. They make informed policy decisions and effectively manage or administer the programs for which they are responsible. Although they may help shape research efforts, they are more often consumers, rather than conductors, of research. Problems and issues they address might include law enforcement, housing, homelessness, transportation, community relations, corporate hiring strategies, health care, education, or other societal problems directly related to their focus on elders.

Clinical sociologists, by contrast, apply sociological knowledge through actual intervention; they use sociological techniques to guide the process of change in a wide variety of social settings. While they sometimes intervene with or on behalf of an individual, they are more likely to work with or through groups, such as elders and their families, to provide support related to counseling, mediation and conflict resolution, and assessment, evaluation, and facilitation.

EDUCATION AND EXPERIENCE REQUIREMENTS

A master's degree in sociology or applied sociology is a minimum requirement; a graduate degree in sociology, applied sociology, demography, criminology, social gerontology, or another subfield of sociology is required for many clinical or applied practice positions (e.g., therapists, counselors, agency directors, researchers, statisticians). Gerontology coursework or a degree component is also strongly recommended.

CERTIFICATION, LICENSURE, AND CONTINUING EDUCATION REQUIREMENTS

Clinical sociologists must meet state licensure requirements, if any, in order to conduct a clinical practice. Requirements for applied sociologists will vary from none to those required in their specific employment settings.

CORE COMPETENCIES AND SKILLS NEEDED

- Good working knowledge of the processes and tools used in research, assessment, evaluation, problem solving, conflict resolution, and policy analysis, development, and enactment
- Excellent written and oral communication skills
- Ability to think through problems, issues, and concerns at the societal level
- Good working knowledge of organization structure and function
- Familiarity with market analysis and focus group techniques

COMPENSATION

This varies by education, experience, the nature of the employment setting, and the level of responsibility.

WORKPLACE(S)

These include social service agencies and corporate, nonprofit, and governmental settings.

EMPLOYMENT OUTLOOK

Promising but difficult to track since relevant positions may be filled by professionals from other applied and clinical fields (e.g., clinical psychology, social work).

RELATED PROFESSIONAL ORGANIZATIONS AND WEBSITES

- American Sociological Association (ASA): www.asanet.org [See entries on Employment and on Jobs and Careers on ASA's website]

ARCHITECT

BASIC DESCRIPTION

A growing sector of the professional field of architecture is devoted to designing home environments that support and aid normal changes in human and family function that occur with aging (including original design, renovation, remodeling, aging-in-place planning, consumer-created co-operatives, and co-housing projects); residential and long-term care facilities that adapt to the changing needs of elders who are physically and/or mentally frail (e.g., continuing care residential communities, assisted living and skilled nursing facilities, adult day program centers, memory care and dementia care settings); and community-based activity centers that serve older adults (e.g., senior centers, wellness therapy, fitness centers).

Tasks for which architects are responsible include site analysis; interviews and questionnaires with intended residents and, for facilities, also with staff members; architectural design and documentation; interior architectural planning and design; structural, mechanical and electrical engineering (along with consultants); construction administration and oversight; and post-occupancy evaluation. For multiunit projects and multiperson residential and care facilities, additional tasks include project architectural research, strategic master planning, strategic program and environment redefinition, project conception and pro forma development (along with consultants), project development, and capital campaign collateral development.

EDUCATION AND EXPERIENCE REQUIREMENTS

A minimum of a Bachelor of Architecture (BArch) degree (5-year first professional degree) is required. A Master of Architecture (MArch) degree is strongly recommended and may be earned by completing one of two optional paths: a 4-year pre-professional degree (BA or BS) plus a 2-year professional architecture degree program or a 4-year non-architecture degree (BA or BS in another field) plus a 3- to 4-year Master of Architecture (MArch) degree. Gerontology coursework or a degree component is recommended.

CERTIFICATION, LICENSURE, AND CONTINUING EDUCATION REQUIREMENTS

Architects must comply with the licensure and registration requirements in the state where the practice occurs. Most states require a postgraduate training period (usually 3 years) under the direct supervision of a licensed architect in order to become eligible to take the Architect Registration Exam. Registered architects are eligible for certification by the National Council of

Architectural Registration Boards (NCARB). Certification requires a professional architecture degree earned from a National Architectural Accrediting Board (NAAB) accredited program, satisfactory completion of the Intern Development Program (IDP) training requirements, passing scores on the nine divisions of the Architect Registration Examination (ARE), application for and receipt of a license to practice from one of NCARB's member registration boards, and application for the NCARB Certificate. Continuing education requirements for registration renewal are set by the state(s) in which the architect is registered and practices.

CORE COMPETENCIES AND SKILLS NEEDED

- Ability to visualize completed structures
- Competence in computer-aided design technology
- Knowledge of person-environment fit conceptual frameworks

COMPENSATION

This varies by the type of practice and position within an architectural firm, the level of professional education and experience, and the geographical location of the practice.

WORKPLACE(S)

These include independent consultancies, sole proprietor practices, architectural firms and studios, corporate architecture departments, and long-term care facilities.

EMPLOYMENT OUTLOOK

Moderate, with excellent potential for expanding opportunities due to an increase in the number and variety of independent living communities, continuum of care residential communities and centers for elders, long-term care facilities (including dementia care units) for frail and at-risk older adults, and free-standing hospice facilities.

RELATED PROFESSIONAL ORGANIZATIONS AND WEBSITES

- The American Institute of Architects (AIA): www.aia.org
- American Institute of Architect Students (AIAS): www.aias.org
- National Architectural Accrediting Board, Inc. (NAAB): www.naab.org
- National Council of Architectural Registration Boards (NCARB): www.ncarb.org

- Association of Collegiate Schools of Architecture (ACSA): www.acsa-arch.org
- Society for the Advancement of Gerontological Environments (SAGE): www.sagefederation.org
- The Environmental Design Research Association (EDRA): www.edra.org
- Environment-Gerontology Network: www.edra.org/content/environment-gerontology
- Institute on Aging and Environment, University of Wisconsin-Milwaukee: www4.uwm.edu/iae

An Interview With ANDREW LEE ALDEN

Living Environments Studio Director
Architecture Firm Studio

Postsecondary educational background, including formal credentials and other education/training in gerontology/geriatrics:
Bachelor's of Science in Psychology
Master's of Architecture, with emphasis in Design for Aging

How and when did you first become interested in gerontology/geriatrics? My formative years were heavily influenced by my aunts and uncles. My father was the youngest of a very large family, so I was surrounded by elders at every stage of my life. One of those elders was Uncle George, who was in his early 70s when I started to get to know him. He was a successful machinist and businessman with a keen interest in architecture. Uncle George made sure to involve me in designing, building, and restoring everything from houses to a 19th-century bank vault. Due to his age, we often talked about how to make things easier and adapt the environment to fit his needs. I always remembered those conversations and my interest in architecture stayed strong in the years that followed, but was not always connected to the various jobs I had. After pursuing paths in psychology, medicine, and business, it seemed I would never find the one profession that encompassed all of my various areas of interest. I must admit that it was upon my wife's suggestion for me to pursue a career in architecture that I started seriously investigating the possibility.

Briefly describe your gerontology/geriatrics-related career path. As an undergraduate psychology student, I was exposed to gerontological issues, but it was not until graduate school that I started to focus my studies on aging. While in graduate school, I got involved with the Institute on Aging and Environment in the School of Architecture and Urban Planning. The primary goal of the Institute was to improve the physical environment for older adults, especially in care settings such as assisted living and skilled nursing communities. I worked with faculty members on consulting projects across the country. Through my involvement at the Institute and the mentoring of the Institute co-director, I gained an understanding of the impact environments can

(*continued*)

An Interview With ANDREW LEE ALDEN *(continued)*

have on the lives and well-being of older adults. I was suddenly able to apply my psychology background to an architectural purpose that focused on older adults. Upon graduation, I worked as a designer for a local architecture firm and, eventually, as a project manager specializing in environments for older adults. During that time, I also continued my strong focus on connecting research and practice by presenting at conferences, writing articles, conducting research at the Institute, and teaching at the local university. A few years ago, I made the transition to my current employer and new position as part of my continued career development.

Briefly describe your current professional position:

Position title: Living Environments Studio Director

Primary role tasks/responsibilities: My duties involve the daily operations, personnel management, and fiscal responsibility for a 22-member architectural studio. The studio has an emphasis on continuum of care—from independent living to skilled nursing—for older adults. I also participate in various roles (e.g., client executive, project manager, or designer) in our project teams.

Type of employment setting: Architecture firm studio

Length of time in this position: 2-1/2 years

How did you first become interested in this position? I was fortunate to be approached by an executive recruiter who was given my name by a colleague. I was intrigued with the idea of leading a group of individuals who were as passionate about design for aging as I was. I have not been disappointed.

Describe a typical workday in your current professional position. Every day has the potential to be very different. Balancing administrative, personnel, and project issues often results in interesting adventures both outside and inside the office. It is hard to describe a typical day

(continued)

An Interview With ANDREW LEE ALDEN (*continued*)

because it varies greatly from day to day. For instance, one day might involve intense client meetings, another day might involve discussing and planning strategies for upcoming projects with my studio members, and yet another day might involve higher level company strategy meetings with the management team. I also find time to focus on my client, executive, or design responsibilities with specific projects. My job is fast paced, and I enjoy using a diverse set of skills to achieve my goals.

What is the time commitment required of your current professional position? My typical work week is around 45 hours, with variations depending on specific initiatives or projects in the studios. My weekly hours might extend considerably beyond that during the conference and trade show seasons that occur during the spring and fall of each year. Conference weeks may result in 65+ hours, depending on the number of scheduled client/future client meetings and the presentations and/or trade show schedules. I try to reserve the weekends for family but typically spend a few hours on Sunday evening getting ready for the next week.

How do you stay up-to-date in your profession?

Professional organization memberships and/or activities? To have a different perspective on issues that impact older adults, it is important for me to be involved with both local and national organizations. I am actively involved and in leadership positions with two national organizations: the American Society on Aging (ASA) and the Society for the Advancement of Gerontological Environments (SAGE). Local organizations include an elder services advisory board and the Home Sweet Home Safety Evaluation Program.

Subscribe to and/or read professional journals and/or newsletters? I read a variety of publications (both print media and electronic format) in the fields of architecture and gerontology. The most helpful architecture publications are produced by the American Institute of Architects (AIA). The resources produced by the American Society on Aging, including

(*continued*)

An Interview With ANDREW LEE ALDEN *(continued)*

Aging Today and *Generations*, are important. The Gerontological Society of America produces *The Gerontologist* and the *Journals of Gerontology*, which also are valuable resources.

Attend professional conferences and/or participate in education/training programs? Environments for Aging (E4A) conference, American Society on Aging (ASA), and Leading Age (national and state chapter).

What are the most rewarding aspects of your current career position? I have the privilege of working with a very talented group of individuals, and it is a pleasure to come to work every morning.

What are the most rewarding aspects of your gerontology/geriatrics-related career path? It is very rewarding to make a difference in the life of an older adult. The physical environment can make a dramatic difference in the experience of residents, family members, and facility staff.

What are the most challenging aspects of your current career position? Time management is always a challenge. I need to ensure that each endeavor receives the appropriate amount of attention, and I must recognize my own chronological limitations.

What are the most challenging aspects of your gerontology/geriatrics-related career path? Due to the dynamic nature of the design-for-aging field, informational overload is always a possibility. The amount of new information available on a daily basis from popular media and research-based periodicals is overwhelming. It is absolutely necessary to prioritize the information you seek and sift through to achieve a manageable amount.

How do you balance career and other aspects of your life? The architecture business is not necessarily a 9 to 5 occupation; it depends on how you manage your time and what priorities you set for yourself. Saturdays are for family; it's my one golden rule. It takes constant

(*continued*)

An Interview With ANDREW LEE ALDEN (*continued*)

effort to strive for balance—my work is my passion, but my family is my life.

What advice do you have for someone contemplating a career in the field of aging? Many factors should be considered when contemplating a career path; the first and probably most important is to ask, "Will I enjoy what I am doing?" Many opportunities exist for exposure to careers in aging; these include mentoring, internships, informational interviews, and exploring media publications. Explore the possibilities to establish a firm footing of what to do next. The field of aging has advantages in comparison to other career possibilities. The first characteristic is job growth and potential. The demographics indicate a dramatic future increase in the number of older adults in the United States. Those older adults will need services. The second characteristic is personal fulfillment—understanding that what you do makes a difference to a community, a family, or an individual. A career that has substantial growth potential and will be personally rewarding seems to be a worthwhile and logical choice.

What advice do you have for someone considering a professional position similar to your current position? The beauty of architecture is that your educational background and experience do not have to be solely architecture related. As an example, my own background in psychology has enriched my interests in the architecture profession. Many universities around the country offer 3-1/2-year master's degrees to students with undergraduate degrees in other fields. Architecture with a gerontological specialty is a fast-growing field and offers many opportunities. My advice is to follow all of your passions, as diverse as they may seem. It is only when we figure out a way to combine all of the things we love in the world that we can truly find that "job" that becomes our passion. Architecture is my passion, but please don't tell my wife since she realized it before I did.

ART THERAPIST

BASIC DESCRIPTION

Art therapy is used predominantly in mental health, human service, educational, medical, and social settings to help clients achieve positive outcomes, such as greater self-awareness and self-esteem, resolution of intra- and interpersonal conflicts, development of new social and coping skills, reduction of anxiety, improvement in how problems are handled, appropriate changes in reality orientation, and acquisition of helpful personal insights. Psychology and human development, especially adult development and aging, provide the theoretical foundation for art therapy. Art therapists draw on this interdisciplinary background for assessment and treatment models, tools, and strategies from cognitive, educational, psychodynamic, transpersonal, and other perspectives. They involve patients and clients in creative art processes (e.g., painting, drawing, creating fiber art, pottery) to encourage self-expression through creation of clients' own artworks. They also observe their clients' reactions to already produced art objects (e.g., sculpture, pottery, paintings) as a way to understand their clients' individual developmental level, personality, interests, abilities, concerns, problems, conflicts, and potential for growth. The professional tasks of art therapists include selection of appropriate materials and interventions; determination of goals and objectives for clients to achieve maintenance of relevant case records; preparation of periodic reports; consultation with clients, family members, caregivers, and professional colleagues; participation in staff meetings and multidisciplinary health care teams; and involvement with professional organizations and conferences. In addition to their direct practice with patients, art therapists may serve as unit supervisors, agency administrators, and expert witnesses in court cases involving their clients.

EDUCATION AND EXPERIENCE REQUIREMENTS

A minimum of a master's degree in art therapy is required for licensure and practice. Acceptance to a graduate degree program in this field requires a bachelor's degree from an accredited college/university and documentation of 15 semester hours in studio art and 12 semester hours in psychology prior to application and submission of a portfolio of original art.

CERTIFICATION, LICENSURE, AND CONTINUING EDUCATION REQUIREMENTS

The Art Therapy Credentials Board Inc. (ATCB) is the credentialing body. Attaining the Art Therapist Registered (ATR) designation requires documentation that the candidate has completed the proper master's degree and the required postgraduate experience. ATRs who pass the ATCB written examination are qualified as Board Certified (ATR-BC). Continuing education is required for recertification every 5 years.

CORE COMPETENCIES AND SKILLS NEEDED

- Familiarity with and skill in the use of an array of art media
- Sensitivity to an array of older adult needs and interests
- Capacity for insight into the psychological processes of older adults
- Attentive listener
- Keen observer
- Emotional stability
- Patience
- Strong interpersonal skills; ability to develop rapport with older clients
- Ability to work effectively with a wide range of mental, emotional, physical, and social health care needs
- Ability to work effectively in a variety of settings
- Flexibility; ability to adapt
- Sense of humor

COMPENSATION

This varies by one's education, experience, licensure, type of practice, and nature of the practice setting.

WORKPLACE(S)

These include hospitals and clinics (medical and psychiatric), hospices, wellness centers, social services agencies, outpatient mental health agencies and day treatment programs, educational programs and services, long-term care and assisted living facilities, senior centers and other community-based programs that serve elders, adult and intergenerational daycare programs and centers, substance abuse and chemical dependency programs and agencies, rehabilitation and residential treatment centers, domestic violence and homeless shelters, community agencies and nonprofit organizations, correctional facilities, and independent private practices or consultancies.

EMPLOYMENT OUTLOOK

Good, with an increasing potential for practice as the population grows older and as older persons become more comfortable with mental health therapies and human service interventions.

RELATED PROFESSIONAL ORGANIZATIONS AND WEBSITES

- American Art Therapy Association (AATA): www.arttherapy.org
- Art Therapy Credentials Board (ATCB): www.atcb.org
- National Coalition of Creative Arts Therapies Associations (NCCATA): www.nccata.org
- International Art Therapy Organization (IATO): www.internationalarttherapy.org

AUDIOLOGIST

BASIC DESCRIPTION

Audiologists are experts in the nonmedical management of the auditory (hearing) and balance systems of the human body. Their work with clients is related to normal and impaired hearing, prevention of hearing loss, identification and assessment of hearing or balance problems and rehabilitation of persons with hearing and balance disorders. Some audiologists also design hearing instruments and testing equipment; conduct research to add to the knowledge about normal hearing, hearing evaluation, and treatment of hearing and balance disorders; manage agencies, clinics, or private practices; or assist in the education of future audiology professionals through their work as professors or clinical supervisors and trainers. Audiologists in clinical practice frequently work with speech-language pathologists and medical specialists; some serve on interdisciplinary health care teams. Some audiologists also hold credentials and practice as speech-language pathologists.

EDUCATION AND EXPERIENCE REQUIREMENTS

A master's degree with an emphasis in audiology or a doctorate in audiology (AuD) is required. Undergraduate students may complete a bachelor's degree in communication sciences that includes audiology coursework, but a degree in audiology is not available at the undergraduate level. Gerontology coursework or a degree component is strongly recommended.

CERTIFICATION, LICENSURE, AND CONTINUING EDUCATION REQUIREMENTS

For licensure, audiologists must meet the regulatory (licensure) standards in the state(s) where the practice occurs. For certification, individuals who hold a graduate degree in audiology are eligible for the Certificate of Clinical

Competence in Audiology (CCC-A), which is issued by the Council for Clinical Certification in Audiology and Speech-Language Pathology (CFCC) of the American Speech-Language-Hearing Association (ASHA). Requirements include a graduate degree in audiology, 375 hours of supervised clinical experience, a 36-week postgraduate clinical fellowship, and a written examination.

CORE COMPETENCIES AND SKILLS NEEDED

- Good listening skills
- Good oral and written communication skills, including the ability to effectively communicate diagnostic test results
- Ability to relate to patients/clients and their caregivers/families about diagnosis and rehabilitation plans
- Ability to explain technology developments and devices that assist patients/clients with hearing loss
- Ability to propose and interpret treatment so that is easily understood by clients and other professionals
- Objective approach to problems
- Patience
- Compassion
- Capable of providing appropriate support for clients/patients and their caregivers/families

COMPENSATION

This varies according to one's educational background, certification, experience, nature of practice, and type of practice setting.

WORKPLACE(S)

These include hospitals, medical centers, rehabilitation centers, residential health facilities, community clinics, private practice offices, long-term care facilities, community hearing and speech centers, physicians' offices, research laboratories, and consultancies with local, state, and government agencies and organizations that serve elders.

EMPLOYMENT OUTLOOK

Excellent; job growth expected to increase 37% between 2010 and 2020 (estimated 4,800 jobs) due to an increase in the elderly population, an increased demand for audiologists in private practice to provide direct services to individuals, and the increased use of contract services by hospitals, medical centers, and long-term nursing care facilities.

RELATED PROFESSIONAL ORGANIZATIONS AND WEBSITES

- American Speech-Language-Hearing Association (ASHA): www.asha.org
- American Academy of Audiologists (AAA): www.audiology.org
- Accreditation Commission for Audiology Education (ACAE): www.acaeaccred.org
- National Council of State Boards of Examiners for Speech-Language Pathology and Audiology: www.ncsb.info

An Interview With KATHLEEN SAWHILL

Audiologist

Postsecondary educational background, including formal credentials and other education/training in gerontology–geriatrics:

BS, Communication Disorders, with Minors in Gerontology and Human Development AuD, Audiology

Audiologist Licensure (issued by state board of audiology)

Certificate of Clinical Competence–Audiology (CCC-A), American Speech-Language-Hearing Association (ASHA)

How and when did you first become interested in gerontology/geriatrics? From very early on in my college career, I knew that I wanted to work in a "helping" profession. I explored different therapeutic professions and found the science of hearing to be incredibly interesting. Part of what drew me to the profession was the ability to make a significant impact in the quality of life of older persons through the fitting of amplification. Through the assistance of hearing aids, I am able to allow older persons to maintain their social connections, and that is something that is extremely rewarding.

Briefly describe your gerontology/geriatrics-related career path. Upon earning my bachelor's degree in communication disorders, I made the decision to further my education with a Doctorate of Audiology. The degree currently requires 3 years of on-campus coursework and a 1-year externship. I completed the 4th-year externship of my doctoral studies at a major medical center. Upon graduating, I was offered a full-time position in the audiology department. Two years later, I made the decision to start a private practice, and I am currently an ownership partner in that practice.

Briefly describe your current professional position:

Position title: Audiologist and private practice owner

Primary role tasks/responsibilities: As a clinical audiologist in private practice, much of my day is spent testing and consulting patients regarding their hearing loss. If hearing aids are appropriate, I am also

(*continued*)

An Interview With KATHLEEN SAWHILL *(continued)*

responsible for making appropriate recommendations and for the fitting of the amplification. An ownership role within the practice also means that I have many responsibilities concerning the general management and daily operations of the office. These responsibilities often include scheduling, marketing, and financial management.

Type of employment setting: Private practice

Length of time in this position: 5-1/2 years

How did you first become interested in this position? I had a desire to provide hearing health care to those in my community and also to achieve personal growth goals of owning my own business.

Describe a typical workday in your current professional position. A typical day currently involves consulting with patients for hearing evaluations and the fitting and adjustment of hearing aids. Between patients, I also help to manage office responsibilities.

What is the time commitment required of your current professional position? I currently work 8:30 a.m. to 3:30 p.m., 4 days a week. As the mom to two young boys, my current position allows me to work a modified schedule to accommodate their needs.

How do you stay up-to-date in your profession?

Professional organization memberships and/or activities?
American Academy of Audiology (AAA), Member
American Speech-Language-Hearing Association (ASHA), Member

Subscribe to and/or read professional journals and/or newsletters? I also stay up-to-date through the use of professional journals. I often enjoy articles from *Audiology Today* and *The Hearing Journal.*

Attend professional conferences and/or participate in education/training programs? Both my ASHA Certification and state licensure require continuing education to maintain those credentials. I also attend conferences at both the state and national level to obtain necessary continuing education credits.

(continued)

An Interview With KATHLEEN SAWHILL *(continued)*

Some hearing aid manufacturers also provide local training sessions when new products and/or software are released. Continuing education credits can also be obtained through online courses.

What are the most rewarding aspects of your current career position? Having a career that offers me the personal reward of making a significant difference in the lives of others.

What are the most rewarding aspects of your gerontology/geriatrics-related career path? I've done similar work in both audiology positions that I have held. The opportunity to assist older adults in hearing well again is very rewarding. After the fitting of an amplification, many are overjoyed at the possibility of hearing the birds again, hearing their grandchildren speak, or hearing music the way it is intended. All of these improvements have a significant impact on individuals' quality of life, and that is something that I am honored to provide them.

What are the most challenging aspects of your current career position? Hearing aids have made tremendous technological improvements in the past few years, but they are still an "aid" and cannot replace the hearing that you originally had as a child. Counseling individuals about the realistic expectations pertaining to this can be challenging. Learning to "hear again" and learning to hear "differently" takes time and a commitment to wearing amplification consistently. In working in partnership with a knowledgeable audiologist, significantly improved hearing and communication with others is achievable.

What are the most challenging aspects of your gerontology/geriatrics-related career path? My career path has led me to a career in private practice. One of the most challenging aspects has been learning to balance the two different roles that I hold, one being clinical audiologist, the other, business owner. Throughout any given day, I have had to learn to step "in and out" of each role so that I can give each my full and undivided attention.

How do you balance career and other aspects of your life? Whenever possible, I try to leave "work" at "work." There certainly are times when I

(continued)

An Interview With KATHLEEN SAWHILL *(continued)*

choose to accommodate a patient's schedule and offer to see them in the evening or on a Saturday morning, but those times are rare, and for the most part, my "work life" does not interfere with my "family life."

What advice do you have for someone contemplating a career in the field of aging? For individuals considering a career within the field of aging, I would suggest that personal qualities of patience and compassion are both very important. A good sense of humor is also very helpful!

What advice do you have for someone considering a professional position similar to your current position? As a private practice audiologist, I feel that patience and good communication skills are extremely important. The interpersonal skills necessary to develop a trusting relationship with the geriatric patient are also essential. Hearing aid technology is changing rapidly. It is important that those in this role can adequately counsel older persons regarding this technology.

CAREER AND EMPLOYMENT COUNSELOR

BASIC DESCRIPTION

Career and employment counselors (sometimes titled "career counselors" or "employment counselors") assist individuals who are seeking employment or assistance with employment or career reentry, career development and transition, and work-to-retirement transitions. Although their clients traditionally have been adolescents and young or middle-aged adults, they now find older adults among their clientele. Using the tools of the professional field in which they were trained, career and employment counselors assess their clients' work-related skills, abilities, and interests, and then assist their clients with work-related training or retraining, career development, job search, and job entry. While they use similar processes with clients of all ages, career and employment counselors who specialize in working with older adults must be sensitive to the factors that shape an older person's need or desire for employment, regardless of whether that need is related to remaining in the workforce rather than retiring, entering the workforce for the first time in later life, reentering the workforce after an extended time out of it, making a work-to-retirement transition, or returning to full- or part-time employment after an earlier retirement. Some career/employment professionals (such as personnel administrators or human resources managers) hold positions in corporate settings where they are responsible for recruitment, hiring, and supervision of older workers; oversight of laws and regulations specific to older workers; and work-to-retirement transitions. Others work with government needs-based employment programs (e.g., Foster Grandparents Program, Senior Companion Program) for older persons.

EDUCATION AND EXPERIENCE REQUIREMENTS

A bachelor's or higher degree in counseling and guidance, personnel administration, adult education, or a closely related field is required. A professional counseling master's or doctoral degree is preferred or required by some employing agencies and for some specializations within the field (e.g., addiction counseling, career counseling, clinical mental health or community agency counseling, marriage and family counseling, and gerontological counseling). Gerontology coursework or a degree component is strongly recommended.

CERTIFICATION, LICENSURE, AND CONTINUING EDUCATION REQUIREMENTS

Career and employment counselors must meet the licensure requirements in the state where the professional practice occurs. Certification is a voluntary option (not mandatory) for counselors in an array of specializations. The National Board for Certified Counselors (NBCC) and the Commission on Rehabilitation Certification (CRCC) are the leading certification organizations for the counseling profession. Continuing education or post-degree supervised clinical training may be required for some professions or employing agencies, licensure, and/or certification/recertification.

CORE COMPETENCIES AND SKILLS NEEDED

- Good understanding of the factors related to older adults' needs and/or desires to work
- Good working knowledge of laws and regulations related to older workers and age discrimination in the workplace
- Respect for the talents and skills of older adults in regard to career
- Ability to establish trusting, open, and helpful relationships with older clients
- Commitment to a client-centered practice
- Ability to facilitate decision making and goal setting
- Computer literacy on relevant software and databases

- Excellent verbal and written communication skills
- Attentive listening skills
- Ability to maintain confidentiality
- Good organizational skills

COMPENSATION

This varies by one's education, experience, type of position, level of responsibility and the nature of employment setting.

WORKPLACE(S)

These include community-based career counseling centers and adult education programs; corporate human resources departments; community college, college, and university career counseling centers; centers and agencies that serve elders; and Senior Community Service Employment Programs (SCSEP).

EMPLOYMENT OUTLOOK

Limited at the current time, but nevertheless promising due to an increase in the size of the older adult population, an increase in the number of older adults who are interested in employment and career development opportunities and new career-focused programs for older adults.

RELATED PROFESSIONAL ORGANIZATIONS AND WEBSITES

- American Counseling Association (ACA): www.counseling.org
- ACA Career Center: www.counseling.org/careers/aca-career-center
- National Employment Counseling Association (NECA): www.employmentcounseling.org
- National Older Worker Career Center (NOWCC): www.nowcc.org
- Senior Community Service Employment Program (SCSEP): www.doleta.gov/seniors
- Encore Careers: www.encore.org
- National Career Development Association (NCDA): www.ncda.org
- National Board for Certified Counselors (NBCC): www.nbcc.org
- Commission on Rehabilitation Counselor Certification (CRCC): www.crcccertification.com

CERTIFIED AGING-IN-PLACE SPECIALIST (CAPS)

BASIC DESCRIPTION

Certified aging-in-place specialist (CAPS) is a certification program administered by the National Association of Home Builders (NAHB). CAPS-certified professionals assist people of all ages to continue living independently, safely, and comfortably in their own homes, regardless of their income, health status, and functional level. Professionals with the CAPS designation include building contractors and remodelers, architects, interior designers, reverse mortgage specialists, environmental gerontologists, certified senior advisors, occupational and physical therapists, and aging consultants.

EDUCATION AND EXPERIENCE REQUIREMENTS

Educational requirements include completion of an appropriate degree or training program for the base profession, completion of the CAPS educational program (courses on working with and marketing to older adults, home modifications, and introduction to business management), and submission of a graduation application to NAHB.

CERTIFICATION, LICENSURE, AND CONTINUING EDUCATION REQUIREMENTS

Additional continuing education and/or participation in community service is required every 3 years.

CORE COMPETENCIES AND SKILLS NEEDED

- Understand the meaning of home to each specific client
- Know and stay updated on relevant building codes, standards, and materials
- Practice excellent interpersonal communication skills
- Recognize impact of physical, mental, and social health on housing needs of aging persons
- Meet requirements for practice in the primary profession

COMPENSATION

This varies by type of career position, nature of the employment setting, educational background, experience, part- or full-time position, and geographical location.

WORKPLACE(S)

These include building and remodeling contract firms, banks, interior design studios, private consulting firms, agencies that serve elders, and community and human service agencies.

EMPLOYMENT OUTLOOK

Good, but varies by type of profession; actual demand is not yet established for professionals with this relatively new certification.

RELATED PROFESSIONAL ORGANIZATIONS AND WEBSITES

- National Association of Home Builders (NAHB): www.nahb.org
- National Aging in Place Council (NAIPC): www.naipc.org

CERTIFIED GERIATRIC PHARMACIST (CPG)

BASIC DESCRIPTION

Certified geriatric pharmacist (CPG) is a voluntary specialization for pharmacists who pass a written examination on geriatric pharmacy practice and principles of geriatric drug therapy. Recognizing that medication for older adults must be tailored to the individual patient's circumstances, including comorbidities, goals of care, patient preferences, and the patient's ability to adhere to medication dosages and instructions, CPGs practice medication therapy management (MTM). Special consideration is given to potentially inappropriate drugs, polypharmacy, prescribing cascade, and impact of medications on geriatric syndromes (e.g., falls, cognitive impairment).

EDUCATION AND EXPERIENCE REQUIREMENTS

Minimum of a bachelor's or master's degree in pharmacy or a PharmD degree from an American Council for Pharmacy Education (APCE)-accredited school of pharmacy.

CERTIFICATION, LICENSURE, AND CONTINUING EDUCATION REQUIREMENTS

To be eligible for CPG certification, a pharmacist must hold a current license to practice pharmacy and have at least 2 years of experience as a licensed pharmacist. CPG status is earned by passing the CPG examination administered by the Commission for Certification of Geriatric Pharmacists (CCGP).

Recertification is required every 5 years and can be earned by retaking the CPG examination or through the Professional Development Pathway by completing 75 hours of designated continuing education over the 5-year cycle.

CORE COMPETENCIES AND SKILLS NEEDED

- Competence in patient-centered practice with older adults and geriatric patients
- Research-based understanding of the aging process and factors that affect the physical, mental, and social health of elders
- Excellent understanding of geriatric pharmacotherapy specific to disease-specific conditions of patients
- Excellent communication and interpersonal skills
- Ability to educate patients and/or their personal and professional caregivers about the proper and safe use of medications and other pharmacy-related therapies
- Commitment to prevention of misuse and abuse of medications and over-the-counter drugs
- Commitment to ethical practice with elderly and frail clients

COMPENSATION

This varies by the type of practice, education, experience, place of employment, level of position held, and geographical location.

WORKPLACE(S)

These include community-based pharmacies, hospital and medical care center pharmacies, nursing facilities, subacute care and assisted living facilities, psychiatric hospitals, hospice programs, and home- and community-based care organizations.

EMPLOYMENT OUTLOOK

Good to very good, but may depend partially on location (both by state and by rural vs. urban/metropolitan) and on consumer awareness of the availability and benefits of using a CPG-certified pharmacist.

RELATED PROFESSIONAL ORGANIZATIONS AND WEBSITES

- American Pharmacist Association (APhA): www.pharmacist.com
- Commission for Certification in Geriatric Pharmacy (CCGP): www.ccgp.org

- American Council for Pharmacy Education (ACPE): www.acpe-accredit.org
- American Pharmacists Association (APhA): www.pharmacist.com
- Accreditation Council for Pharmacy Education (ACPE): www.acpe-accredit.org
- National Association of Boards of Pharmacy (NABP): www.nabp.net

CONSULTANT OR SENIOR CARE PHARMACIST

BASIC DESCRIPTION

Consultant pharmacists and senior care pharmacists provide expertise on the use of medications by individuals or through pharmacy services in health care institutions. They commonly work as a member of a health care team to practice patient-centered pharmacotherapy that recognizes the complexity of interrelationships among disease states, injury statuses, nutrition, medications, and other variables. Working with and on behalf of patients, consultant pharmacists provide information and recommendations to subscribers and caregivers; review patients' drug regimens; educate and counsel patients about appropriate and safe use of medications; present in-service educational and training programs for facility staff members, family caregivers, and the lay public; oversee medication distribution services in the facility; provide related services such as pain management counseling, pharmacokinetic dosing services, intravenous therapy, nutrition assessment and support, and durable medical equipment; and identify, resolve, and prevent medication-related problems.

EDUCATION AND EXPERIENCE REQUIREMENTS

Minimum of a bachelor's or master's degree in pharmacy, although a PharmD degree is strongly recommended and is required by some employing agencies and consultation settings.

CERTIFICATION, LICENSURE, AND CONTINUING EDUCATION REQUIREMENTS

Consultant pharmacists and senior care pharmacists must have a valid pharmacy license in the state(s) where the practice occurs; stay current with changing laws and regulations about medications and the settings in which they practice; and maintain or improve their level of knowledge and practice competence through postgraduate residencies, experiential traineeships, and continuing pharmaceutical education.

CORE COMPETENCIES AND SKILLS NEEDED

- Knowledge and skills in geriatric pharmacotherapy and the unique medication-related needs of elders and long-term care residents
- Expertise in long-term care settings for frail and at-risk elders
- Patient-centered advocacy skills
- Current knowledge of state and federal pharmacy laws applicable to practice setting(s)
- Ability to work collaboratively as a member of an interdisciplinary health care team
- Good organizational skills
- Good written and oral communication skills

COMPENSATION

This varies by education, experience, practice setting, type and level of professional position, geographical location, and negotiation skills, and may be affected by fluctuations in the economy.

WORKPLACE(S)

These include hospitals, medical centers and clinics, long-term care and nursing facilities, subacute care and assisted living facilities, psychiatric hospitals, hospice, and home- and community-based care programs.

EMPLOYMENT OUTLOOK

Good to very good, depending on location. As medical and health care systems use more contractual services, employment outlook for consultant pharmacists may improve. Growth in the elderly population should help to increase the demand for senior care pharmacists.

RELATED PROFESSIONAL ORGANIZATIONS AND WEBSITES

- American Society of Consultant Pharmacists (ASCP): www.ascp.com
- American Pharmacists Association (APhA): www.pharmacist.com
- Accreditation Council for Pharmacy Education (ACPE): www.acpe-accredit.org
- National Association of Boards of Pharmacy (NABP): www.nabp.net

An Interview With MARY SCOTT

Certified Geriatric Pharmacist and Consultant Pharmacist

Postsecondary educational background, including formal credentials and other education/training in gerontology/geriatrics:
BS, Pharmacy Certification in Geriatric Pharmacy (CGP)

How and when did you first become interested in gerontology/geriatrics? About 5 years after graduating from pharmacy school, I started working in a long-term care pharmacy and decided to become a consultant pharmacist.

Briefly describe your gerontology/geriatrics-related career path. I worked as a consultant pharmacist for a few long-term care pharmacies and decided to become certified in geriatric pharmacy in 1998. I have recertified every 5 years since 1998.

Briefly describe your current professional position:
Position title: Pharmacist (part-time) and consultant pharmacist on pro re nata (PRN, as needed) basis

Primary role tasks/responsibilities: When I work as a consultant pharmacist, I review the medication sheets and charts for every resident in the nursing facility, making notes on drug interactions, incorrect times when medications are given, improper storage of medications, incorrect dosages of medications for a particular resident, and other tasks specific to residents' medications. I write a report detailing my findings and provide a copy of the report to the director of nursing and facility administrator. I also write a recommendation letter to physicians if I feel a resident's medication needs to be adjusted. At some facilities, I am asked to assist with drug disposal. I also provide nursing in-service training sessions on new medications, changes in state survey regulations, and medication documentation. A family member of a resident may also request a meeting with me to go over medications prior to a resident's discharge.

Type of employment setting: Health maintenance organization (HMO-managed care, for part-time pharmacist position); long-term care facilities, hospices, assisted-living centers (for consultant pharmacist work)

(*continued*)

An Interview With MARY SCOTT *(continued)*

Length of time in position: 5-1/2 years

How did you first become interested in this position? I was downsized from my part-time position as a consultant pharmacist in 2010. I had been working part-time for the HMO, so they offered me more hours. I first became interested in being a consultant pharmacist when I was searching for a position that would allow me to use my clinical expertise in geriatric medicine.

Describe a typical workday in your current professional position. I am responsible for dispensing medication for the HMO members, I monitor the members who are on specialty medications, and I attend medication meetings with other staff members (e.g., physicians, physician's assistants, health coaches, and nurses).

What is the time commitment required of your current professional position? I work 3 days per week for 8 hours each day. The health center is open 8:30 a.m. to 5:30 p.m., Monday through Friday only. Evening/weekend work is not required.

How do you stay up-to-date in your profession?

Professional organization memberships and/or activities? American Society of Consultant Pharmacists (ASCP)

Subscribe to and/or read professional journals and/or newsletters? The ASCP journal, *The Consultant Pharmacist*, is the most helpful. The *Pharmacist's Letter* (monthly newsletter available in the mail and online) is also very useful.

Attend professional conferences and/or participate in education/training programs? I have attended ASCP conferences, both the yearly meetings and their mid-year regional meetings that are locally based.

Other? I keep up with pharmacy-related websites, such as Drug Topics and Pharmacy Times. There also are several LinkedIn groups that I converse with on a weekly basis.

(continued)

An Interview With MARY SCOTT (*continued*)

What are the most rewarding aspects of your current career position? The feeling that I am helping people manage their medications.

What are the most rewarding aspects of your gerontology/geriatrics-related career path? It is most rewarding to me to feel that by helping people manage their meds, I am helping them avoid having to go to a long-term care facility. By avoiding polypharmacy, people often can remain in their homes and experience a greater quality of life.

What are the most challenging aspects of your current career position? I can't really think of anything really challenging in my current career position.

What are the most challenging aspects of your gerontology/geriatrics-related career path? Right now, because of the economy, it is hard to find a position in long-term care in my geographical area.

How do you balance career and other aspects of your life? It is relatively easy for me since I only work 8:30 a.m. to 5:30 p.m. 3 days a week. It was harder when my kids were small and I worked full-time.

What advice do you have for someone contemplating a career in the field of aging? Do not wait until you graduate from pharmacy school to start working in a pharmacy. Many pharmacies would welcome a pharmacy intern. Working even a few hours a week will allow you to experience the "real work" in a pharmacy. In a pharmacy environment, the majority of your patients/customers are elderly, and you can learn what problems with medications are particular to this age group. Upon graduation, your clinical expertise is at the embryo stage. You will learn much more after you graduate and start working fully as a professional pharmacist.

What advice do you have for someone considering a professional position similar to your current position? Stay open to learning from the pharmacy technicians who are working with you. A team approach makes for the best working environment. Make yourself available for consultation with other team members (e.g., physicians, physician assistants, and nurse practitioners). Pharmacists are the medication experts, and the other

(*continued*)

An Interview With MARY SCOTT *(continued)*

team members can always use your expertise when it comes to changing a patient's medication to avoid a particular drug interaction or side effect. Don't be afraid to question the dosing of a medication. By determining the biometrics of a particular patient, the pharmacist and physician can arrive at the optimal dose of a medication for patients with, for example, serious kidney or liver problems.

CERTIFIED SENIOR ADVISOR (CSA)

BASIC DESCRIPTION

Certified senior advisors (CSAs) are professionals from a wide variety of fields (e.g., accounting, law, business, clergy, medicine, nursing, pharmacy, financial planning, funeral services, geriatric care, home health care, insurance, realty, mortgage lending, housing, social work) who have earned the CSA designation to add to the credentials they hold in their primary professional field(s). The CSA education program integrates the social, health, and financial aspects of aging to help professionals focus on people rather than products. By having a better understanding of their aging and elderly clients, CSAs fit their products and services to the needs and interests of the clients.

EDUCATION AND EXPERIENCE REQUIREMENTS

Applicants for CSA training must hold valid credentials in their field(s) of practice.

CERTIFICATION, LICENSURE, AND CONTINUING EDUCATION REQUIREMENTS

To complete CSA program requirements, applicants must pass the CSA exam (150 multiple choice questions: Social Aspects of Aging [25%]; Health Aspects of Aging: Physical and Mental [25%]; Financial and Legal Aspects of Aging [20%]; Government Assistance to Seniors [10%]; and Understanding and Communicating with Seniors [20%]). CSA certification is good for 3 years, during which CSAs must present a yearly recertification statement, pay the annual certification fee, and complete 30 CSA continuing education credits in courses that are directly related to seniors and ethical issues.

CORE COMPETENCIES AND SKILLS NEEDED

- Good written and communication skills
- Attentive listener
- Good interpersonal skills
- Good organizational skills
- Commitment to client-centered practice
- Ethical conduct of business/professional practice
- Competencies specific to primary professional field(s) and practice standards

COMPENSATION

This varies by the type of professional practice, educational background, experience, and geographical location.

WORKPLACE(S)

This varies by the type of professional practice.

EMPLOYMENT OUTLOOK

Moderate to high, depending on the type of professional practice.

RELATED PROFESSIONAL ORGANIZATIONS AND WEBSITES

- Society of Certified Senior Advisors: www.csa.us

CONTINUING CARE RETIREMENT COMMUNITY (CCRC) ADMINISTRATOR

LONG-TERM CARE FACILITY ADMINISTRATOR

BASIC DESCRIPTION

Administrators of residential care facilities, such as continuing care retirement communities (CCRCs) and long-term care facilities, direct or oversee all operational aspects of the facility, including personnel and labor assessment, training, human resources, and evaluation; labor union relationships; regulatory, licensure, and organizational/facility policies and procedures compliance; property assessment and management; supervision of resident care; food services; risk management; physical plant maintenance; facility/community operating systems; marketing and public relations; budget and revenue; and reporting and liaison functions with community or facility boards and corporate leadership. Administrators are also responsible for long-term strategic planning and initiatives.

EDUCATION AND EXPERIENCE REQUIREMENTS

A bachelor's degree or higher is the minimum requirement; a master's degree in health care administration, long-term care administration, hospital administration, or a closely related field is preferred. Also, a minimum of 3 to 5 years of health care administrative experience is required.

CERTIFICATION, LICENSURE, AND CONTINUING EDUCATION REQUIREMENTS

Administrators must meet nursing home administrator licensure in the state where the professional practice occurs. Continuing education may be required for licensure renewal, job tenure, or advancement.

CORE COMPETENCIES AND SKILLS NEEDED

- Understanding of long-term care market and operations
- Strong financial acumen
- Sensitive to labor issues
- Knowledge of state and federal regulations specific to type of facility
- Genuine passion for improving quality of life for older adults
- Commitment to client-centered care
- Demonstrated leadership capacity and ability
- Strong team orientation
- Demonstrated credibility, discipline, follow-through, and consistency
- Enthusiasm and energy
- Self-motivated
- Excellent oral and written communication skills
- Attentive listener
- Excellent interpersonal skills

COMPENSATION

This varies by education, experience, the nature of the employment setting, the level of responsibility within the total organization, and geographical location.

WORKPLACE(S)

These include assisted living and long-term care facilities, continuum of care communities, long-term care corporations, and dementia care units.

EMPLOYMENT OUTLOOK

Good, but may be influenced by the increasing focus on aging in place in independent living situations (such as age-friendly neighborhoods), growth of the in-home care industry, and the legislative focus on deinstitutionalization.

RELATED PROFESSIONAL ORGANIZATIONS AND WEBSITES

- Commission on Accreditation of Rehabilitation Facilities (CARF International); now includes Continuing Care Accreditation Commission (CCAC): www.carf.org

COUNTY COMMISSION ON AGING DIRECTOR

BASIC DESCRIPTION

A county commission on aging (COA) is a county-level governmental unit that is charged with providing Older Americans Act programs and services to persons who are 60 years of age and older. Although "county commission" is the commonly used term, some county units are titled differently (such as county department or bureau of aging), and some are multicounty units (such as a tri county commission on aging). Regardless of the name of the unit, the directors of units are responsible for the overall administration of the agency. They prepare and administer grants related to aging services and programs; develop and oversee the commission's budget; oversee the recruitment, hiring, supervision, evaluation, and discipline of commission employees; serve as the primary liaison to the area agency on aging and the state office on aging; and serve as the primary representative for the agency on county and state governing boards and committees. Additional responsibilities vary from one commission to another and may include working to establish and maintain a county-wide senior services millage or other local fundraising efforts, editing an agency newsletter, and other tasks related to meeting the needs of the agency's clients.

EDUCATION AND EXPERIENCE REQUIREMENTS

A master's degree in public administration, social work, gerontology, or a closely related human service field is required. Coursework or degree components in gerontology, community organization and leadership, or public administration are recommended. A minimum of 3 to 5 years of administrative leadership experience in human service field or an aging network agency is required.

CERTIFICATION, LICENSURE, AND CONTINUING EDUCATION REQUIREMENTS

None are required, but staying current is vital and can be obtained through either formal or informal continuing education.

CORE COMPETENCIES AND SKILLS NEEDED

- Ability to work with and relate to older adults, and address their needs and their concerns
- Ability to work with clients from diverse backgrounds
- Good working knowledge of the formal aging network
- Good working knowledge of regulations related to the commission's programs and services
- Ability to supervise others, including staff, volunteers, and clients
- Working knowledge of committee and board structures, functions, and processes
- Good written and oral communication skills
- Public speaking skills
- Grant writing skills
- Good financial management skills
- Good organizational skills

COMPENSATION

This varies according to one's educational background, amount of field service and administrative experience, and the geographical location.

WORKPLACE(S)

These include county or multicounty units on aging, which are usually located in the largest city within the county(ies) served.

EMPLOYMENT OUTLOOK

Good, but may be limited by the longevity of some COA directors (especially in more rural counties). Job prospects are also dependent on continued federal, state, and county funding for COAs.

RELATED PROFESSIONAL ORGANIZATIONS AND WEBSITES

- State organization for directors of services to the aging units

An Interview With CRAIG ZEESE

County Commission on Aging Director

Postsecondary educational background, including formal credentials and other education/training in gerontology/geriatrics:
Bachelor of Social Work (BSW), with Minors in Gerontology and Psychology

How and when did you first become interested in gerontology/geriatrics? I really didn't know that I was interested in working with older adults, but just by chance, I volunteered for part of a day at a local nursing home when I was in high school. This simple action made such an impact on my life that from that moment on I knew I wanted to work with senior citizens in some capacity. Early in my college career, I did more volunteer work with senior citizens, and that confirmed that I wanted to work with older adults. I found it interesting that this became my career choice because I really did not have contact with older adults in my family because all of my grandparents were deceased before I was born.

Briefly describe your gerontology/geriatrics-related career path. While attending college, I was able to obtain a wide variety of volunteer opportunities with senior citizens in several different settings. In addition, through class projects I also was exposed to the legislative process and grant writing aspects in the human service field. Having a variety of experiences allowed me to evaluate the type of gerontology setting that was best suited for me. Through my volunteer experiences, I found that I preferred to work within an agency providing services that would help keep senior citizens in their own homes. While I was a volunteer, my supervisor became the director of a county commission on aging. She was aware of my passion to work with older adults, and I had proven my abilities and work ethic as a volunteer. She hired me; I worked as a case manager for that county commission on aging for 4 years, and I thoroughly enjoyed the one-to-one experience with the clients. During that time, I also was able to take on various middle management–type responsibilities. I found that I enjoyed the challenge of the management role as long as I could still have some direct contact with older adults. I realized this could take place if I remained within a small agency. It was extremely beneficial that I was able to work on various regional planning projects involving other

(*continued*)

An Interview With CRAIG ZEESE (*continued*)

case managers and directors within our region. This allowed others to become aware of my abilities and allowed me to learn about job openings that might be of interest, including the opening for a case manager in another county commission on aging. Fortunately, I was hired for that position. I made it very clear early in my tenure with the agency that I was interested in becoming the director when the current director retired, and that is exactly what happened.

Briefly describe your current professional position:

Position title: Director of a county commission on aging

Primary role tasks/responsibilities: I administer, oversee, manage, and coordinate an agency whose major function is to provide direct services to residents throughout the county age 60 and over that allow them to remain independent and safe within their own homes. My responsibilities include developing and monitoring the agency budget, overseeing all agency programs and service, hiring and supervising all personnel, writing grants, serving as agency liaison for community projects, developing strategies to address community needs, overseeing the maintenance of necessary records for all funding sources, and reporting to the board of directors of the agency and to the county board of commissioners. One very important responsibility I have is developing and overseeing the senior millage campaign that provides the majority of the funding for the agency every 4 years.

Type of employment setting: Commission on aging (a unit of county government)

Length of time in position: 28 years

How did you first become interested in this position? While I was working as a case manager for another commission on aging, I had contact with other case managers and administrators from other counties throughout the state. One connection was with the former case manager for my current county commission on aging, and she was being promoted to be the

(*continued*)

An Interview With CRAIG ZEESE *(continued)*

director of the agency. Therefore, the agency would be hiring a new case manager to replace her. I did some homework and found that the county commission on aging was the size and type of agency that I was looking for. I also learned that the newly hired director would be retiring after a few years. I thought this would be the perfect opportunity to establish myself as a case worker and then, hopefully, be promoted into the director's position when she retired. This would not only give the board of directors and the community a chance to know my skills, but it also would give me the time to see if the agency was where I wanted to move into a permanent management position.

Describe a typical workday in your current professional position. There isn't a typical workday. In the course of a week, however, I usually spend some time on either the research and/or preparation of a grant or at least working with existing grants and the regulations associated with them; preparing and working with the agency budget and other financial matters; attending work groups, committees, boards, and community activities where representation of older adults and/or the commission on aging is needed and expected; informing elected officials, at all levels of government, of the needs and concerns of older adults; and dealing with personnel issues, such as unplanned illnesses, and trying to coordinate activities so that our services to clients are not disrupted. Work is completed weekly on articles submitted to newspapers and preparing/giving presentations in the community. I frequently meet with funding providers to work on issues at hand or with county administrators who are working on a multitude of policies that impact county government. Every day, though, there seem to be unexpected challenges that arise. It could be problems due to weather when volunteers are delivering meals or transporting clients to medical appointments. It could be an in-home service worker finding that a client has fallen and immediate medical action is necessary. It could be a mechanical problem at one of the nutrition sites, and action is required to see that the programs for the day are not canceled, or it could be a local food pantry calling to say that they have an overabundance of perishable food and they would like us to get it out to our elderly clients before it spoils. It is the unexpected situations needing immediate attention that cause the greatest stress, but

(continued)

An Interview With CRAIG ZEESE (*continued*)

in the end, more satisfaction is achieved when an unexpected problem is resolved.

What is the time commitment required of your current professional position? On average I work about 50 hours a week. There are frequent evening meetings and group presentations and, usually, some project or fundraising event, on an average of one weekend a month.

How do you stay up-to-date in your profession?

Professional organization memberships and/or activities? The only continuous and (to me) the most important gerontology group that I belong to is the State Directors of Services to the Aging, which is the best group to consult to have questions answered because the association is able to obtain information directly from state officials. Involvement in this group is also a great way to get information, share ideas, and obtain input from other directors throughout the state.

Subscribe to and/or read professional journals and/or newsletters? Within the aging network, there is a great deal of information regarding grants and other funding sources passed along through the Area Agency on Aging and the State Office of Services to the Aging. Whenever I am looking for aging information on a specific topic, I simply seek out information from journals and articles that can be found on the Internet.

Attend professional conferences and/or participate in education/training programs? I am always looking for appropriate opportunities for my staff and I to obtain good information that will help with our professional responsibilities. The State Office of Services to the Aging and the regional Area Agencies on Aging sponsor helpful trainings. I also have found it helpful to attend public speaking seminars and various management training seminars that are offered throughout the state by independent businesses.

Other? I believe it is very important to be an active participant in local, regional, and state endeavors. It allows others to realize that you are a

(*continued*)

An Interview With CRAIG ZEESE *(continued)*

team player, and you never know what contacts you will make and how they might be of assistance to you and your organization in the future.

What are the most rewarding aspects of your current career position? The most rewarding aspect of my position is knowing that because of my leadership older adults are being assisted every day in some way by a dedicated and caring staff. Hearing comments from clients and their families as to how helpful our agency is or has been to them makes the job all worthwhile. Knowing that we are able to make a difference in individuals' lives and help to keep them independent and in their own homes is very rewarding.

What is the most rewarding aspect of your gerontology/geriatrics-related career path? Over the decades of working with older adults, I believe I have gained a greater appreciation of their accomplishments, not only as individuals, but as a generation. By accomplishments, I mean the extremely hard, physical work older adults had to do and the stress they endured when they were younger. They lived through some very tough times. I have visited with many who lived through the Great Depression and became stronger and more independent because of it. Their sense of pride and respect for others is unmatched, and I believe I am a better person because I have learned and continue to learn from those who are much wiser and more experienced than I.

What are the most challenging aspects of your current career position? One of the most challenging aspects is trying to figure out what is the best way to educate and influence the elected officials who make the financial decisions about the allocation of government funds for programs and services for older adults. Another challenge is trying to educate younger people, to enlighten them regarding how their actions and behaviors of today will influence how they age physically and their outlook on aging.

What are the most challenging aspects of your gerontology/geriatrics-related career path? I would have to say what *was* my most challenging aspect when choosing gerontology as a career was the fact that I was young. Clients would look at me and wonder how I could help them

(continued)

An Interview With CRAIG ZEESE *(continued)*

because I was so much younger than they were, and I certainly could understand their concern. What I could offer to them was my knowledge of resources and options.

How do you balance career and other aspects of your life? It is extremely important to balance my family life and career. First, it is okay to say "no" to some projects, but I do believe it is important to be active with civic groups and community organizations. I try to volunteer, as time permits, for various functions and exercise several hours a week. There are several community groups that I belong to, and while not intended, it is amazing how those social contacts can come back to reward the agency.

What advice do you have for someone contemplating a career in the field of aging? Complete as much volunteer work as you can, even if it is not aging related, so it can be placed on your resumé. Even more importantly, any contact you have with older adults will help you decide if gerontology is the best career choice for you. Get honest feedback from others who know you to see if they agree that you would be good working with older adults.

What advice do you have for someone considering a professional position similar to your current position? Work as a staff member first, preferably in a casework-type setting or direct care aide position to obtain more practical experience, and then work your way up the ladder into administration. This is the only way you can have an appreciation of what others do and to earn the respect that is so important, not only from the staff, but from clients and community members. Make sure you are comfortable speaking in front of groups and are willing to be a team player with other community organizations.

DANCE/MOVEMENT THERAPIST (DMT)

REGISTERED DANCE/MOVEMENT THERAPIST (R-DMT)

BOARD CERTIFIED DANCE/MOVEMENT THERAPIST (BC-DMT)

BASIC DESCRIPTION

Dance/movement therapy (DMT) is the psychotherapeutic use of dance and movement as a process and tool to assist and support integration of an individual's physical, cognitive, emotional, and social aspects of life. DMT is one of several creative arts therapies used with older adults to help improve their self-esteem, body image, balance, communication, and relationships; gain new insights into both positive and negative behaviors; and cope with the problems they face in one or more aspects of their lives. DMTs use movement expressed through dance as an observational and assessment tool and as a therapeutic and intervention process. Use of the language of the body—not just verbal communication—is a unique asset of DMTs. They usually work with both individual clients and groups.

EDUCATION AND EXPERIENCE REQUIREMENTS

A master's degree in dance/movement therapy from an American Dance Therapy Association (ADTA)-approved program is required. Graduate students accepted for a DMT master's program usually have a bachelor's degree in liberal arts, extensive dance experience, and some coursework in psychology. Gerontology coursework or a degree component is encouraged for those who intend to work primarily with older adult clients.

CERTIFICATION, LICENSURE, AND CONTINUING EDUCATION REQUIREMENTS

Registered Dance/Movement Therapist (R-DMT) is the basic level of preparedness and competence to be employed in an educational or clinical setting. R-DMT status can be obtained by completing a graduate degree in dance/movement therapy from an ADTA-approved graduate program and completion of the R-DMT Application for Approved Program Applicant. An alternative is to earn a master's degree from an accredited institution of higher education and complete specific general training in dance/movement therapy coursework, a fieldwork experience, and a DMT internship. To maintain their registration, R-DMTs must complete 50 clock hours of continuing education every 5 years. Earning the Board Certified Dance/Movement Therapy (BC-DMT) credential recognizes attainment of an advanced level of practice and preparedness to engage in private practice, offer training, and provide supervision. Recertification requires 100 clock hours of continuing education every 5 years.

CORE COMPETENCIES AND SKILLS NEEDED

- Working knowledge of aging processes and how they impact the body's ability to move
- Working knowledge of psychotherapeutic, counseling, and rehabilitation interventions and strategies
- Self-discipline
- Good interpersonal skills
- Good observation and assessment skills specific to dance/movement therapy
- Physically and emotionally fit

COMPENSATION

This varies by one's education, experience, level of registration, or certification and the nature of the workplace.

WORKPLACE(S)

These include long-term care and assisted living facilities, hospitals/medical centers, wellness centers, alternative health care centers and programs, substance abuse and chemical dependency treatment facilities and centers, counseling centers, senior centers, retirement communities and residences, crisis centers, and medical and psychiatric rehabilitation centers.

EMPLOYMENT OUTLOOK

Limited, primarily due to a limited number of ADTA-approved master's degree programs (only five programs currently exist at colleges in Colorado, Illinois, New Hampshire, New York, and Pennsylvania). This outlook may be improved by increased interest in wellness and fitness among persons now entering elderhood.

RELATED PROFESSIONAL ORGANIZATIONS AND WEBSITES

- American Dance Therapy Association (ADTA): www.adta.org
- Dance/Movement Therapy Certification Board (DMTCB): www.adta.org/DMTCB
- Marian Chace Foundation of the American Dance Therapy Association: www.adta.org/Marian_Chace_Foundation
- National Coalition of Creative Arts Therapies Associations (NCCATA): www.nccata.org

DRAMA THERAPIST

REGISTERED DRAMA THERAPIST (RDT)

BOARD CERTIFIED TRAINER (BCT)

BASIC DESCRIPTION

Drama therapists and registered drama therapists (RDTs) intentionally employ the processes of drama or theater (e.g., improvisation, storytelling or enactment, theater games, puppetry, role-playing, pantomime, mask work, theatrical production) to help their clients and patients meet individual or group therapeutic goals. To identify appropriate prevention, intervention, and treatment goals, they first assess clients' needs. Next, they devise a plan of action and use appropriate strategies to help their clients build interpersonal and personal skills, change negative or inappropriate behaviors, integrate their physical and emotional selves, and achieve personal mental and emotional growth. Text (e.g., literary dialogues, poetry, play scripts), performance, and ritual are among the "tools of the trade" used by drama therapists. Also, drama therapists sometimes work collaboratively with professionals from other creative arts (e.g., music, dance/movement, art therapy) to facilitate positive outcomes for their clients. Board certified trainers (BCTs) are RDTs who work as clinicians, trainers, supervisors, and teachers.

EDUCATION AND EXPERIENCE REQUIREMENTS

Becoming a RDT requires a master's or doctoral degree in drama therapy from a program accredited by the North American Drama Therapy Association (NADTA). An alternate route to registration requires a master's or doctoral degree in a field related to drama therapy (e.g., drama/theater, psychology, counseling, social work, occupational therapy, recreational therapy, art therapy, music therapy, dance/movement therapy) from an accredited college/university, completion of Alternative Training Education requirements under the supervision of a RDT or board certified drama trainer (BCT), a drama therapy internship, and additional work/training experience. BCTs are members of the NADTA faculty who have worked in the field for at least 5 years and have mentoring experience.

CERTIFICATION, LICENSURE, AND CONTINUING EDUCATION REQUIREMENTS

Licensure is required in some states, especially for RDTs who practice in health care and mental health settings. RDTs must complete 30 hours of continuing education within every 2-year cycle. BCTs must provide proof of attendance at a BCT training or NADTA-sponsored meeting at least once in every 2-year cycle.

CORE COMPETENCIES AND SKILLS NEEDED

- Expertise in dramatic, theatrical, and performance media
- Demonstrated competence in use of an array of drama/theater processes with diverse clients
- Understanding of psychotherapeutic processes with different populations in a variety of settings
- Knowledge of theories related to personality and group processes
- Experience with integration of the artistic and psychological aspects of drama therapy
- Commitment to patient-centered care
- Excellent interpersonal and communication skills
- Ability to be creative and innovative
- Ability to blend verbal and nonverbal components of drama therapy
- Ability to involve sometimes reluctant participants in therapy processes

COMPENSATION

This varies by education, experience, registration as an RDT or certification as a BCT, type of professional practice, and the nature of the employment setting. Some positions may be part time and wage based or on a contractual fee-for-service basis.

WORKPLACE(S)

These include mental health facilities, hospitals, rehabilitation programs, private practice clinics, medical programs (e.g., chronic pain, cancer,

HIV/AIDS), substance abuse treatment centers, adult daycare/service centers, correctional facilities, shelters, long-term care and assisted living facilities, corporations, theaters, housing projects, medical schools, training organizations, memory loss/dementia care programs and residential settings, senior centers, and other organizations or programs for older adults.

EMPLOYMENT OUTLOOK

Limited, partially due to only a few NADTA-accredited degree programs, but the potential for improvement exists with the anticipated growth in the older adult population and as elders become more comfortable with seeking or accepting therapeutic intervention and treatment.

RELATED PROFESSIONAL ORGANIZATIONS AND WEBSITES

- North American Drama Therapy Association (NADTA): www.nadta.org
- National Coalition of Creative Arts Therapies Association (NCCATA): ww.nccata.org
- The Drama Therapy Fund: www.dramatherapyfund.org
- American Society of Group Psychotherapy and Psychodrama (ASGPP): www.asgpp.org
- American Board of Examiners in Psychodrama, Sociometry and Group Psychotherapy: www.psychodramacertification.org

DRIVER REHABILITATION SPECIALIST (DRS)

CERTIFIED DRIVER REHABILITATION SPECIALIST (CDRS)

BASIC DESCRIPTION

Driver rehabilitation specialists (DRS) are health care and/or driver education professionals with added training/education who help individuals and their families adjust to driving challenges and explore alternative transportation solutions. They provide driver rehabilitation services for individuals who are disabled but are still able to drive if appropriate rehabilitation, equipment, and support are made available. A DRS first does clinical (predriving) evaluations and/or behind-the-wheel driving evaluations before developing and implementing a driving rehabilitation or mobility intervention plan specific to the client's needs. This plan may include recommendations for adaptive equipment, counseling related to a transitional return to driving, training toward the goal of driving independence, or identification of alternative transportation programs. The Association of Driving Rehabilitation Specialists (ADED) currently is the credentialing agency. While driver rehabilitation specialists come from many professional fields, many are occupational therapists. The American Occupational Therapy Association (AOTA) offers a Specialty Certificate in Driving and Community Mobility to occupational therapists (OTs) and occupational therapy assistants (OTAs) who meet certification eligibility requirements.

EDUCATION AND EXPERIENCE REQUIREMENTS

Candidates are eligible for the Driver Rehabilitation Specialist Certification (CDRS) exam if they meet one of the following educational and/or experience requirements specified by the ADED:

- Undergraduate degree or higher in a health-related field,[1] plus 1 year of full-time work experience in the degree field and 1 additional year of full-time work experience in driver rehabilitation
- Four-year undergraduate degree or higher, with a major or minor in traffic safety and/or driver and traffic safety endorsement, plus 1 year full-time of work experience in traffic safety and 2 additional years of full-time work experience in driver rehabilitation
- Two-year degree in a health-related field,[1] with 1 year full-time work experience in the degree field and 3 additional years of full-time work experience in driver rehabilitation
- Five years of full-time work experience in the field of driver rehabilitation

CERTIFICATION, LICENSURE, AND CONTINUING EDUCATION REQUIREMENTS

DRS certification good for 3 years is granted to candidates who meet specified education and/or work experience requirements, pay the required examination and application processing fees, and pass the CDRS exam. Recertification is based on the accumulation of continuing education credits (points) for approved professional activities. Candidates must possess a valid driver's license in the state where the practice occurs.

CORE COMPETENCIES AND SKILLS NEEDED

- Excellent personal driving skills
- Knowledge of relevant state laws

---

[1]Health-related fields include occupational therapy, physical therapy, kinesiotherapy, speech therapy, therapeutic recreation, or other fields approved by the ADED Certification Committee.

- Good written and oral communication skills
- Knowledge of and competence in administering the required clinical and behind the wheel driving evaluations
- Understanding of the various disabilities experienced by clients
- Good teaching and training skills
- Patience

COMPENSATION

This varies by the type of professional practice, the nature of the workplace and employing agency, one's educational background, the amount and type of work experience, and the geographical location.

WORKPLACE(S)

These include rehabilitation clinics, hospitals/medical centers, organizations that offer driver retraining programs (e.g., AARP's 55 and Alive program), state departments of motor vehicles, and senior centers.

EMPLOYMENT OUTLOOK

Good, with increasing opportunities as governmental programs are made available to meet the mobility and transportation needs of the rapidly growing older adult population.

RELATED PROFESSIONAL ORGANIZATIONS AND WEBSITES

- The Association for Driver Rehabilitation Specialists (ADED): www.driver-ed.org
- American Occupational Therapy Association (AOTA): www.aota.org
- AOTA Driving and Community Mobility Specialists: www.aota.org/Practice/Productive-aging/Driving.aspx

EDUCATIONAL GERONTOLOGIST

GERONTOLOGY EDUCATOR

BASIC DESCRIPTION

Education about elders, education for elders, and education by elders is how Howard Y. McClusky defined educational gerontology, the field for which he is considered to be the founding father. From this perspective, educational gerontologists would include gerontology and geriatrics program administrators and faculty members in higher education, administrators and facilitators of older learner programs in a variety of settings, and older adults who serve as teachers and facilitators of learning for other older adults. From an academic perspective, an educational gerontologist most likely would be someone who has earned a degree in educational gerontology, even though there currently are no degree programs in educational gerontology. An alternative, however, does exist in one gerontology doctoral program. Recognizing that many of their graduates would become classroom instructors, those who designed the curriculum for this degree program built in a teaching seminar in gerontology and a teaching practicum in gerontology. Most of those in academe who teach about aging and administer gerontology programs come from a vast array of disciplines and professional fields where the focus is on what to learn/teach rather than on how to learn/teach it. Because of this, the label of gerontology educator may seem more appropriate. Regardless of their educational backgrounds, gerontology educators develop, implement, and evaluate educational programs, courses, and other learning experiences about aging in a wide variety of settings. They prepare educational materials about aging and older adults (e.g., textbooks, professional handbooks, and encyclopedias, journal articles, print materials for consumption by the general public, educational films, and other audiovisual teaching/learning tools). Some gerontology educators are theorists and researchers who work to better understand adult learning processes and to develop curriculum models and methodologies that are appropriate for adult and older adult learners.

EDUCATION AND EXPERIENCE REQUIREMENTS

These vary by the type of position and the nature of the employment setting. For most administrative and teaching positions at colleges, universities, and professional schools (e.g., medical schools), a doctoral degree in a discipline (e.g., anthropology, sociology, psychology, biology) or in a professional field (e.g., social work, geriatric medicine, nursing, physical or occupational therapy, interior design, family studies, gerontology) is required. For teaching at community colleges, a minimum of a master's degree is required, although doctoral-level preparation is increasingly preferred.

CERTIFICATION, LICENSURE, AND CONTINUING EDUCATION REQUIREMENTS

Currently, educational gerontologists/gerontology educators in higher education have no certification or licensure requirements, although they must meet employment standards and requirements related to reappointment, tenure, and promotion or advancement from teaching to administrative positions. These requirements may vary across academic departments and other units within the same institution of higher learning and from one college/university to another.

CORE COMPETENCIES AND SKILLS NEEDED

- Updated understanding of research-based knowledge about aging processes and the elderly population
- Specialized education and/or training in subject matter to be taught
- Good working knowledge of learning and/or adult learning theories and methodologies
- Demonstrated ability to develop, implement and evaluate appropriate curriculum design and methodologies
- Demonstrated ability to facilitate learning for learners from a variety of backgrounds and with varying interest in specific courses and course content
- Good working knowledge of research design and methodology
- Familiarity with relevant professional resources
- Good interpersonal skills
- Excellent communication skills (written, oral, listening)
- Working knowledge of the process of preparing grant applications in support of research studies and academic projects is increasingly important

COMPENSATION

This varies by education, experience, type of position, level of responsibility, nature of the employment setting, and the geographical location. Some positions are part time and may be paid by hourly wage or per credit hour taught rather than by salary with a benefit package.

WORKPLACE(S)

These include community colleges, colleges, universities, professional schools; geriatric education centers; institutes for learning in retirement and other older learner programs; visiting professor and adjunct teaching positions in higher education; and consulting opportunities in corporate and other noneducational settings.

EMPLOYMENT OUTLOOK

Varies, usually related to the stability of the gerontology/geriatric education program(s) within a given institution of higher education. It is thought that several factors—the potential of accreditation for gerontology programs, the anticipated rapid growth of the older population, retirement of long-term faculty members, the expanding number of venues for older learner programs and educational services for older persons—will improve the employment outlook for educational gerontologists/gerontology educators.

RELATED PROFESSIONAL ORGANIZATIONS AND WEBSITES

- Association for Gerontology in Higher Education (AGHE): www.aghe.org
- Gerontological Society of America (GSA): www.geron.org
- American Association for Adult and Continuing Education (AAACE): www.aaace.org
- Lifetime Education and Renewal Network (LEARN), American Society on Aging (ASA): www.asaging.org/learn

An Interview With MICHAEL A. FABER

Gerontology Educator
Higher Education: Community College

Postsecondary educational background, including formal credentials and other education/training in gerontology/geriatrics:

AA, Social Science
BS, Gerontology
MA, Sociology, specializing in Aging and the Life Course
Certificate in Mental Health and Aging
Fellow in Gerontology/Geriatrics, Association for Gerontology in Higher Education (AGHE)
Licensed Bachelor's Social Worker (licensed by state)

How and when did you first become interested in gerontology/geriatrics? Like most freshmen, my first year of college was a time of exploration and discernment. I knew that I wanted to do something with people, perhaps teaching, but had no clear direction. That is, until one day in a health education class when the graduate assistant teaching the course mentioned something to do with aging that caught my attention and prompted me to have a conversation with him after class. In this conversation, I asked if there was any type of job working with older people and that was when I first learned about gerontology. The next semester, I took my first gerontology course and I never looked back. I had found my passion—what I was born to do. I think the positive experiences that I had with older people earlier in my life helped to set the stage for this decision. This included positive experiences with my grandparents and also the job of delivering daily newspapers in a subsidized senior apartment complex. This paper route was considered a sweet assignment since one could deliver all of the papers in 15 minutes or less. However, it took me nearly 3 hours to complete the route each day. I loved spending time with the seniors who lived there—hearing their stories and enjoying all the wonderful milk and cookies.

Briefly describe your gerontology/geriatrics-related career path. Knowing early in my college experience that gerontology was the career path for me, I was able to begin my career by working as a home health care aide while I was still in college. As a professional caregiver, I had

(*continued*)

An Interview With MICHAEL A. FABER *(continued)*

the privilege of working with frail, homebound, and terminally ill older adults in their own homes. After completing graduate school, my first job was working for a county-based council on aging to provide case coordination and support to frail, homebound seniors. This job was followed by a position as a long-term care ombudsman, advocating for the needs and rights of nursing home residents within a nine-county region. I completed my first decade in the field of aging as a dementia specialist working to support and educate families caring for loved ones with Alzheimer's disease and related forms of dementia. For the past 16 years, I have held my dream job as a gerontology educator at the local community college.

Briefly describe your current professional position:

Position title: Associate Director, Older Learner Center, and Adjunct Instructor of Gerontology

Primary role tasks/responsibilities: Like many professionals today, I wear many different hats. As a full-time administrator, I am responsible for the development and implementation of a nationally recognized Older Learner Center. In this capacity, I provide staff supervision and oversee the daily operations of the center, administer a number of grant-funded initiatives, oversee program budgets, write grant proposals and report on grant projects, and coordinate a wide variety of community-based educational outreach activities. I also develop, coordinate, facilitate, market, and implement a number of noncredit life enrichment and educational outreach programs for older persons, their families, and caregivers. I also do those same functions for the continuing education training we provide for professionals working in the field of aging. As a part-time adjunct instructor, I am responsible for curriculum development, classroom instruction and student evaluation for the 32-credit undergraduate gerontology certificate program that I developed.

Type of employment setting: Community college

Length of time in this position: 16 years

(continued)

An Interview With MICHAEL A. FABER *(continued)*

How did you first become interested in this position? I have always been interested in the teaching aspect of gerontology. In every position I have held, there have been opportunities for either one-on-one or group education/teaching, and I always have enjoyed this component of my work. There also has been some type of administrative program development and implementation component that interested me. My current administrative position with the Older Learner Center did not exist prior to my employment at the college; it was an opportunity made available to me by a former gerontology instructor at a time when my grant-funded position with the local aging network was eliminated. This is a perfect example of why it is important to network and maintain past educational and professional connections. In my case, it resulted in the perfect position to complement my education, knowledge, skills, and interests.

Describe a typical workday in your current professional position. Although each day is different, a typical workday may include activities related to program development, marketing, facilitation, evaluation, and/or reporting. This requires fielding frequent phone calls and e-mail messages, supervising staff, attending and/or facilitating planning meetings, and other administrative activities. On the days that I teach, my work also includes curriculum review/development, preparation of classroom activities, interaction with students, and classroom instruction.

What is the time commitment required of your current professional position? My full-time administrative position requires an average of 40 to 50 hours per week. This work is primarily limited to Monday through Friday during daytime hours ranging from 7 a.m. to 6 p.m. My part-time adjunct instruction occurs two evenings per week during each fall and spring term and, with preparation and grading, adds approximately 10 to 15 additional hours to my average work week.

How do you stay up-to-date in your profession?

Professional organization memberships and/or activities? Association for Gerontology in Higher Education (AGHE), Institutional Member

(continued)

An Interview With MICHAEL A. FABER (*continued*)

Representative; I also have served as chair/tri-chair of the Community College Task Force/Standing Committee, on the Membership Committee, and as an Associate Editor of the *AGHExchange*.

Subscribe to and/or read professional journals and/or newsletters? The *AGHExchange* (professional newsletter) is a very useful resource in staying up-to-date on educational gerontology. I also enjoy reading the *Teaching Gerontology Newsletter* (monthly e-newsletter published through AARP's Office of Academic Affairs).

Attend professional conferences and/or participate in education/training programs? The conference that I find most useful for networking, information sharing, and learning related to classroom-based gerontology instruction is the AGHE Annual Meeting and Educational Leadership Conference. I highly recommend AGHE Institutional Membership and participation in the annual conference for anyone involved in educational gerontology.

What are the most rewarding aspects of your current career position? There are many things that I find rewarding about my current position. Sometimes I am just amazed at the fact that I get paid for doing what I love to do. I find the creative aspects of my work especially rewarding. In this respect, I love to develop innovative new programs and services, encourage and sustain community-wide collaboration, and inspire students' interest and passion in the field of gerontology.

What are the most rewarding aspects of your gerontology/geriatrics-related career path? One of the aspects of gerontology that has always been attractive to me is the fact that it is still a relatively new and evolving field where one can be a trailblazing pioneer. Being free to think outside the box, dream, and create your own career path has always been rewarding to me. Whenever someone has said to me "You can't do that," I have always responded, "Why not?" I truly believe that where there is a will, there is a way, and I find it very rewarding and satisfying to be able to overcome obstacles and make new and exciting things happen.

(*continued*)

An Interview With MICHAEL A. FABER *(continued)*

What are the most challenging aspects of your current career position? Finances and budget development are definitely the most challenging aspects of my current position. Unfortunately, public and private funding of programs and services geared to older persons is limited. The need is great and ever-growing at a time when funding options and levels are decreasing. In this respect, programs serving older adults are asked to do more and more with less and less funding to support this important work.

What are the most challenging aspects of your gerontology/geriatrics-related career path? I believe that one of the most challenging aspects related to educational gerontology as a career path is the fact that there are fewer college- and university-based gerontology programs today than there were in the 1970s and 1980s. This trend really makes no sense based on the rapidly increasing aging demographics driven by the baby boomer and centenarian populations. Unfortunately, many of these gerontology programs also lack institutional support and are championed by only one or two passionate individuals and, all too often, are no longer sustained when something happens to these key individuals.

How do you balance career and other aspects of your life? It isn't always easy, and unfortunately, I haven't always been successful in doing so. I think that when you are passionate about what you do, it is very easy to get overly absorbed in your work. To the detriment of my wife and family, this is what happened to me. Only in recent years have I come to realize and regret the extent to which I have wounded my wife and children by not having my priorities straight. Certainly, it is okay to be passionate about what you do, but not to the extent that your work and home life are not in balance. I now work to create this balance by limiting my work hours in order to be home with my family on the evenings that I do not teach and by better managing my work schedule so that I do not exhaust myself physically or mentally before it is time to leave for home. This new balance priority is probably best summed up by a small note that I now keep fixed to my computer monitor visibly reminding me to "Save some for Home." It took me a lot of years to learn this lesson, and so I now try to pass this advice on to my students whenever possible.

(continued)

An Interview With MICHAEL A. FABER (*continued*)

What advice do you have for someone contemplating a career in the field of aging? Choose to pursue a career in aging based on genuine interest and passion for improving the lives and condition of older persons. If you are uncertain of this passion, I recommend that you take an introductory gerontology course, do informational interviews with those working in the field, and volunteer to work with older persons to check out your interest and passion level. Although very few people get rich working in the field of aging, many, including myself, find personal and social satisfaction in this important work.

What advice do you have for someone considering a professional position similar to your current position? Meet with and job shadow someone already working as a gerontology educator and/or program administrator. As you pursue your education, take every opportunity to connect with your professors and network with other professionals in the field of aging. The single most helpful thing to my entry into the field of educational gerontology was the relationships that I had established and maintained with my former gerontology professors and the connections that I had made throughout the years within the local aging services network.

An Interview With LISA M. CURCH

Educational Gerontologist
Higher Education: University

Postsecondary educational background, including formal credentials and other education/training in gerontology:
BA, Psychology
MA, Gerontology
PhD, Gerontology

How and when did you first become interested in gerontology/geriatrics? The focus of my BA in psychology was child psychology, and I intended to work with children. I moved back to where I am originally from, got married, and procured a job at a preschool. I started out as an assistant but soon got my own classroom with young toddlers, ages 18 to 24 months. After a year, I realized that early childhood education was not for me, and I was not particularly interested in other child-related work possibilities. So I once again turned to my old friend higher education. I looked into graduate school at a university that was within commuting distance for me. I initially looked at psychology programs, but I had received information about all available graduate programs, and a master's program in gerontology caught my eye. After conferring with my husband and getting more information about the program, we decided I would go back to school and try gerontology. It seemed a practical thing to do. After all, we lived in a retirement town, and certainly, I could find a good job there with a degree in the field of aging. It also resounded with me on a personal level; my grandmothers and great aunt had always been important role models for me. Plus, I had always liked school. It turned out that I loved to study aging.

Briefly describe your gerontology/geriatrics-related career path. The master's program in gerontology culminated in a semester-long, 40-hour-per-week internship in the gerontology department of the local public hospital. My responsibilities included shadowing the department manager and other department personnel, representing the department at hospital and community meetings/events, providing administrative assistance, attending hospital training seminars, exploring community resources for older adults, and providing community education and

(*continued*)

An Interview With LISA M. CURCH *(continued)*

service. Within 2 weeks of graduation, I was hired as the admission and marketing director for a nursing and rehabilitation health care facility. About 6 months later, dissatisfaction with the job led me to reconsider my career goals. This time, I seriously considered what I enjoyed doing in life and how I could integrate that with my interest in aging and older adults. The one thing I always enjoyed was education. I enjoyed being a student, but I also found through community education projects during my internship and my job at the nursing home that I also enjoyed educating. So, I decided that academics would be my goal. I applied and was accepted into the second cohort of students for the university's new PhD program in gerontology. Throughout my time there, I knew that getting an academic position was my goal, and through participation in the Preparing Future Faculty program, I knew that a position at a teaching-oriented college or university was my ultimate goal. I even took some courses on college teaching, had a graduate assistantship at the university's Teaching and Learning Center, and taught two undergraduate courses in aging. When I began the job search process, I found my forthcoming degree in gerontology to be an advantage in that a number of different types of departments and programs were looking for experts in aging (though, admittedly, there was some proving of myself because gerontology is a degree in a nontraditional discipline). It provided me flexibility in that sense and I also knew that should I come up empty-handed in the education arena, there were other positions in research and administration that I could apply for. Fortunately, I was invited to interview at three different schools whose emphasis was on teaching. I accepted a position as assistant professor in sociology at a state college, where I would teach courses in aging, life course, and medical sociology.

Briefly describe your current professional position:

Position title: Chair and Associate Professor of Sociology

Primary role tasks/responsibilities: Teaching: The teaching load is 21 credit hours (about seven courses, with four one semester and three in the other), but as department chair, I get course reductions due to the added

(continued)

An Interview With LISA M. CURCH (*continued*)

responsibilities and teach nine credit hours (three courses) per academic year. In addition to Introduction to Sociology, I teach courses on social aspects of aging, health, policy, and social psychology. This includes courses such as Aging, Generations and Society, Sociology of Aging and Health, Sociology of Death and Dying, Society and the Individual, and Social Policy and Life Course Studies. Administration: As department chair, my many and varied tasks include facilitating curriculum development; overseeing departmental assessment activities; course scheduling; student advising; responding to student issues/requests (e.g., requests for transfer credit reevaluation, course waivers); reviewing/approving faculty-supervised student projects (e.g., internships, assistantships, and independent studies); reviewing/approving faculty requests (e.g., travel); preparing reports; administering the budget; facilitating personnel actions; managing the office, staff, and facilities; facilitating information flow at various levels; representing the department at various college meetings and functions; being a department liaison to administration; and communicating with prospective students and parents.

Type of employment setting: A mid-sized public college that is part of a state higher education system

Length of time in this position: Chair, 2 years; professor, 12 years

How did you first become interested in this position? I had served as interim department chair for one semester while the regular chair was on sabbatical and thought then that I would serve, at some future time, as the department chair (if elected). It seemed a dutiful way to serve the department, and I also felt I had skills and talents that could contribute to the department's welfare. I am organized and good at developing structures/systems; I thought I could help make a difference in department operations. Then, 2 years ago, my time to be elected chair arrived.

Describe a typical workday in your current professional position. A typical day starts anywhere from 7:30 a.m. to 9:00 a.m., depending on whether there are early meetings. I usually start with checking e-mail and

(*continued*)

An Interview With LISA M. CURCH *(continued)*

responding to issues that I can do quickly, prioritizing responses to students first. How the day goes from there can be quite variable. Days tend to be fragmented, first tending to any "fires" that have to be immediately addressed (e.g., the part-time faculty were mistakenly locked out from their e-mail accounts), working on tasks that have imminent deadlines (e.g., the next semester's course schedule), dealing with constant interruptions from staff (e.g., need to sign paperwork), faculty (e.g., questions about whether the budget has money for some equipment), and students (e.g., questions about course credit, internships, graduation), and in between, working as I can on longer term tasks (e.g., the self-study for a program review). There are usually meetings throughout the day; these can include individual meetings with students and faculty, department meetings, divisional meetings with other chairs and the dean, academic affairs meetings, and college committee meetings. Occasionally, there are meetings with prospective students and parents. I also teach one or two courses a semester, so the day might also include a class (which means I also spend time on course preparation and grading). A little bit of time might be spent on professional obligations (e.g., professional committees, conference calls). Meanwhile, the e-mail inbox constantly fills!

What is the time commitment required of your current professional position? On average, I work about 38 hours a week (about 30 hours in office and 8 hours at home). I have lots of autonomy regarding my work schedule, although I try to structure my work time to help establish boundaries and keep it from overtaking my life. Generally speaking, I work roughly 8:30 a.m. to 4:30 p.m., 4 days a week, plus 1 day working from home. On occasion, I work a little in the evening (mainly checking e-mail) or on weekends.

How do you stay up-to-date in your profession?

Professional organization membership and/or activities?
Gerontological Society of America (GSA), Member
Association for Gerontology in Higher Education, Institutional Representative; Immediate Past Editor, *AGHExchange*; Publications

(continued)

An Interview With LISA M. CURCH *(continued)*

and Resources Committee Member State Society on Aging (SSA), newly involved Member; Visions Task Force Member
Sigma Phi Omega, Gerontology National Honor Society, Member

Subscribe to and/or read professional journals and/or newsletters? I find the following publications to be very helpful: *The Gerontologist, Journals of Gerontology: Series B* (psychological and social sciences), and *AGHExchange*.

Attend professional conferences and/or participate in education/training programs?
AGHE Annual Educational Conference and Business Meeting, attend regularly
GSA Annual Scientific Research Meeting, sometimes attend
SSA Annual Meeting, regularly attend

Other? I also try to keep up by reading relevant news items in newspapers and credible websites.

What are the most rewarding aspects of your current career position? I get to work with students (mostly young adults, but a few are middle-aged) who are just starting to explore the possibilities of study and work in gerontology and are excited about it. That I can in some way contribute to their futures and improve the quality of life for the elders they work with or on behalf of is rewarding. I also find it very rewarding when I get students taking a course on aging who are in other fields but discover there is a lot to the field that it is much more interesting than they ever thought! What they learn can be taken with them into their careers and personal lives.

What are the most rewarding aspects of your gerontology/geriatrics-related career path? Over the years I have met so many interesting people—young, middle-aged, and old alike—who have a common interest in aging and in furthering the field in some way. It is encouraging and motivating!

(continued)

An Interview With LISA M. CURCH *(continued)*

What are the most challenging aspects of your current career position? Because things are always evolving in the aging field, keeping current can be a challenge, but it is necessary when you teach and do research. Also, moving into an administrative position reduces time available to spend on teaching, research, and professional development, and this is a real challenge. I have to really manage my time and priorities in a different way.

What are the most challenging aspects of your gerontology/geriatrics-related career path? It was very challenging to work in a nursing home, but I believe the experience was worth the stress. In addition to learning a lot, it helped me figure out what I really did want to do. While I like having many options in this field, it also was difficult for me to identify the particular direction to go. While getting a PhD in gerontology, I knew that I wanted to work in academia, but being in an interdisciplinary field meant that finding an academic "home" was not as easy.

How do you balance career and other aspects of your life? It takes a conscious effort because it's easy for career to take over. Keeping to a structured work schedule is one way to make sure that I make time for other aspects of my life. I also have a great, supportive spouse who, among his many contributions to our lives, regularly reminds me of the need to take time for him and for myself (which I also schedule!). I remind myself that while my career is important, there are other things in life that are also important to me, are worth my time, and help me to keep my sanity.

What advice do you have for someone contemplating a career in the field of aging? There is a wide range of options in the field, so you need to research those options and the requirements for each position (e.g., education, training, experience). Also think about whether you want to work directly with older adults or on behalf of older adults. Getting experience in the areas you are considering, even if it just to shadow or interview someone who works in the particular area or position, gives you a good idea of the day-to-day aspects of the job, which is as important to understand as the overall purpose of the job and its role in the field of aging

(continued)

An Interview With LISA M. CURCH *(continued)*

and society. That understanding also should inform your decision about a career direction to pursue.

What advice do you have for someone considering a professional position similar to your current position? Being a professor is a great job, but not all professor jobs are the same. You need to know whether you want to be involved primarily in teaching or research. Almost all professor positions will involve both, but the emphasis is usually on one over the other. If you end up at a teaching institution, be sure that you really like to teach and interact with students. If your preference is to do research, you will not be as happy at a teaching institution. You also have to be willing to invest the time and effort, as most full-time professor positions require a PhD. To get to be a faculty member at a college/university, you should enjoy being a student. Being a department chair is an administrative position, and not everyone is suited for such positions. It requires doing much more paperwork and being in more meetings than being a regular faculty member. It requires working with people and data and being an analyst, manager, leader, and diplomat. You have to be organized and familiar with policies and procedures. You get to make a difference and have a positive impact on your department, department faculty, and students, but you do not have as much time for teaching and research.

ELDER LAW ATTORNEY

CERTIFIED ELDER LAW ATTORNEY

ELDER CARE ATTORNEY

BASIC DESCRIPTION

Elder law attorneys specialize in the practice of law related to legal matters of specific concern to older/elderly persons, their families, caregivers, and legal representatives. These law matters include health and personal care planning; pre-mortem legal planning; fiduciary representation; legal capacity counseling; public benefits advice; advice on insurance matters; resident rights advocacy; housing counseling; employment and retirement advice; income, estate, and gift tax advice; public benefits advice; counseling related to age or disability discrimination in employment and housing; and litigation and administrative advocacy. A certified elder law attorney has enhanced knowledge, skills, experience, and proficiency in elder law practice and has met the requirements for certification set out by the National Elder Law Foundation (NELF). Certification, however, is voluntary and is not required for an attorney to practice elder law. An elder law attorney who specializes in matters specific to the care of elders who are at risk due to physical and/or mental frailty may prefer to be called an elder care attorney.

EDUCATION AND EXPERIENCE REQUIREMENTS

This profession requires a law degree (JD) and coursework specific to the field and practice of elder law. Gerontology coursework is strongly recommended in an undergraduate degree or as continuing education addition to the law degree.

CERTIFICATION, LICENSURE, AND CONTINUING EDUCATION REQUIREMENTS

To become a certified elder law attorney, a candidate must be licensed to practice law in at least one state or the District of Columbia, have practiced law for the 5 years immediately prior to application for certification, be a member in good standing with the bars in all states where he or she is licensed, have averaged at least 16 hours per week in elder law practice, have handled at least 60 elder law matters during each of the 3 years immediately prior to application, have participated in at least 45 hours of continuing legal education in elder law during the preceding 3 years, submit 5 references from attorneys who can attest to his or her competence and qualifications in elder law, and sit for the certification examination within 2 years of filing the certification application. Certification is good for 5 years. Recertification requires the candidate to meet the same standards required for the original certification.

CORE COMPETENCIES AND SKILLS NEEDED

- Ability to recognize issues of concern that arise during counseling and representation of older persons or their representatives on relevant law matters
- Familiarity with public and private, professional, and nonlegal resources and services that are available to meet the needs of older persons

- Ability to recognize professional conduct and ethical issues that arise during representation of older persons
- Good listening and oral and written communication skills

COMPENSATION

This varies by the type of practice, the nature of the practice setting, education, experience, NELF certification, and geographical location.

WORKPLACE(S)

These include independent practices, law firms, medical centers or long-term care facilities, legal aid clinics, law schools, and consultation opportunities with health care systems, mental health facilities, and community-based public and private agencies that serve elders.

EMPLOYMENT OUTLOOK

Excellent, with anticipated growth in employment opportunities due to the increase in the elderly population and new laws and regulations that have legal implications for elders and their representatives, caregivers, and families.

RELATED PROFESSIONAL ORGANIZATIONS AND WEBSITES

- American Bar Association (ABA): www.americanbar.org
- ABA Section of Family Law (includes elder law): www.americanbar.org/groups/family-law
- ABA Commission on Law and Aging: www.americanbar.org/aging
- National Elder Law Foundation (NELF): www.nelf.org
- National Academy of Elder Law Attorneys (NAELA): www.naela.org

An Interview With ROXANNE J. CHANG

Elder Care Attorney and Counselor

Postsecondary educational background, including formal credentials and other education/training in gerontology/geriatrics:
BS, Psychology
MS, Clinical-Behavioral Psychology
Graduate Certificate in Gerontology
JD, Law

How and when did you first become interested in gerontology/geriatrics? I have always felt a connection with older adults. I became interested in gerontology/geriatrics when I was attending graduate school. A professor in the psychology department introduced me to the field.

Briefly describe your gerontology/geriatrics-related career path. After graduate school, my specialty was working with individuals with memory loss. I was an instructor for the gerontology program at a local university, where I taught classes related to dementia care and designed therapeutic activities for individuals with dementia. In addition, I was practicing as a limited licensed psychologist consulting with long-term care facilities and providing psychological service to older adults, including the development of behavioral care plans. I subsequently decided to pursue a career in elder and special needs law.

Briefly describe your current professional position:

Position title: Attorney and counselor

Primary role tasks/responsibilities: Advising and counseling for clients on legal matters and long-term care issues related to elder care and for persons with special needs; training and education in elder and special needs law; and mediation and conflict resolution coaching with persons who are older or with special needs and their families.

Type of employment setting: Self-employed

Length of time in this position: 11 years

How did you first become interested in this position? I learned about elder and special needs law as a practice area when I met another attorney

(*continued*)

An Interview With ROXANNE J. CHANG *(continued)*

who practiced in this field while I was working as a limited licensed psychologist.

Describe a typical workday in your current professional position. A typical workday includes meeting with clients and their families to assist with estate planning, planning to pay for long-term care (e.g., Medicaid eligibility), and advocacy for quality of life and care, drafting pleadings and other documents, educating older adults and individuals with special needs and their families on legal issues and care matters, and attending probate court proceedings.

What is the time commitment required of your current professional position? The time commitment required really varies depending on the needs of my clients and workflow. I typically work approximately 50 hours a week. I try to accommodate my clients by being available for evening appointments and weekends, but I do try to limit my hours to weekdays and during the day as much as possible.

How do you stay up-to-date in your profession?

Professional organization memberships and/or activities?

Elder Law and Disability Rights, Probate and Estate Planning, and Alternative Dispute Resolution Sections of the State Bar, Member

National Academy of Elder Law Attorneys (NAELA), Member

I frequently review the e-mail listservs available for section members of both organizations to obtain updated information and to bounce ideas off of other attorneys and professionals.

Subscribe to and/or read professional journals and/or newsletters? The Sections of the State Bar of which I am a member and NAELA frequently publish journals and newsletters for updates and continuing education that are very helpful. I also have a membership with the Institute of Continuing Legal Education to access resources and written handbooks and manuals to assist me with my law practice.

Attend professional conferences and/or participate in education/training programs? I frequently attend conferences and education/training

(continued)

An Interview With ROXANNE J. CHANG (*continued*)

programs on elder care law and advocacy—specifically, the semi-annual conferences put on by the Elder Law and Disability Rights Section of the State Bar, along with the conferences, seminars, and workshops through the Institute of Continuing Legal Education and NAELA. I also enjoy attending conferences related to aging issues and memory loss to stay abreast of clinical issues and innovations in care.

What are the most rewarding aspects of your current career position? The most rewarding aspects of being an elder care attorney relate to the satisfaction I derive from advising and assisting older adults and their families to advocate for quality of life and care, plan for long-term care, and other aging-related issues. I really enjoy problem solving and resolving conflicts. I also find it extremely rewarding to assist vulnerable adults and ensure they are protected to the greatest degree possible while I also am promoting independence and self-determination.

What are the most rewarding aspects of your gerontology/geriatrics-related career path? The most rewarding aspect of working in gerontology/geriatrics-related career path is interacting with older adults, especially those with memory loss, and their caregivers. I have personally gained so much wisdom about life in general from these individuals, particularly in regard to staying focused on what is truly important in life.

What are the most challenging aspects of your current career position? The most challenging aspects of my current career position are related to the barriers of quality care within the long-term care and legal system; the potential or actual abuse, neglect, or exploitation of a vulnerable adult; and working with others in the field who do not have the same philosophy of care when working with older adults.

What are the most challenging aspects of your gerontology/geriatrics-related career path? The most challenging aspects of my gerontology/geriatrics-related career path relates to how services are provided to older adults, particularly with how quality of care is defined and the current medical model of care.

(*continued*)

An Interview With ROXANNE J. CHANG *(continued)*

How do you balance career and other aspects of your life? I balance my career with other aspects of my life by being able to set boundaries with clients, using time management skills, having a sense of humor, being creative, practicing mindfulness and acceptance skills, and living in the present moment.

What advice do you have for someone contemplating a career in the field of aging? I suggest to anyone interested in exploring a career in the field of aging to do some volunteer work with persons who are older. In particular, it may be helpful to volunteer in a variety of long-term care settings to become familiar with the resources and services available to individuals and their families. In addition, it is important to determine early on whether a person is comfortable in interacting and working with individuals with cognitive disabilities or impairment (e.g., dementia, memory loss) by getting exposure through volunteer work. If there is a particular setting or service that someone is interested in, it also would be helpful to do a practicum or internship experience within that setting. Nothing matches the learning gained from direct, hands-on experiences in the field.

What advice do you have for someone considering a professional position similar to your current position? Volunteering or clerking at an elder care firm can be very helpful in becoming familiar with the field of elder care law. In addition, joining professional organizations like the Elder Law and Disability Rights section of the State Bar or the National Academy of Elder Law Attorneys as a student member can also be very helpful. It is important to note, however, that elder law does not involve just Medicaid planning and asset protection and estate planning. An elder care attorney should have experience in and be well-versed with the long-term care system. Being knowledgeable of clinical issues, the personal experiences of older adults and their caregivers, and innovations in care, particularly related to individuals with memory loss, also is important. Obtaining hands-on experiences and education in the long-term care system or advocacy organizations for older adults (e.g., volunteer facilitator for an Alzheimer's Association caregiver support group, attending conferences on dementia care) are crucial to providing holistic elder care law services.

ENTREPRENEURIAL GERONTOLOGY: AN EMERGING FIELD

ENTREPRENEURIAL GERONTOLOGIST

GERONTOLOGICAL ENTREPRENEUR

BASIC DESCRIPTION

Opportunities abound for gerontological specialists, gerontologists, and others from outside the field of aging to develop products and deliver services for needs of older adults that are unmet or not yet met adequately through existing avenues. Simply put, an entrepreneur identifies one of these needs for a defined target audience, creates appropriate products or services to meet the need, designs an appropriate delivery system, and then delivers these products or services to the target audience. In fact, many gerontological specialists and gerontologists already carry out this process as part of their full-time positions when they deliver their knowledge through speaking engagements, training programs, and consultations with organizations, agencies, and facilities external to their regular employment setting. In these situations knowledge is their "product." In some cases, however, the "product" might be an item that they design or help to design or a service they provide. It is quite likely that at least one entrepreneurial opportunity exists in relation to each of the career position profiles and in the ". . . and More" section of this book. With the population of elders growing, an economy that has led to downsizing in both the private and public sector, and more individuals wanting more control over their work worlds, there is an increased focus on entrepreneurship as a response for mid-career changes among undergraduate and graduate students in a variety of fields and for older adults seeking what have become known as "encore careers." It also appears that the developmental midlife shift is ripe for an entrepreneurial mindset, and it has been observed that certain attitudes and personality types are more likely to embrace entrepreneurship, which makes this a more suitable career path for those individuals. Finally, while entrepreneurial gerontology seems to be a good fit with a positive, optimal, and healthy aging approach, it seems not to be a good fit with geriatrics and a problem-based, pathological aging approach. Many colleges and universities have opened centers for entrepreneurship, sometimes in collaboration with community-based partners (e.g., chambers of commerce, corporations, or community foundations) that offer training and support for those interested in developing entrepreneurial startups. More recently, the first courses specific to entrepreneurial gerontology are being offered at two universities—Long Island University and Virginia Commonwealth University (and, perhaps, at others not yet identified)—and a college in Canada has a complete curriculum "stream": Studies in Aging Business and Entrepreneurship. For now, the title "entrepreneurial gerontologists" is used for individuals who have earned a degree, certificate, or similar gerontology/geriatrics-specific academic credential. For all others, the title "gerontological entrepreneur" is used.

EDUCATION AND EXPERIENCE REQUIREMENTS

Variable, but not yet clearly defined

CERTIFICATION, LICENSURE, AND CONTINUING EDUCATION REQUIREMENTS

None yet known

CORE COMPETENCIES AND SKILLS REQUIRED

- Ability to identify a viable niche product, service, program, or business
- Patience, persistence, and perseverance
- Flexibility and adaptability
- Ability to identify and access an appropriate target market
- Willingness to learn, as needed, in regard to knowledge, skills, and outcomes
- Ability to edit, as needed, to refine the product, service, program, or business
- Open to feedback from colleagues, mentors, professionals in the field of aging, and potential older adult consumers/clients
- Adequate financial base (for both personal purposes and development of entrepreneurial intent)
- Strong support system
- Physical, mental, and emotional strength to move from vision to success

COMPENSATION

This will vary by stage in development, availability and/or success of the entrepreneurial product, business, or service, and other factors specific to each venture.

WORKPLACE(S)

Wide variation, but many work from a home-based setting

EMPLOYMENT OUTLOOK

Promising, but not yet verified

RELATED PROFESSIONAL ORGANIZATIONS AND WEBSITES

- Consortium for Entrepreneurship Education, based at Ohio State University: www.entre-ed.org
- Program for Acquiring Competence in Entrepreneurship (PACE), Ohio State University, College of Education and Human Ecology: http://cete.osu.edu/products-services/pace

An Interview With RYAN DUFFY

Entrepreneurial Gerontologist and Owner/President, Fitness and Wellness Business

Postsecondary educational background, including formal credentials and other education/training in gerontology/geriatrics:
BA, Psychology
BA, Philosophy
MSG, Gerontology

Certificate to work with older adults in a group residential setting (issued by the State Department of Social Services)

How and when did you first become interested in gerontology/geriatrics? In my last undergrad semester, I took an adult developmental psychology course. We examined basic psychological concepts of aging from a developmental perspective and compared research against popular perceptions of aging. After I graduated, my professor asked me to participate in a research group on aging issues with an emphasis on Alzheimer's disease. We had a "guest educator," the program director of the area Alzheimer's Association, who helped guide and inform the theory and research we did. I ended up primarily working with a friend on a paper about reminiscence therapy. During the semester, the guest educator invited us to an in-state caregiver conference. The experience was not only mind opening; it also resonated in my heart. Caregivers and educators were all there for each other and their care recipients, with compassion as the driving force. At that time in my life, I wanted to be able to have a positive impact on the lives of others and was looking for a particular part of the population with whom to work. I had considered working with older adults, but when I experienced the dedication and compassion of everyone at the conference, I had made up my mind. To get some experience regarding working with individuals with Alzheimer's, I took a class offered by the Department of Social Services on working with groups of older adults and individuals with dementia. Part of the class involved hands-on volunteering with seniors and individuals with dementia; this solidified my desire to work with older adults, perhaps even focusing on dementia or individuals who were dying. Shortly thereafter, I prepared to apply for graduate school and found the gerontology program at a local university to be a good fit for me.

(*continued*)

An Interview With RYAN DUFFY *(continued)*

Briefly describe your gerontology/geriatrics-related career path. My goal as a graduate student was to help seniors improve their quality of life and well-being. Initially, I wanted to work with seniors who had dementia or were dying or near death and also to help their families cope with grief and loss. I had recently dealt with major losses in my family; thus, I had in mind a goal to improve the end-of-life quality of life and well-being of individuals and their families. I considered taking courses in patient counseling to help me with this goal, but the classes weren't offered during my first two graduate semesters. I adapted by deciding to combine my interest in working with seniors with my passion for physical fitness and alternative mind–body practices. I also decided to create my own business based on Tai Chi, Chi Kung, and meditation practices that I had been learning for about 5 years. As part of my MSG practicum, I compiled research articles about Tai Chi and Chi Kung practices and how they benefit older adults. I presented the research at a gerontological conference and constructed a long list of exercises and practices that can benefit seniors who may have several physical and mental issues. Additionally, I wrote a basic manual for teaching such exercises to older adults. Learning to teach out-of-the-ordinary exercises to seniors occurs through gaining experience; I had done this before, but not in the various contexts in which I was planning to work once I graduated. I was limited with my experience, so before starting my business, I volunteered my services with adult day centers and assisted living facilities. After several months, I became a better, more versatile teacher and group fitness instructor. I wanted to make sure I worked with people of all different abilities, limitations, and conditions so I could understand which exercises were best for them and how to best teach them. Eventually, I was working with senior facilities, gyms, churches, yoga studios, and community organizations. I also decided to offer in-home personal training after just a few months of opening my business.

Briefly describe your current professional position:

Position title: Owner/president

(continued)

An Interview With RYAN DUFFY *(continued)*

Primary role tasks/responsibilities: My primary roles are to advertise, market, and network; contact businesses that might be interested in my services or have clients who would be interested; complete mundane tasks necessary with owning a business (e.g., collecting receipts, budgeting, balancing the books); and teaching group classes and personal training sessions, primarily in the modalities of Chi Kung, Tai Chi, and meditation.

Type of employment setting: As the sole proprietor of an aging fitness and wellness business, I travel to churches, gyms, community centers, individual residences, and other places that hold or would like to offer group fitness classes for seniors. Otherwise, I work at home.

Length of time in this position: 2-1/2 years

How did you first become interested in this position? I became interested in creating my own fitness and wellness business when I was studying for my MSG. I didn't see anything else like it, and no other fitness or wellness businesses in the area focused solely on seniors. Also, being my own boss is great!

Describe a typical workday in your current professional position. My typical workday consists of preparing for and teaching group classes and personal training sessions. Because every group is different, I consistently rework the curricula based on the abilities and limitations of class participants. I also come up with ideas for classes I would like to teach and for classes that are needed, but for which there are no current venues. To expand my business, I am always calling or e-mailing different institutions and facilities to see if their residents/clients would be interested in my services. I occasionally attend networking events and social gatherings of gerontological professionals and organizations. Every month or so, I teach a seminar or give a talk on meditation, fitness for seniors, or Tai Chi or Chi Kung. I currently am planning on expanding my business by opening a fitness and wellness facility for folks 50 and older, so creating a new business plan and model are a part of my daily work.

What is the time commitment required of your current professional position? Forty hours per week reflects my total hours, regardless of the time or day. I have worked weekends in the past and still work evenings.

(continued)

An Interview With RYAN DUFFY (*continued*)

How do you stay up-to-date in your profession?

Professional organization memberships and/or activities? I currently am not a member of any particular organizations.

Subscribe to and/or read professional journals and/or newsletters? I read up on Tai Chi, Chi Kung, yoga, and anything related to physical therapy and physical training with older adults. I often go to PubMed (www.ncbi.nim.nih.gov/pubmed) for articles, and I receive articles from colleagues and fellow professionals on a regular basis. For anything that is written in newspapers or on websites, I usually try to find the article or at least the abstract to verify the information. This is helpful for me because I can share those articles that are more accessible to the average person (than research articles), with clients or participants. Occasionally, I write a brief column for a gerontology newsletter.

Attend professional conferences and/or participate in education/training programs? Currently, I do not attend any conferences.

Other? When I encounter physical conditions I have not worked with before, I discuss them with physical therapists, massage therapists, and physical trainers. I also try to read up on the condition and find videos by health professionals on YouTube that address the condition, along with beneficial practices and exercises. I am undergoing certification to become a health and wellness coach because many of my clients and participants expressed or implied the need for such a service. I'm always learning as I teach, and I try to improve my teaching methods. I have personal guidance from a few mentors, which helps me improve my own practice and my business.

What are the most rewarding aspects of your current career position? Watching people discover more about themselves and watching them become more physically functional (e.g., stronger, more flexible, less pain, regain an ability), thus improving their mood and everyday life.

What are the most rewarding aspects of your gerontology/geriatrics-related career path? Many older clients come to my class with an intention of improving their physical health and quality of life. What is most rewarding

(*continued*)

An Interview With RYAN DUFFY *(continued)*

about working with them is that they value what I am teaching and put to work what they learn; they put energy and focus into what they are doing because they have a purpose behind it. They have achieved a certain level of appreciation and understanding that the subtleties and often neglected parts of our lives need work if we want to continue to be healthy and thrive.

What are the most challenging aspects of your current career position? The most challenging aspect of my current position is self-direction. Because I did not get an MBA or any business-related degree, I have had to learn the ropes of running my own business. I had no interest in marketing or networking when I started, but I knew it was necessary, so I've gotten used to it and much better at communicating who I am and what I do to different audiences.

What are the most challenging aspects of your gerontology/geriatrics-related career path? It is difficult to address everyone's needs in group classes. My clientele includes yoga practitioners, runners, gardeners, former laborers, sedentary people, and individuals with joint replacements, arthritis, cardiovascular issues, depression, anxiety, and other specific health concerns. The range of abilities and limitations is quite wide; even within one class, I sometimes have people who are nothing alike. I cannot cater to everyone, which results in exclusion. Additionally, there are people who become pushy when I don't address all of their needs. It becomes even more difficult when clients want or expect me to work with them beyond my expertise. Some individuals even demand such attention in group scenarios, which usually bothers most of the other participants. Sometimes, I just can't avoid the occasional "bad apple" that makes things difficult for me and for the other class participants.

How do you balance career and other aspects of your life? Working on my own schedule facilitates overall balance in my life. I sometimes work late, but I still get to spend time with my wife during the week. I used to teach weekend classes, but I stopped because I wanted to keep my weekends open for my wife and friends. The main issue I have balancing my career and other aspects of my life is physical burnout from all of the movement

(continued)

An Interview With RYAN DUFFY (*continued*)

that I do as a fitness and exercise professional. Occasionally, I need to rest my body, so I take a week or two off from teaching or reduce my workload by removing a class from my schedule for a month or so and then add it back to my schedule when I am ready.

What advice do you have for someone contemplating a career in the field of aging? Investigate the options you have, and spend time in the field to learn more about what careers might interest you. Hands-on work is important because you may learn that something you thought would be a great career is not what you thought it was; on the other hand, you may be intrigued by a position that you didn't even consider as a valid option. Experiencing different career options is important because each career has academic and training paths that properly prepare you. If you are already in another profession and want to focus on seniors, then consider a certificate or a degree in gerontology.

What advice do you have for someone considering a professional position similar to your current position? Volunteer your services at different facilities and institutions to improve your abilities to work with older adults. Find a mentor or two to help you with the business aspects, group teaching, and personal sessions with clients. Networking with professionals and other businesses in the aging community is important to help spread the word about what you do, but you also need to reach out to people and businesses who don't work primarily with aging individuals. Because you will be marketing yourself to both gerontological and non-gerontological professionals, you will need to develop different presentations and vocabularies that cater to their perspectives and needs. Creating an "elevator speech" for both audiences is important because their clientele, services, and environment are different from each other even though the services you are offering them are the same.

An Interview With SONYA BARSNESS

Entrepreneurial Gerontologist, Consultant and Business Owner

BS, Psychology, with minors in Biology and Gerontology
MS, Gerontology, with concentration in Psychogeriatrics

How and when did you first become interested in gerontology/geriatrics? When I was a child, we lived with my grandparents. My experience with aging has always been that it is a normal part of life. I also have been volunteering with elders since I was 11 years old, and I was a "friendly visitor" for elders living in my neighborhood. In college, I was involved in numerous service learning projects, and some were in nursing homes. Through these experiences, I learned that there was a field of study called gerontology, which I then pursued. As an undergraduate, my intent was to become a psychologist or neuropsychologist, but my path took a different direction.

Briefly describe your gerontology/geriatrics-related career path. After my undergraduate degree, I worked in social services at a nursing home and then as a neuropsychological test technician. As I explored graduate school options, I realized that I did not want to pursue psychology; rather, I wished to pursue gerontology and enrolled in a master's degree program in gerontology. My passion had always been in working with people living with dementia, and my concentration in psychogeriatrics facilitated this focus. After graduate school, I worked in assisted living. Through these continued experiences in long-term care, I became increasingly concerned with the philosophy and practice of care for elders, particularly people with dementia, in long-term care. This led me to seek a position in policy, with the intention of being able to effect change in long-term care at the federal policy level. I continued to work in federal and state policy and program development in both residential and community-based care. In working with people in the early stages of dementia, I learned about person-centered care, which was the articulation of what I had been practicing and advocating. Recognizing my interests in policy, research, practice, and education related to person-centered care, I decided my best career path would be to start my own consulting business through which I could promote and operationalize my interests and preferred practice modes. A large focus of my work is

(*continued*)

An Interview With SONYA BARSNESS *(continued)*

person-centered dementia care, but I also work to change the culture of aging and how we care for each other as we age.

Briefly describe your current professional position:

Position title: Consultant and business owner

Primary role tasks/responsibilities: As a consultant, I work with organizations to promote and operationalize person-centered care through education, policy, research, and practice. My specific focus is with people living with dementia.

Type of employment setting: Limited liability company (LLC) consulting firm

Length of time in this position: Approximately 6 years

How did you first become interested in this position? In self-evaluating that I hold both diverse skills and a specific niche focus, I did not see a traditional employment position that would be a good fit for my goals. I wanted to have more autonomy in focusing on projects for which I was passionate and felt I could effect change. I also saw an unmet need to include gerontologists in various aspects of long-term care and dementia care. For this reason, I began to refer to myself as a "rent-a-gerontologist," with the thought that organizations would hire me for my gerontological expertise and experience.

Describe a typical workday in your current professional position. There is truly no typical day in my position, which is something I enjoy. Because I work for multiple organizations and have various projects, each day depends on those factors. Some of this work is directly with long-term care providers and some is with organizations that somehow are related to long-term care or dementia care. I travel fairly often and operate "virtually" for most of my projects. I often have conference calls with clients and partners. Although I am an independent consultant, I never work alone; I always work in collaboration with a client team or with other

(continued)

An Interview With SONYA BARSNESS (*continued*)

consultants. I usually work on a few grant-funded projects along with typical "fee-for-service" consulting jobs. My projects are both short-term (e.g., a conference presentation) and long-term (a year or longer). One aspect of my business model is partnering with nonprofits in developing proposals to fund a common goal or idea. We come up with an idea in collaboration, I help write the proposal, and I am written into the proposal as a consultant for project implementation.

What is the time commitment required of your current professional position? Having my own consulting business affords some flexibility so that I can schedule my own hours, although I still maintain a typical business hours—9 a.m. to 5 p.m.—schedule. That being said, I often work much more than 40 hours a week because having my own business means not just doing the actual gerontology work but also maintaining a business (e.g., billing, marketing, contracts, proposals). I do have to work additional hours at times to accomplish this. I have established a fairly strict "no working on weekends" rule. I generally do not check e-mail on the weekends. There are exceptions when I travel, as I sometimes have conferences or events that fall on weekends.

How do you stay up-to-date in your profession?

Professional organization memberships and/or activities? Gerontological Society of America (GSA), Member

Subscribe to and/or read professional journals and/or newsletters? I receive the GSA journals and have access to many other professional journals, as needed. I receive many newsletters from organizations focused on aging, person-centered care, and dementia care and from foundations/funders; I try to read as many as I can. I love *Changing Aging*, a multiblog platform; the *Current Awareness Aging Research (CAAR) Report*, a daily E-Clippings service of the Center for Demography of Health and Aging (CDHA) at the University of Wisconsin-Madison; and *Human Values in Aging*, a monthly e-newsletter.

(*continued*)

An Interview With SONYA BARSNESS (*continued*)

Attend professional conferences and/or participate in education/training programs? I try to attend and/or present at national or state conferences whenever possible, but because I am paying for them out of my own pocket I am not always able to attend. I have attended the Pioneer Network conference every year for the past 5 years. I also participate in quite a few webinars offered by various organizations, including the Pioneer Network, the Administration for Community Living, and other state or local organizations.

What are the most rewarding aspects of your current career position? I am able to work on a variety of projects, have a good bit of autonomy yet work in collaboration with others, and mostly focus on projects for which I am passionate. I am constantly challenged by my work. I love the fact that one day I am facilitating a training with professionals, the next day I am working with people with early stage dementia to understand their condition, and another day I am developing a survey instrument.

What are the most rewarding aspects of your gerontology/geriatrics-related career path? I feel like I have had a real opportunity to make a positive difference in the lives of elders and people with dementia by being able to help change the way we care for each other as we age. I have had the opportunity to meet many leaders in this field who are true visionaries and are changing the world.

What are the most challenging aspects of your current career position? The amount of travel can be challenging on a personal level. The responsibility of owning a business and not having a consistent income can be stressful. Because I have to pay travel expenses myself, I have to be very selective about the conferences I can afford to attend. It is sometimes difficult to balance multiple projects from different clients at the same time. In a typical work situation, you might be able to say to your boss, "I have too much on my plate; help me prioritize my work." As an independent consultant with multiple bosses (who often do not know of each other and rightly want each of their projects to be my priority), it can be difficult to balance this.

(*continued*)

An Interview With SONYA BARSNESS *(continued)*

What are the most challenging aspects of your gerontology/geriatrics-related career path? Change takes a long time, and changing the culture of aging will likely not happen in my lifetime. It takes patience to recognize that I am chipping away in meaningful ways, but that I might not see monumental shifts I would like to see. It takes humility to recognize that we are all in this together and each have an important, yet, perhaps, incremental role. It is difficult for me to consider the untapped potential of elders in our society, particularly those living with dementia.

How do you balance career and other aspects of your life? I am pretty strict with my "no working on the weekend" rule. I try not to work too often in the evenings and try to balance evening work by taking time for myself and my family at other times during the week. It is important for me to have interests and experiences outside of gerontology. Although I love to read books on aging and dementia, I make sure I read all sorts of literature. I find this invigorates me all around and gives me a wider perspective on my work.

What advice do you have for someone contemplating a career in the field of aging? Expose yourself widely to opportunities to learn about what the professionals who work in this field do in their work. Do as much service-learning and volunteering as you can in various aspects of the field. Volunteer in a nursing home, senior center, and with other programs/services for older adults. Visit or volunteer with and shadow professionals who work in different ways in the field—such as researchers, educators, writers, volunteer coordinators, and therapists of one kind or another. Unlike other job roles (such as teacher or physical therapist), many gerontology jobs and career paths do not have a straight path that is clearly defined. The opportunities lie in a range of possibilities, but you have to actively seek them. Also, consider the various types of career paths—research, policy, direct practice, education—available. If you then choose a career path in this field, you need to be ready and willing to convince others that your expertise on aging is necessary.

What advice do you have for someone considering a professional position similar to your current position? There are certainly pros and cons to

(continued)

An Interview With SONYA BARSNESS *(continued)*

being a consultant in aging. Talk to as many people as possible who are in consultant roles so you can better understand the pros and cons. Consultants generally need a certain level of experience in their particular niche, so in thinking about your consulting interests, consider your specific expertise and how this will be valuable to others. Be thoughtful in considering your skills, talents, interests, and what you can share with the world. Do not be afraid to take risks and know that it takes a good bit of patience and perseverance to work as a consultant and to own a consulting business.

EXECUTIVE DIRECTOR, AREA AGENCY ON AGING

BASIC DESCRIPTION

As the lead administrator for an Area Agency on Aging (AAA), the executive director is responsible for the overall strategic and operational planning, delivery, and evaluation of programs and services mandated by the Older Americans Act, the state office of services to the aging, and/or within the counties covered by the AAA. Although the specific responsibilities may vary from one agency to another, the executive director generally provides leadership for and management of personnel, oversight of program planning and delivery, financial health and budgeting, fundraising and development initiatives, internal and external organizational communication, relationships with governing boards and external partnerships, and acquisition and maintenance of the agency's physical structures/equipment and contractual processes. The executive director is the "public face" of the agency and serves as its primary liaison with other governmental agencies (local, county, state and federal) and other related organizations.

EDUCATION AND EXPERIENCE REQUIREMENTS

Bachelor's degree required, although a master's or higher degree in social work, gerontology, public administration, business administration, or related fields is preferred. Minimum of 5 to 7 years of demonstrated successful management and leadership experience in nonprofit and/or human services is required.

CERTIFICATION, LICENSURE, AND CONTINUING EDUCATION REQUIREMENTS

None required, but staying current with changes in policies on aging and regulations related to delivery of programs and services to older adults is vital. Some AAAs may institute specific requirements and/or strong recommendations for specific continuing education goals, objectives and/or activities.

CORE COMPETENCIES AND SKILLS NEEDED

- Demonstrated success in community and organizational development
- Ability to envision and communicate the agency's current and future mission and goals
- Ability to create and nurture an intra-agency culture that recognizes the strengths, talents, and contributions of each team member
- Sound decision maker
- Willingness and ability to delegate appropriately
- Ability to improve and sustain performance
- Develop and follow through on priorities, both role specific and with staff/volunteers
- Policy development knowledge and skills
- Good written and oral communication skills, including public speaking
- Excellent interpersonal communication skills—exhibits openness and approachability
- Sensitivity to cultural diversity and competency
- Commitment to ethical and appropriate practice for self, staff, and agency
- Knowledge of budgets and accounting processes
- Able to work collaboratively with other agencies
- Successful grant application, award, and oversight record
- Information technology expertise

COMPENSATION

This varies with the educational and experience background of the executive director, geographical location (within a state), factors related to the specific coverage area of the AAA, and continued funding of AAA programs and services from federal, state, regional, and county sources.

WORKPLACE(S)

This is typically the AAA regional headquarters/office, which usually is located in the county in the AAA's coverage area with the largest elderly population.

EMPLOYMENT OUTLOOK

Good, but limited in number per state and the tendency toward longevity in the position. In some states, the number of positions has been narrowed by mergers that lowered the number if AAAs within the state.

RELATED PROFESSIONAL ORGANIZATIONS AND WEBSITES

- National Association of Area Agencies on Aging (n4a): www.n4a.org
- Administration on Aging (AoA): www.aoa.gov
- State organization for Directors of Area Agencies on Aging

An Interview With ROBERT C. SCHLUETER

Executive Director, Area Agency on Aging

Postsecondary educational background, including formal credentials and other education/training in gerontology/geriatrics:
BS, Sociology
BPh, Philosophy

How and when did you first become interested in gerontology/ geriatrics? Since my parent were both older when they married and my grandparents on both sides were already well into their 70s when I was very young, I have been surrounded by elderly people my entire life. I am the third of four boys. Because of this life experience, I have always felt at ease around elderly people and in their environments. I believe this living experience has helped me understand the importance of older persons' contributions to our social fabric and how they fit into our lives as naturally as the newborn baby.

Briefly describe your gerontology/geriatrics-related career path. When I was first hired at the Area Agency on Aging, I provided employment-related services to businesses in our 10-county region. I also assisted individuals who were at least 55 years old in their efforts to obtain employment. This included all aspects of a job search effort and, in many cases, enrollment in education classes to upgrade existing skills. My responsibilities, along with one-on-one general problem solving and counseling, included extensive program support, grant writing, employee supervision, personnel problem-solving, budgeting, and technical report writing. Within 5 years, this position developed into an agency-wide personnel management position, in which I was responsible for developing a positive and productive employee team. It was important that I learned about the various programs the agency ran so that I could appreciate and assist employees with their concerns. As our office became more reliant on electronic information management and more computers and related items were purchased, I developed into the IT management person. It became important for me to develop relationships with a wide variety of professionals involved in aging and related services. Through these relationships, I was put more frequently into a decision-making role and after 7 years, I was named the deputy director.

(*continued*)

An Interview With ROBERT C. SCHLUETER (*continued*)

Briefly describe your current professional position:

Position title: Executive Director

Primary role tasks and responsibilities: Working closely with a policy board and also with an advocacy board, I oversee operations of a large aging and health care organization. I also work very closely with local, state, and federal elected officials, educating them in the areas of needed services and funding to assist our elderly and disabled citizens.

Type of employment setting: Area Agency on Aging that serves 10 counties

Length of time in this position: 4 years

How did you first become interested in this position? I applied initially to the Area Agency on Aging for an economic development position they were seeking to fill. This position worked with regional businesses and unemployed seniors. I grew into my current position through several advancement opportunities offered to me within the agency. As my professional management skillsets and relevant talents improved, so did my work responsibilities and opportunities. As my mother in-law always pointed out, "When the tarts are passed, take one."

Describe a typical workday in your current professional position. I typically start my day by 7 a.m. I am responsible for many of the IT needs of the organization, so I try to take care of these tasks before the office opens for business. With a small organization, I have many of the responsibilities that a home owner might have. I oversee all the maintenance of our two buildings and need to know early if there are problems that would delay the opening of the office. This "quiet time" frequently allows me to focus on paperwork-type efforts without being interrupted by others. Again, being a small organization without many of the maintenance support staff enjoyed by larger structures and businesses, I frequently assist employees with issues related to their work sites (such as technology issues and environmental work space issues). No two days have the

(*continued*)

An Interview With ROBERT C. SCHLUETER *(continued)*

same problems and I find that to be of my liking. I frequently have staff members come into my office to discuss problems, concerns, ideas, and other relevant topics. I consider it of utmost importance to give them the time they need for these discussions. We run many different programs, so the questions vary greatly. I also spend a great deal of time following up on local, state, and federal programs that are available to help us better serve our consumer base. It is very important to create an environment that is flexible and able to respond quickly to the many political and programmatic winds that blow. It also is very important to establish various "game plans" that assist me in staying ahead of the aging information curve and to continually improve the future of our aging services capabilities. I meet on a regular basis with administrative staff, service providers, grantors and grantees, local and state government officials, and anyone else I can think of who will make the provision of services to the aging and disabled communities better.

What is the time commitment required of your current professional position? My work day starts before 7 a.m. and frequently runs until 6 p.m. or later. Most times, this work schedule is Monday through Friday, but on occasion, there are weekend commitments. There are frequent night meetings of local organizations and county commissions to attend.

How do you stay up-to-date in your profession?

Professional organization memberships and/or activities?

Statewide association of Area Agencies on Aging: I represent my agency and their lobbyist helps to keep us up to speed on what is happening with state legislative initiatives.

Michigan Society of Gerontology (MSG): I serve on the board of directors. MSG focuses on bridging the gaps between research, practice, and advocacy in regard to aging issues.

National Area Agency on Aging Association (n4a): I am a member and have participated in many conference calls, online surveys, and in-person conferences. This organization is very active in regard to legislation, as I am at the state level.

(continued)

An Interview With ROBERT C. SCHLUETER *(continued)*

Subscribe to and/or read professional journals and/or newsletters? I receive many very helpful publications, including newsletters, through these organizations and also from various other aging-focused associations.

Attend professional conferences and/or participate in education/training programs? Because of the expenses involved, I am very conservative when it comes to attending any conference outside of the state. I have not attended any in recent years. I do count on staff members from our agency to attend important national conferences and report back their findings. From time-to-time, conferences and related workshops are offered in our geographical region and I do attend those.

What are the most rewarding aspects of your current career position? I feel that I can make a real difference in improving the services provided to our consumers. My role as executive director opens many doors of leadership and allows my thoughts and ideas to be presented in a forum where others will listen and take note. It is very important to be well informed of my topic since my credibility is always on the line.

What are the most rewarding aspects of your gerontology/geriatrics-related career path? I love people of all ages, but I am especially drawn to older adults due to their life experiences and what I can learn from them.

What are the most challenging aspects of your current career position? Establishing stable program funding and keeping up with all the new program initiatives coming out of state and federal governments.

What are the most challenging aspects of your gerontology/geriatrics-related career path? Staying up with all the new research findings, health and economic initiatives, and political priorities that involve the aging population, especially specific to those served by my agency.

How do you balance career and other aspects of your life? Having a "life" outside of work has always been a priority. I learned a long time ago that you need to have a balance between work and play, or both will suffer. I

(continued)

An Interview With ROBERT C. SCHLUETER *(continued)*

usually do not work in a "crisis management" position, so maintaining the balance is not difficult if I indeed keep my priorities in front of me.

What advice do you have for someone contemplating a career in the field of aging? Talk to as many people as possible who work in the various academic and service provision areas of the aging world. Understand that in many ways, because of what is occurring today in this area of study, the aging field is very much a "new frontier" in the vast world of human services. Find your comfort level in working with elders. Not everyone can do it, just like not everyone can work with a newborn baby. Again, though, talk to as many people as possible from the different areas of the aging world so that you have a good picture of what you are considering.

What advice do you have for someone considering a professional position similar to your current position? Learn from the ground up ... get your hands dirty in the real world of providing services to the aging so that you know how it looks and feels. Learn about the many financial matters of local, state, and federal funders. Search out best practices in both service providing and business operations. Make friends at all levels. Don't be afraid to say, "I don't know that. Would you please help me?" Obtain appropriate educational degrees so that doors are more easily opened ... especially if you don't have the practical experience to sell.

FOSTER GRANDPARENT PROGRAM (FGP) DIRECTOR

FOSTER GRANDPARENT PROGRAM (FGP) COORDINATOR

BASIC DESCRIPTION

The Foster Grandparent Program (FGP) is a Senior Corps Program affiliated with the Corporation for National and Community Service (CNCS). Through FGP, persons 55 years of age and older work one-on-one with disabled or disadvantaged youth in schools, hospitals, juvenile correctional institutions, daycare facilities or Head Start centers. FGP directors manage the overall operation of the program, including the following tasks: developing and monitoring the program budget; writing, monitoring and managing grants; supervising paid staff (FGP coordinators and clerical staff); identifying volunteer stations that fit FGP guidelines and meet community needs in the program's service area; recruiting, training, placing, and evaluating the foster grandparents; maintaining open communication with and responding to issues, concerns and problems that arise among program staff, volunteers, and volunteer station personnel. FGP coordinators work directly with foster grandparents on a daily basis and assist the FGP director with budget and grant preparation; volunteer recruitment, training and evaluation; maintenance of the required schedule, volunteer hours, performance and other records for individual volunteers; and other tasks as requested by the director.

EDUCATION AND EXPERIENCE REQUIREMENTS

The FGP director position requires a bachelor's degree or higher in a related field (e.g., education, human development, social work); a master's degree is preferred by most employing agencies. Coursework or a degree component in gerontology and coursework in program management or volunteer agency administration are desirable. The FGP coordinator position also requires a bachelor's degree in a related field (e.g., education, human development, social work). Coursework or a degree component in gerontology is encouraged.

CERTIFICATION, LICENSURE, AND CONTINUING EDUCATION REQUIREMENTS

Directors and coordinators must meet all state licensure requirements related to Foster Grandparent Program (FGP) administration and to their base professional field. Continuing education requirements may be specified by their employing agency or as a FGP mandate.

CORE COMPETENCIES AND SKILLS NEEDED

- Firm knowledge of state and federal policies, guidelines, and procedures for FGP
- Good organizational skills
- Good time- and budget-management skills
- Knowledge of school-based programs for disabled and disadvantaged youth
- Comfortable with working in disadvantaged communities or community settings
- Good interpersonal communication skills
- Good observational and listening skills
- Grant writing skills

COMPENSATION

This varies by type of position, the nature of the employing agency, and the geographical location. The position may be part time or combined with another part-time position, such as directing or coordinating another older adult volunteer program (e.g., Senior Companions) or doing case/care management.

WORKPLACE(S)

These include county commissions on aging or other aging-specific human service agencies and settings in which they supervise foster grandparents.

EMPLOYMENT OUTLOOK

Moderate, but contingent upon continued FGP funding and longevity of some directors/coordinators.

RELATED PROFESSIONAL ORGANIZATIONS AND WEBSITES

- Corporation for National and Community Service (CNCS): www.nationalservice.gov
- National Association of Foster Grandparent Program Directors (NAFGPD): www.nafgpd.org

FUNDRAISER

DEVELOPMENT DIRECTOR

BASIC DESCRIPTION

Professionals in fundraising and development are responsible for the design, implementation and evaluation of fund-raising programs (often called "campaigns") intended to supplement or enhance the basic operational budget of a nonprofit organization, agency, or facility. The funds raised may be for the general operational fund or earmarked for specific programs or special projects. Although the titles of fundraiser and development director are sometimes used synonymously, the title of fundraiser might be used for entry-level paid professionals and for volunteers for fundraising efforts. Fundraisers assist in the development of a fundraising campaign, make direct contact with potential donors through a variety of strategies, and report to the development director. Essentially, fundraisers are the "front-line" workers for a campaign. Development directors are responsible for the development, planning, and execution of a development program that may include multiple fundraising campaigns and strategies. They identify and cultivate new and existing donors; implement the fundraising program so as to maximize the gift giving and stewardship for specific organization programs and projects; are responsible for gift management, fundraising events, and recognition of donors; maintain the development program database; create and/or oversee public and community relations, outreach, and marketing; create, oversee, and adhere to the development program budget; recruit, train, supervise, and evaluate development program staff members and volunteers; and report on development program activities to higher-level organizational administrators and boards. Some development directors have responsibilities related to the organization's grants program.

EDUCATION AND EXPERIENCE REQUIREMENTS

Fundraisers need a bachelor's degree or higher in a field related to professional practice or equivalent work experience. Gerontology coursework or a degree component is encouraged. Development directors require a master's degree or higher, preferably in a field related to professional practice, and at least 3 to 5 years relevant fundraising/development experience. Gerontology coursework or a degree component also is encouraged for directors.

CERTIFICATION, LICENSURE, AND CONTINUING EDUCATION REQUIREMENTS

Two voluntary certifications are available through the Association of Fundraising Professionals (AFP):

- Certified fund raising executive (CFRE) candidates must have at least 5 years of paid professional practice in fundraising and meet the minimum point requirements in four categories: education (continuing education workshops, seminars, conferences, and/or academic degree), professional practice (paid professional experience on a philanthropic fundraising staff or as a consultant to a nonprofit organization), professional performance (communications projects, management projects, and/or actual funds), and service (participation in professional and/or community organizations). Once these eligibility requirements are met, a candidate must pass the standardized written exam (225 multiple-choice questions in core knowledge areas: Prospect Identification, Solicitation, Donor Relations, Volunteerism, Management, and Stewardship), agree to adhere to the CFRE Donor Bill of Rights and sign an agreement with the CFRE Program's Accountability Standards. Recertification is required every 3 years and is based on an update of education, professional practice, professional performance, and service activities.

- Advanced certified fundraising executive (ACFRE) candidates must currently be working in the profession, have accumulated 10 or more years of professional fundraising experience, and hold a CFRE credential or be a Fellow of the Association of Healthcare Philanthropy (FAHP). They must have a BS/BA degree or equivalent, completed at least 15 contact hours of senior-level management and 15 contact hours of senior-level leadership seminars/courses, and participated in at least 10 hours of ethics courses within the previous 5 years. Active membership in at least one field-related professional organization, demonstrated volunteer service to nonprofit organizations, and adherence to the Donor Bill of Rights and its Code of Ethical Principles and Standards are mandatory. Upon successful completion of the written application attesting to the previous requirements, candidates sit for an oral peer review specific to fundraising ethics, management, leadership, planning, and problem solving in at least two of their specialty areas.

CORE COMPETENCIES AND SKILLS NEEDED

- Thorough working knowledge of fundraising/development processes and strategies
- Excellent verbal and written communication skills; excellent oral presentation skills
- Excellent interpersonal skills
- Good organizational and administrative skills
- Demonstrated leadership skills (for development director); emerging leadership skills and ability to work well in a team (for fundraiser)
- Familiarity with relevant software, including spreadsheets and database management
- Positive personality
- Self-starter
- Committed to ethical and legal practice

COMPENSATION

This varies by one's education, experience, level of certification, level of responsibility, and the nature of the employing agency/organization. Some positions may be part time and wage based or on a contractual fee-for-service basis.

WORKPLACE(S)

These include community-based nonprofit organizations, agencies, and facilities that serve older persons; governmental agencies/programs that serve and support older adults; and community-based foundations and organizations that raise funds to support programs and services for older adults.

EMPLOYMENT OUTLOOK

Good, especially due to shifts in governmental funding priorities and budget reductions related to programs and services for older adults as the elderly population expands.

RELATED PROFESSIONAL ORGANIZATIONS AND WEBSITES

- Association for Fundraising Professionals (AFP): www.afpnet.org
- Certified Fund Raising Executive (CFRE International): www.cfre.org
- Association of Healthcare Philanthropy (AHP): www.ahp.org

GERIATRIC CARE MANAGER (GCM)

PROFESSIONAL GERIATRIC CARE MANAGER (PGCM)

CERTIFIED GERIATRIC CARE MANAGER (C-GCM)

FELLOW CERTIFIED GERIATRIC CARE MANAGER

BASIC DESCRIPTION

Geriatric care managers (GCMs) are health and human services professionals with backgrounds in nursing, social work, gerontology, or psychology whose private professional practice is based on issues of aging and elder care. Their clients are ill, frail, and disabled elders and their families. The goal of their practice is to help their clients to achieve maximum potential function. In providing their professional services, GCMs might conduct care planning assessments and offer solutions to problems that are identified; screen, arrange, and monitor in-home help or other services; review financial, legal, or medical issues and make referrals to geriatric specialists; provide crisis intervention; assist with client relocation; serve as a liaison with family members at a distance; provide consumer education and advocacy; and connect clients and their caregivers to appropriate services. In general, GCMs manage care rather than providing direct care to their clients, although some GCMs hold professional credentials and licenses that allow them to provide individual or family therapy, assist with financial management, serve as a conservator or guardian, and/or provide direct caregiving services.

A certified geriatric care manager (C-GCM) is a member of the National Association of Professional Geriatric Care Managers (NAPGCM) who has made a commitment to adhere to the NAPGCM Standards of Practice and Pledge of Ethics. "Fellow of the Academy" designation is conferred to recognize C-GCMs who have demonstrated their ability as advanced practitioners and experts in the field of geriatric care management.

EDUCATION AND EXPERIENCE REQUIREMENTS

A baccalaureate, master's, or PhD, with at least one degree held in a field related to care management (e.g., in nursing, social work, gerontology, psychology, mental health, counseling). Alternative routes to certification, based on 2 or more years of direct practice of services to elders and their families, are available. Gerontology coursework or a degree component is strongly recommended for those who do not have a degree in gerontology. Membership in relevant professional organizations is strongly encouraged.

CERTIFICATION, LICENSURE, AND CONTINUING EDUCATION REQUIREMENTS

These professionals must meet all the requirements specified by the geriatric care manager's base profession and by federal, state, county, and local laws that govern the practice of care/case management. All certified members of NAPGCM must hold at least one of the following certifications: Care Manager Certified (CMC) from the National Academy of Certified Care Managers (NACCM), Certified Case Manager (CCM) from the Commission for Case Manager Certification (CCMC), Certified Advanced Social Work Case Manager (C-ASWCM) from the National Association of Social Workers (NASW), or Certified Social Work Case Manager from NASW. Ongoing, self-directed continuing education (e.g., conference, workshop, and seminar attendance; participation in webinars and self-study programs; reading current professional literature) is expected of all certified case managers.

CORE COMPETENCIES AND SKILLS NEEDED

- Commitment to client-centered practice, including client self-determination and provision of care to the entire "client system"
- Understanding of the client's right to privacy and the ability to maintain confidentiality

- Commitment to practice with integrity and ethical behavior
- Awareness of own personal and professional value system and beliefs and willingness to go through a continuous process of self-reflection and/or case consultation to maintain objectivity in work with clients, their families, and other caregivers
- Ability to maintain appropriate boundaries, professional discretion, and impartial judgment
- Excellent written, listening, and oral communication skills
- Ability to translate medical and consumer information to clients in terms they understand
- Good working knowledge of care needs assessment tools and procedures
- Good working knowledge of laws and regulations that govern geriatric care/case management
- Familiar with medical care, human service, and aging organizations/agencies in the community
- Ability to work collaboratively and cooperatively with both client system and other professionals involved in the plan of care
- Willingness to seek supervision and/or consultation, as needed, to develop, coordinate, and/or manage the care plan
- Knowledge of laws and regulations related to employment practices

COMPENSATION

This varies by one's education, experience, the specific nature of the professional practice, and practice setting. Some hold salaried positions, while others work on a contractual basis with a negotiated or standardized fee for service.

WORKPLACE(S)

Most GCMs work in private or group practices, and some serve as consultants to medical centers, long-term and assisted living facilities, mental health clinics, hospice programs and facilities, or agencies and organizations that serve older adults.

EMPLOYMENT OUTLOOK

Excellent, with anticipated increase in demand due to the rapid growth of the older adult population and more persons living long enough to require caregiving and care management needs.

RELATED PROFESSIONAL ORGANIZATIONS AND WEBSITES

- National Association of Professional Geriatric Care Managers, Inc. (GCM): www.caremanager.org
- Commission for Case Manager Certification (CCMC): www.ccmcertification.org
- National Academy of Certified Care Managers (NACCM): www.naccm.net
- National Association of Social Workers (NASW): www.socialworkers.org

GERIATRIC DENTIST

BASIC DESCRIPTION

Dentists diagnose and treat individual patients for conditions that affect the teeth, tongue, gums, lips, and jaw and often are the first health care professionals to detect an array of other diseases (e.g., diabetes, cancer, osteoporosis, some cardiovascular problems). They may perform surgeries to repair, restore, and maintain teeth (e.g., dental implants), gums, and oral structures that were damaged or lost due to accidents, disease, and other traumas. Recently, dentists have become more involved in cosmetic dental procedures. Dentists also are involved in education and prevention programs to improve dental health for their patients in the communities where they practice. Some dentists with advanced education become researchers and faculty members in dental schools and allied health departments of colleges/universities. Geriatric dentists have acquired specialized knowledge about aging and work primarily with patients who are older adults, usually in private practice or through consultation with other medical and health care professionals. Some become researchers or academicians. Increased interest in geriatric dentistry is evident in the creation of a Gerontology and Geriatrics Education Section within the American Dental Education Association (ADEA) and the Fellowship in Geriatric Dentistry by the American Society for Geriatric Dentistry (ASGD). In 2007, ASGD joined with two other organizations, the American Association of Hospital Dentists (AAHD) and the Academy of Dentistry for Persons with Disabilities (ADPD), to form a new joint organization, the Special Care Dentistry Association (SCDA). Fellows from all three organizations who complete additional requirements may achieve Diplomate status in Special Care Dentistry.

EDUCATION AND EXPERIENCE REQUIREMENTS

Geriatric dentistry requires a Doctor of Dental Medicine (DDM) from an accredited dental school.

CERTIFICATION, LICENSURE, AND CONTINUING EDUCATION REQUIREMENTS

Geriatric dentists must meet licensure requirements in the state where the professional practice occurs. Continuing education is required for license renewal in most states, and some states specify the type of continuing education required.

CORE COMPETENCIES AND SKILLS NEEDED

- Commitment to evidence-based practice
- Scientific knowledge about aging processes, factors that influence individual aging, acute and chronic health conditions/diseases prevalent among elders in relation to dental health and dental care needs of older adults
- Keen visual memory
- Excellent judgment of space and shape
- High degree of manual dexterity
- Literacy related to computer applications for dental and geriatric dental practice
- Demonstrated ability to use technologies (e.g., digital radiography and laser systems) specific to dental care practice
- Good interpersonal and oral communication skills
- Good oral and body hygiene

COMPENSATION

This varies by one's education, experience, attainment of Fellow and/or Diplomate status, type of professional practice, the nature of the employment setting, and the geographical location.

WORKPLACE(S)

These include individual or group private practices, institutional settings (e.g., long-term care and assisted living facilities), academia, and consultancies to community organizations, agencies, and programs that serve older adults.

EMPLOYMENT OUTLOOK

Excellent, especially due to the anticipated rapid growth of the elderly population and increased interest among dentistry educators, practitioners, and students.

RELATED PROFESSIONAL ORGANIZATIONS AND WEBSITES

- American Dental Association (ADA): www.ada.org
- Special Care Dentistry Association (SCDA): www.scdaonline.org

- American Dental Education Association (ADEA): www.adea.org
- American Student Dental Association (ASDA): www.asdanet.org
- Interest Group on Oral Health, Gerontological Society of America (GSA): www.geron.org

GERIATRICIAN

BASIC DESCRIPTION

Geriatric medicine is a subspecialty of two medical specializations—internal medicine and family medicine. The American Board of Internal Medicine (ABIM) and the American Board of Family Medicine (ABFM) offer a Certificate of Added Qualifications in Geriatric Medicine upon successful completion of the Geriatric Medicine exam. Geriatricians are internists or family practitioners who have earned voluntary certification in geriatric medicine. They have been trained in the processes of aging and have acquired special diagnostic, therapeutic, preventive, and rehabilitative skills to use in their professional practice with elderly patients. The American Geriatrics Society (AGS) was the first medical organization to recognize the value of comprehensive assessment of elderly patients. This approach requires assessment by a team of medical and allied health professionals (e.g., physicians, social workers, nurses, pharmacists, occupational therapists, physical therapists, dietitians, psychologists, psychiatrists) and other professionals (e.g., spiritual advisors), who address the older person's physical, mental, and social needs from a holistic perspective. In 1994, AGS, with support from the John A. Hartford Foundation, launched the Geriatrics for Specialists Initiative (GSI) to expand geriatric expertise in 10 surgical and related medical specialties: anesthesiology, emergency medicine, general surgery, gynecology, ophthalmology, orthopedic surgery, otolaryngology, physical medicine and rehabilitation, thoracic surgery, and urology. To encourage early career physicians with an interest in aging/geriatrics research and trained in medical and surgical subspecialties, the National Institute on Aging provides awards (up to $150,000 in direct costs over a 2-year period) for research on geriatric aspects of their specialty. Through its Dennis W. Jahnigen Career Development Award (JCDA), AGS offers supplemental funding for GEMSSTAR projects.

EDUCATION AND EXPERIENCE REQUIREMENTS

Geriatricians require a bachelor's degree (BA or BS), with a strong emphasis on basic sciences, a Doctor of Medicine degree (MD) from a medical school (4-year undergraduate medical education) accredited by the Liaison Committee of the Committee on Medical Education (LCCME), a residency program (3-year graduate medical education for internal medicine or family medicine), and a Fellowship (subspecialty training in geriatric medicine). A PhD may be required for geriatricians who become researchers or faculty members in medical schools or other institutions of higher education.

CERTIFICATION, LICENSURE, AND CONTINUING EDUCATION REQUIREMENTS

Geriatricians require licensure to practice in the state or jurisdiction of the United States in which their professional practice occurs. Continuing medical education (CME) varies by state, professional organizations, and medical staff organizations. The Certificate of Added Qualifications in Geriatric Medicine must be renewed periodically and may be accomplished through CME credit and retesting on the Geriatric Medicine exam.

CORE COMPETENCIES AND SKILLS NEEDED

- Commitment to an interdisciplinary teamwork and ability to work well in a team process
- Commitment to practice of comprehensive geriatric assessment
- Commitment to a holistic health approach
- Excellent listener and observer
- Excellent communication and interpersonal skills
- Patience
- Ability to work with and on behalf of patients, as well as their family members and other caregivers

COMPENSATION

This varies by one's education, experience, specific type of practice, the nature of the practice setting, and the geographical location. Geriatricians are the lowest paid category of medical/surgical physicians, although they also report higher job satisfaction than is found among other specializations.

WORKPLACE(S)

These include private practices, medical care centers and hospitals, clinics, long-term care facilities, medical schools, colleges and universities, research centers and institutes, and consultancy practices (e.g., with hospice programs and facilities, assisted living facilities, and health care "senior living" corporations).

EMPLOYMENT OUTLOOK

Excellent, due to a growing national shortage of certified geriatricians and the need for more surgical and related specialists with geriatric-specific training.

RELATED PROFESSIONAL ORGANIZATIONS AND WEBSITES

- American Medical Association (AMA): www.ama-assn.org
- American Board of Internal Medicine (ABIM): www.abim.org
- Geriatrics Task Force, Society of General Internal Medicine (SGIM): www.sgim.org/communities/task-force/geriatrics
- American Board of Family Medicine (ABFM): www.theabfm.org
- American Geriatrics Society (AGS): www.americangeriatrics.org
- Geriatrics for Specialists Initiative (GSI), American Geriatrics Society (AGS): www.americangeriatrics.org/gsi/who_is_gsi/gsi_mission_goals
- Early Medical/Surgical Specialists' Transition to Aging Research (GEMSSTAR), NIA and AGS: www.americangeriatrics.org/gsi/gemsstar_jahnigen
- John A. Hartford Foundation: www.jhartfound.org

An Interview With ELIZABETH ECKSTROM

Geriatrician and Director of Geriatrics

Postsecondary educational background, including formal credentials and other education/training in gerontology/geriatrics:

BS, Mathematics
MD
Master's in Public Health (MPH)
Geriatric Fellowship
Board-Certified in Internal Medicine/Geriatrics

How and when did you first become interested in gerontology/geriatrics? I have been drawn to older people since I was about 12 years old and my grandfather, who had Alzheimer's disease, lived with us for a while.

Briefly describe your gerontology/geriatrics-related career path. I didn't start as a geriatrician. I started my career as a general internist doing primary care practice with a wonderful group of patients. I also was getting my MPH at the time and I chose to do a research project on counseling people with chronic diseases, like diabetes and arthritis, to start an exercise program. Not surprisingly, the average age of people in the study was over 70, so I learned a lot about how older people think about their health and about exercise. I also was invited to be part of a project studying tai chi to prevent falls for older adults. Through these projects, I absolutely fell in love with older people. I recognized, however, that I lacked sufficient geriatric training during medical school and residency, so I decided to do a formal geriatrics fellowship so that I could teach geriatrics and, hopefully, give students a better exposure to older adults than I had while in school. It was the best decision of my life. I now lead an academic geriatrics program through which I see patients and teach learners from many professions on a regular basis.

Briefly describe your current professional position:

Position title: Director of Geriatrics

(*continued*)

An Interview With ELIZABETH ECKSTROM *(continued)*

Primary role tasks/responsibilities: I lead the geriatrics practice within the internal medicine clinic and teach internal medicine residents and geriatric fellows in the geriatric consult clinic. My research focuses on promoting a healthy lifestyle for older adults and educating all health professionals to be competent in the care of older adults. I conduct studies to enhance interprofessional teamwork in community practices, including clinics, hospitals, and long-term care facilities. I am principle investigator for the state's Geriatric Education Center (GEC), where I work with colleagues in my institution's School of Nursing, the School of Social Work at another local university, and the School of Pharmacy at another state university to find solutions to challenges facing older adults.

Type of employment setting: Academic medical center

Length of time in this position: 7 years

How did you first become interested in this position? I was invited to apply.

Describe a typical workday in your current professional position. Each day is a little different. I spend some days in clinic, talking with my nurse care manager and social work colleagues, and teaching students and residents. Some days, I do formal teaching or work on research projects.

What is the time commitment required of your current professional position? 70+ hours per week, including many evenings and weekends.

How do you stay up-to-date in your profession?

Professional organization memberships and/or activities? I am active in both the Society of General Internal Medicine (SGIM), where I am part of the Geriatrics Task Force, and the American Geriatrics Society (AGS). I participate in committees, submit workshops and research abstracts to their national meetings, and work on numerous projects with colleagues from these organizations.

(continued)

An Interview With ELIZABETH ECKSTROM (*continued*)

Subscribe to and/or read professional journals and/or newsletters? I read many journals regularly, including the *Journal of the American Geriatrics Society*, the *Journal of General Internal Medicine*, the *New England Journal of Medicine*, and others. All are critical to my work.

Attend professional conferences and/or participate in education/training programs? Yes, as already noted.

What are the most rewarding aspects of your current career position? There are many rewarding aspects. It is an absolute joy to provide longitudinal, team-based care to older adults, many of whom I have known for years and who teach me amazing things every day. Sometimes people ask me how I can keep working with people when so many of them die, but I think the rewards of helping patients and families have the best possible quality of life and die peacefully far outweigh the sadness of losing these treasured individuals. It is also incredibly rewarding to see students understand the value of caring for older adults and then choose to go into geriatrics themselves.

What are the most rewarding aspects of your gerontology/geriatrics-related career path? In addition to the rewards of caring for older patients, it is extremely rewarding to help new research findings get implemented in clinical settings with interprofessional teams. Caring for complex older patients is challenging, but systems, teams, and great communication can make it work. I am delighted to be part of that process.

What are the most challenging aspects of your current career position? The biggest challenge is probably just the lack of geriatricians. There are far more older adults than there are geriatricians, so it is hard to provide optimal care to everyone. My goal is both to help expand the pool of geriatrics-trained health professionals (such as geriatricians), but also ensure that nongeriatrics trained health professionals have some additional training in the care of older adults.

What are the most challenging aspects of your gerontology/geriatrics-related career path? One of the most important aspects of caring for older

(*continued*)

An Interview With ELIZABETH ECKSTROM *(continued)*

adults is having an infrastructure in place to ensure adequate resources to promote health and independence. This includes both health care infrastructure (a team that includes nurses, therapists, social workers, and other relevant professionals) and a community infrastructure (such as safe sidewalks, places to exercise, resources for food, low-income senior housing). Since governmental systems don't adequately support these infrastructures, I often struggle to help patients, caregivers, and colleagues provide an ideal opportunity to age successfully.

How do you balance career and other aspects of your life? Even though I work a lot, a fair bit of my time is flexible, so I can always carve out time for exercise and time with my family, even though I work most evenings and weekends. I love to be outdoors and my family shares my love of hiking, cycling, skiing, and windsurfing, so we can be together and enjoy an active lifestyle, eat from our garden, and stay healthy.

What advice do you have for someone contemplating a career in the field of aging? If you are considering medical school and possibly becoming a geriatrician, volunteer in a hospital, hospice, senior center, or other settings that will give you experience with older adults. Many pre-medical students also work in long-term care settings or other elder communities to gain additional experience in caring for older adults. Once you are in medical school, there are lots of opportunities to work with a geriatrician and get a much deeper understanding of our field.

What advice do you have for someone considering a professional position similar to your current position? Geriatric leaders can influence the health of older adults in many settings—from being chief medical officer at a hospital to being medical director of a long-term care facility or the leader of an academic geriatrics program like I am. If your goal is to impact the care of older adults in a broader way than just being a good doctor, I strongly encourage you to gain extra leadership training through either informal courses or a formal degree, such as a master's in public health. At every step of the way, consider the systems challenges of your environment and engage your colleagues to think about how to make changes to improve the system. You will find endless opportunities for individual growth and will gradually gain the skills to become a leader who can make a positive impact.

GERONTECHNOLOGY: AN EMERGING FIELD

GERONTECHNOLOGIST

ERGONOMIST

HUMAN FACTORS ENGINEER

BASIC DESCRIPTION

Gerontechnology is one of the newest subspecializations within the field of aging, and as such, it is still in the process of being defined at the same time that a wide variety of technological devices and processes are currently being used to meet the goals and objectives of this newly emerging field. Early theoretical work by Herman Bouma in the Netherlands and James Fozard in the United States suggest that systems, person–environment fit, social ecological, healthy aging, and successful aging theoretical models offer a sound basis upon which to build relevant research. Fozard outlines four "classes" of technology—prevention and engagement, compensation and assistance, care support and organization, and enhancement and satisfaction—that have a direct impact on five broad "domains" of human activity—health and self-esteem, housing and daily living, mobility and transportation, communication and governance, and work and leisure—that are of special concern for aged and aging persons. This makes it clear that gerontechnology, at minimum, is a multidisciplinary field and, more likely, an interdisciplinary field as the disciplines of gerontology (e.g., physiology, psychology, sociology) and the technology disciplines (e.g., chemistry/biochemistry, architecture/building, information/communication, mechatronics/robotics, ergonomics design, business management) interconnect and collaborate to create technological responses to needs that arise as humans age and to prevent negative outcomes (e.g., falls, automobile accidents). For example, the Gerontechnology Core Group at a Center for Healthy Aging Research includes faculty members/researchers from electrical engineering, computer science, design and environment, design and mechanics, and the college of business who work collaboratively in interdisciplinary teams to develop and examine innovative support technologies that increase independence and provide support for older adults living in their own homes or in residential facilities. Human factors engineering and ergonomics are closely related fields with considerable overlap in goals and outcomes for older persons. The work of human factors engineers, ergonomists, and gerontechnologists is similar in many ways in that each is based in a systems approach that is user centered. As researchers with gerontology interests, they seek to understand the impact of age-related changes on the daily task and activity performance of elders; identify human, environmental, and product problems and difficulties that affect task and activity performance; and discover solutions to these problems and difficulties. As designers, they may create new products or redesign existing products, modify environments, develop intervention strategies, or provide training to change personal or staff behaviors that prevent or limit optimal performance for older persons. For example, this approach is being applied to elders' living and work environments (e.g., fall prevention, workplace ergonomics), mobility, and transportation (e.g., vehicle design, modification of roadway signage, traffic lights), and use of technology in everyday life (e.g., interactive communication systems, monitoring devices, entertainment devices). Emphasizing the international community involved in gerontechnology, the primary professional organization is the International Society of Gerontechnology (ISG) that has seven international chapters, including a student chapter. ISG publishes a quarterly journal, *Gerontecholology*, and holds a biennial conference. It appears, however, that most individuals now involved in gerontechnology do not identify themselves as gerontechnologists; instead they continue to retain professional identities connected to the discipline(s) or professional field(s) in which they earned their degrees. A search for degree programs in gerontechnology showed a master of science degree offered by the Graduate School of Gerontic Management at Nan Kei Institute of Technology in Taiwan, an interuniversity graduate diploma in gerontechnology at the universities of Grenoble in France, and gerontechnology tracks as part of gerontology graduate certificates at several colleges/universities in the United States.

EDUCATION AND EXPERIENCE REQUIREMENTS

Not yet clearly identified; however, graduate degree programs with an interdisciplinary approach to both aging and technology seem to be a good place to start.

CERTIFICATION, LICENSURE, AND CONTINUING EDUCATION REQUIREMENTS

None yet identified for gerontechnologists, although professionals must meet requirements specified by their professional fields, employers, and/or the state(s) in which their practice occurs.

CORE COMPETENCIES AND SKILLS NEEDED

- Commitment to an interdisciplinary approach to learning about aging and professional practice with or on behalf of aged and aging persons
- Commitment to a user-centered approach
- Willingness to work cooperatively and collaboratively
- Creative and innovative approach to problem solving
- Competence in use of assessment methods and skills
- Competence in research methodologies and statistical analyses
- Good understanding of changes in human function with age
- High level of technology literacy

COMPENSATION

No data yet available

WORKPLACE(S)

Although individuals doing gerontechnological work do so in a wide variety of settings, it appears that more professionals in gerontechnology currently tend to be attached to academic institutions and research centers than in other professional roles.

EMPLOYMENT OUTLOOK

Promising, but still to be determined for this emerging interdisciplinary subspecialization as part of the field of aging.

RELATED PROFESSIONAL ORGANIZATIONS AND WEBSITES

- International Society of Gerontechnology (ISG): www.gerontechnology.info
- Human Factors and Ergonomics Society (HFES): www.hfes.org
- HFES Aging Technical Group (ATG): www.psychology.gatech.edu/atg
- Center for Research and Education on Aging and Technology Enhancement (CREATE): www.create-center.org
- International Ergonomics Association (IEA): www.iea.cc
- Herman Bouma Fund for Gerontechnology Foundation: gerontechnologie.ni
- Network on Environments, Services and Technologies for Maximizing Independence (NEST), American Society on Aging (ASA): www.asaging.org/nest

An Interview With JENNIFER DAVIDSON

Human Computer Interaction PhD Candidate

Postsecondary educational background, including formal credentials and other education /training in gerontology/geriatrics:

Bachelor's degree, Computer Science

PhD Candidate, Computer Sciences, with emphasis in Human Computer Interaction

Graduate Minor, Aging Sciences (included courses related to aging in biochemistry, human development and family sciences, cognition, and computer science)

National Science Foundation—Integrative Graduate Education and Research Traineeship (IGERT) 2011–2013: This fellowship is awarded to 5 to 6 students per year who are doing work related to healthy aging. The students come from a variety of disciplines. Each year's cohort works on a year-long project together, in addition to earning a Minor in Aging Sciences and conducting their own research related to healthy aging. In my cohort, the year-long project was to do a critical review of the literature around circadian rhythms and emotion regulation with older adults. Our deliverable for the project was a symposium (a series of three talks) at the 2013 Gerontological Society of America Annual Scientific Meeting.

How and when did you first become interested in gerontology/ geriatrics? My interest started before I knew what "gerontology" meant. When I was a Girl Scout in 7th grade (11 years old), I went camping at Palomar Mountain near San Diego. The camp host was in his 80s at the time and he had the best stories. For my Girl Scout Silver Award project, I decided that his story needed to be told. So I interviewed him and put his interview on a homemade website, thus preserving his story for years to come. Little did I know I was doing research! Fast forward to college. I worked at a large printer company and noticed that many of my colleagues were of retirement age. A question came to mind: What are they going to do when they retire? Their brains don't shut off just because someone isn't paying them to think. I saw this firsthand a few years ago when my family bought my grandpa an iPad and he went wild with it. He now has a nicer computer than me and is busy working on digitizing all of the family photos and creating sophisticated slide shows

(*continued*)

An Interview With JENNIFER DAVIDSON *(continued)*

with them. My grandpa and those coworkers helped to inspire my dissertation idea of "Involving Older Adults in the Design and Development of Free/Open Source Software." That idea, plus a funding opportunity in healthy aging, was a match made in heaven.

Briefly describe your gerontology/geriatrics-related career path. The first step in my career path was to obtain 2 years of funding related to healthy aging through the IGERT. Then, I completed coursework for a minor in aging sciences. Throughout this time I became more familiar with age-related research and designed my dissertation research study. Currently, I am a PhD candidate, which means that my dissertation proposal is approved and I'm in the process of conducting the related research. Thankfully, I already have accepted a professional position in the industry as a user experience researcher. While my job will not be focused solely on gerontology, I plan to use everything I have learned doing age-related research to guide my path forward. For example, I will specifically ask research questions related to age/experience (e.g., "Do older workers prefer different features in project management software than younger workers?" and "Would workers benefit from a mentoring program where older workers and younger workers mentor each other?"). I will also be sure to recruit computer-user study subjects from a broad range of ages in my research studies because we know there are age-related differences in learning, processing information, and computer use. Overall, my background in gerontology will prepare me to conduct research studies to improve software for older people.

Briefly describe your current professional position:

Position title: Human–Computer Interaction PhD Candidate

Primary role tasks/responsibilities: Design and conduct research studies with computer users and developers

Type of employment setting: I work in the computer science department at a state university. Because my IGERT Fellowship Program funding has ended, I now work as a teaching assistant and as the instructor for an online course; this covers tuition and provides a stipend. I share an office with another graduate student. In Human–Computer Interaction,

(continued)

An Interview With JENNIFER DAVIDSON *(continued)*

we interview individual participants quite frequently and our office is used sometimes as a "lab" for that purpose. We also have a separate computer lab for user studies when we work with a group of people at the same time.

Length of time in this position: 5 years

How did you first become interested in this position? I first became interested in doing a PhD when I had the opportunity to be involved in a National Science Foundation Research Experience for Undergraduates summer internship. Before doing that internship, I thought I hated research. Because of that experience, now I know that I thoroughly enjoy research—there's always something new to discover and I love that. After 2 years of being a doctoral student, I discovered the IGERT fellowship program through my advisor and a collaborator in another department.

Describe a typical workday in your current professional position. For me, a typical workday always involves sending e-mails to research study participants, collaborators, and/or my advisor. When I am running a research study, I oftentimes conduct interviews. Some of my research studies are done in person and some are done virtually (e.g., via Skype or e-mail). Most days, I do data analysis or planning for data analysis. I write every day—sometimes it is just a clarification of my research plan and other times it's an entire conference paper about a research study. Additionally, I have weekly meetings with the Human–Computer Interaction research group and my advisor to get updated on everyone's research. I also often participate in outreach activities. I am program manager for ChickTech, a nonprofit organization to get more women and girls interested and retained in technology. The biggest outreach event I have helped with was to organize a day-long series of workshops held at the university for 100 high school girls. Other than that large event, I help in day-to-day tasks of proofreading communications to the press, budgeting, planning meetings, and related tasks. I am thankful that my advisor is supportive of these outreach efforts, as I feel that they are important for the sustainability of the computer science profession.

(continued)

An Interview With JENNIFER DAVIDSON *(continued)*

What is the time commitment required of your current position? I work about 30 hours a week on my PhD research. I try to keep my working hours to daylight hours, unless there's a conference deadline—then it's pedal to the metal until the conference paper is finished. In computer science, our typical mode of publication is in the form of 10-page conference papers. Our conference papers report on fully completed research studies, are peer-reviewed, and are of publication quality. In my case, my dissertation will be a portfolio of my conference papers. In general, I like that I can structure my work time around other activities and needs.

How do you stay up-to-date in your profession?

Professional organization memberships and/or activities?
Gerontological Society of America (GSA), Student Member
Association of Computing Machinery (ACM), Student Member
Institute of Electronics and Electrical Engineers (IEEE), Student Member

Subscribe to and/or read professional journals and/or newsletters?
IEEE Spectrum magazine
The Gerontologist (GSA)
ACM conference proceedings on *Human Factors in Computing Systems*
Conference proceedings from SIGACCES International Conference on Computers and Accessibility

Attend professional conferences and/or participate in education/training programs? Gerontological Society of America Annual Research Meetings, attended past 3 years; presented a paper and a poster at 2013 meeting.

Other? Systems Member, mailing list (support group) for women in technology; Program Manager of ChickTech, a nonprofit organization whose aim is to create a multigenerational community of women and girls who are technology creators; and Community Manager of Privly, an open source software community whose aim is to inform people and provide tools related to internet privacy.

(continued)

An Interview With JENNIFER DAVIDSON *(continued)*

What are the most rewarding aspects of your current career position? The most rewarding part of my current position is when I get to see older adults engage positively with technology. One of my favorite recent memories of my graduate work was when I held a technology design workshop with 18 older adults (4 to 5 older adults at a time) and multiple participants asked if they could come back! How often do participants ask to participate in your research study again? If you want a way to break down ageist stereotypes about older adults and technology, I encourage you to conduct user research studies with them. My participants were excited, active, creative, and passionate. I have such a great time when I'm in the lab with them and when I'm listening to their stories during the interview process.

What are the most rewarding aspects of your gerontology/geriatrics-related career path? My new professional position as a User Experience Researcher for a large microprocessor manufacturing company is not directly a "gerontechnologist" position, but my background with aging sciences and conducting user studies with older adults not only helped me get the job, but it will also inform how I conduct research studies in the future. Thus far, I will say that the most rewarding part of my career path is that I have been offered a position well in advance of graduation because of my experience studying gerontechnology.

What are the most challenging aspects of your current career position? The hardest part of my position is combating ageist stereotypes about older adults and technology. There is a huge assumption that older adults don't use technology because they don't want to, which leads many developers to think that older adults aren't their "target audience." This is an issue that I have to combat often when talking with computer scientists. Another issue is convincing computer science academics (who review papers) that caring about older adults and age diversity in our developer communities is both worth it and appropriate.

What are the most challenging aspects of your gerontology/geriatrics-related career path? I think the most challenging part is to convince industry to fund research studies that explicitly focus on older adults.

(continued)

An Interview With JENNIFER DAVIDSON (*continued*)

Most industry folks seem only to focus on the 20-something market or perhaps the student market rather than the fastest growing population segment of older adults.

How do you balance career and other aspects of your life? Work–fun balance (not to say that my work isn't fun) is of the highest importance in my life. I strongly believe that I am not as productive if I don't take some time for me and my passions outside of research. I plan weekends away, nights to go to concerts, and sometimes I'll take an extended lunch just to have a long walk and clear my head. A good, full night's sleep helps me to be productive during work hours and have enough energy to do a fun activity—maybe just watching a movie or something else where I can "turn my brain off" after work. Work hard, play hard!

What advice do you have for someone contemplating a career in the field of aging? Know that you will face adversity and you will need to help break down some of our society's deeply ageist views, but it's worth fighting for.

What advice do you have for someone considering a professional position similar to your current position? There are many aspects of research and you won't like every one of them. For example, scheduling participants is one of my least favorite activities. My advice would be to ask for help (even if you don't think you need it). Having a research team is important—a research study cannot be done all by yourself. Also, talk to as many people about your ideas and work as possible. The more you talk about it, the more feedback you'll get and this leads to new ideas. You'll think of a career full of research studies if you take the time to talk with people—offer to speak at your undergraduate university, go to conferences, go to career fairs. Networking pays off. Finally, stand up for what you believe in. Even if your advisor doesn't do work in gerontology or even if your workplace doesn't have an interest in gerontology, keep your interest in gerontology and weave it into your work. Seek out experts for advice and you'll be surprised how successful you can be. Many experts love to mentor passionate emerging scholars, so keep at it!

GERONTOLOGICAL/GERIATRIC OPTOMETRIST

LOW VISION REHABILITATION SPECIALIST

BASIC DESCRIPTION

Optometrists are primary eye care providers who examine the eye structure (internal and external) to diagnose vision conditions (e.g., near or farsightedness, presbyopia, astigmatism), eye diseases (e.g., cataracts, glaucoma, retinal disorders), and systemic diseases (e.g., diabetes, hypertension). Following diagnosis, they treat and manage diseases, injuries, and disorders of the visual system, eyes, and associated body structures. They are licensed to prescribe spectacle and contact lenses, low vision aid rehabilitation, vision therapy, and medications, and to perform some surgical procedures. Optometrists counsel patients regarding treatment plans and procedures. A unique aspect of optometry is the advanced study of optics—the science of light and vision—and extensive training related to corrective lens design, construction, application, and fitting. Gerontological/geriatric optometrists have completed an optional residency in gerontological/geriatric optometry and practice in settings where their primary clients are older adults. Low vision rehabilitation specialists work with clients, including older adults, who are experiencing low vision problems that are treatable or correctable.

EDUCATION AND EXPERIENCE REQUIREMENTS

A Doctor of Optometry (OD) degree from an accredited school/college of optometry is mandatory. Gerontology coursework or a degree component in a pre-professional undergraduate program is strongly recommended and an optional residency in low vision rehabilitation and/or gerontological/geriatric optometry is strongly recommended.

CERTIFICATION, LICENSURE, AND CONTINUING EDUCATION REQUIREMENTS

These professionals must meet state licensing requirements, including a state board examination and annual state-mandated continuing education requirements for optometrists.

CORE COMPETENCIES AND SKILLS NEEDED

- Strong science foundation (including biology, chemistry, biochemistry, human anatomy, physiology, and physics) in pre-professional undergraduate degree program

- Ability to differentiate between age-related visual changes and pathological eye diseases/conditions and to understand the implications of each for the patient
- Commitment to patient-centered care
- Commitment to evidence-based professional practice
- Strong knowledge of the concepts and principles of the public health care system
- Good working knowledge of laws and regulations that govern optometric patient care
- Business management training and skills (e.g., personnel management, business finances)
- Good oral and written communication skills; good listening skills
- Commitment to ethical professional practice

COMPENSATION

This varies by one's educational background, the type of practice, the nature of the employment setting, and the geographical location.

WORKPLACE(S)

These include private practices, multidisciplinary medical practices, hospitals, teaching institutions, research positions, community health centers, retail chains, military, public health, or government services, and the ophthalmic industry.

EMPLOYMENT OUTLOOK

Very good, especially due to the current and future growth of the elderly population, more individuals living long enough to experience more advanced normal aging changes, and the increasing impact of social and environmental factors on vision.

RELATED PROFESSIONAL ORGANIZATIONS AND WEBSITES

- American Optometric Association (AOA): www.aoa.org
- American Optometric Student Association (AOSA): www.aoa.org/students
- American Academy of Optometry (AAO): www.aaopt.org

An Interview With JOHN E. KAMINSKI

Doctor of Optometry

Postsecondary educational background, including formal credentials and other education/training in gerontology/geriatrics:
BS, Applied Biology
Doctorate of Optometry
Low Vision Specialist Certification (awarded by state Optometric Association)
Graduate Interdisciplinary Specialization in Aging
Fellow in the American Academy of Optometry

How and when did you first become interested in gerontology/geriatrics? Through mentorship. I knew someone who was an optometrist and his professionalism inspired me to become an optometrist. I observed different eye doctors in their offices to survey what appealed to my career goals. I spent time researching which subspecialties would be in need with the anticipated rapid growth of the elderly population. It was apparent to me early on in college that the health care needs of older adults are significantly underserved.

Briefly describe your gerontology/geriatrics-related career path. My initial experience with work in geriatrics was during undergraduate school when I worked as a Certified Nurse's Aide (CNA) and a Certified Phlebotomist. While completing my Doctorate in Optometry, the Office of Gerontology Studies promoted the Graduate Interdisciplinary Specialization in Aging program to professional students in the medical, law, social work, optometry, dentistry, and pharmacy programs. I entered practice emphasizing geriatrics and low vision rehabilitation. Also, I have had academic opportunities to contribute to the gerontology program at a nearby university. Combining the clinical and academic experiences, I now present geriatric and aging courses at continuing education conferences around the country.

Briefly describe your current professional position:

Position title: Doctor of Optometry

Primary role tasks/responsibilities: General/Family Practice. I specialize in geriatrics and low vision as a smaller part of my practice.

Type of employment practice: Private practice

(*continued*)

An Interview With JOHN E. KAMINSKI (*continued*)

Length of time in this position: 15 years

How did you first become interested in this position? I wanted to be a business owner or full partner in an eye care practice.

Describe a typical workday in your current professional position. On average, I see about 20 patients a day. I conduct routine eye exams, urgent care for eye conditions, follow-up care for managing eye disease conditions, low vision rehabilitation, and fitting contact lenses. I have responsibilities in managing a 12-member staff, preparing reports, and making financial/purchasing decisions for the practice.

What is the time commitment required of your current professional position? I see patients Monday through Friday, 8 a.m. to 5 p.m. I spend, on average, 1 to 2 hours a week with practice management. Through our on-call system, I occasionally see a patient after hours during the week or on weekends.

How do you stay up-to-date in your profession?

Professional organization memberships and/or activities? Vision and Aging group and Low Vision Section, American Academy of Optometry, Member; I also help develop annual symposia and position papers on geriatric themes.

Subscribe to and/or read professional journals and/or newsletters? Publications from the American Optometric Association, American Academy of Optometry, or Michigan Optometric Association.

Attend professional conferences and/or participate in education/training programs? I attend symposia and continuing education programs at the American Optometric Association, the American Academy of Optometry, or Michigan Optometric Association.

Other? I still find myself using my course notes and textbooks from my graduate work. I have added several textbooks or new editions along the way.

(*continued*)

An Interview With JOHN E. KAMINSKI *(continued)*

What are the most rewarding aspects of your current career position? Helping patients see better, preventing vision loss by managing ocular disease, and overall making a difference in patients' lives.

What are the most rewarding aspects of your gerontology/geriatrics-related career path? Regularly having an opportunity to get optimal outcomes in patient care by applying my geriatric/gerontology education and training.

What are the most challenging aspects of your current career position? Keeping up with the rapid changes in health care to properly manage a practice.

What are the most challenging aspects of your gerontology/geriatrics-related career path? Enduring, on a day-to-day basis, the intensive needs of older patients and demands of a geriatric/low vision practice.

How do you balance career and other aspects of your life? A great spouse and family. I attend regular workout classes. Our family is frequently involved in outdoor sports and going to our cottage.

What advice do you have for someone contemplating a career in the field of aging? Do the strategic analysis on the career you consider. Look for opportunities where you have a rewarding career for the long haul while helping your colleagues meet the many underserved needs of older adults.

What advice do you have for someone considering a professional position similar to your current position? While going through graduate school, think of an emphasis in geriatrics/gerontology as a way to bring added value to a practice. You will make yourself a more competitive and valuable member of the health care team wherever you decide to work after college.

GERONTOLOGICAL NURSE

GERONTOLOGICAL NURSE SPECIALIST

GERONTOLOGICAL NURSE PRACTITIONER

BASIC DESCRIPTION

Five levels of nursing education and licensure are recognized by the American Nurses Association (ANA) and the American Nurses Credentialing Center (ANCC):

- Diploma in Nursing (from a hospital-based school of nursing)
- Associate Degree in Nursing (ADN; 2-year degree from a community college or hospital-based school of nursing)
- Bachelor of Science in Nursing (BSN; 4-year degree from a college/university)
- Master of Science degree in Nursing (MSN)
- Doctor of Nursing Practice (DPN)

Nurses from the first three levels provide basic nursing practice, with advancing roles and increasing responsibilities as more education is acquired. With graduate degrees earned, MSNs tend to move into nursing administration (e.g., Director of Nursing [DON] and nursing education roles) and DPNs move into Advanced Practice Registered Nurse (APRN) clinical practice and leadership roles. Through ANCC, nurses who wish to focus on gerontological nursing practice can be certified at three different levels:

- Specialty Certification in Gerontological Nursing as a Registered Nurse–Board Certified (RN-BC)
- Clinical Nurse Specialist (CNS) as a Gerontological CNS (GCNS-BC) or as an Adult-Gerontology CNS (AGCNS-BC)
- Nurse Practitioner (NP) as a Gerontological NP (GNP-BC), an Adult-Gerontology Primary Care NP (AGNP-BC), or as an Adult-Gerontological Acute Care NP (AGACNP-BC)

Gerontological nurses (RN-BCs) work directly with older patients in a variety of clinical settings. Using their gerontological training and nursing care skills, they assess direct care needs and situations; manage and implement medications, treatments, and other health care services ordered by other health care professionals; and participate in evaluating the effectiveness of these services. Whenever possible, they involve their elderly patients, family members and caregivers, and others in the processes of care. Clinical nurse specialists (GCNS-BCs and AGCNS-BCs) have advanced clinical skills that allow them to provide primary care to older patients, independently or as members of interdisciplinary health care teams, and to serve as resource persons for other staff members in their care of elderly patients. They consult with and guide family caregivers and significant others in the patient's social support network, serve as leaders and supervisors in their work settings, conduct staff and patient education, and are authorized (in some states) to order diagnostic and lab tests, treatments, and medications. Nurse practitioners (GNP-BCs, AGNP-BCs, and AGANCP-BCs) have advanced knowledge, clinical skills, and certification that allow them to provide a full range of health care services related to wellness and illness for older patients. They have the training and authority to make differential diagnoses; manage acute and chronic diseases; carry out evidence-based practice; participate in the conduct of research studies; consult with others, including family and caregivers, in the care and support network of older patients; and serve as case managers for their patients. They also provide leadership for nursing and other staff members in their work setting and within the nursing profession. They are nursing educators and participate in health policy development and implementation. NPs are authorized to prescribe medications and treatments in most states.

In order to produce expert academicians, practitioners, and researchers with a commitment to gerontological/geriatric nursing, the National Hartford Centers on Gerontological Nursing Excellence (NHCGNE) funds Hartford Centers of Geriatric Nursing Excellence and their Scholarships and Fellowships Awards Programs.

EDUCATION AND EXPERIENCE REQUIREMENTS

A Diploma, ADN, or BSN degree is required for certification as a gerontological nurse. A MSN is required for certification as a clinical nurse specialist or nurse practitioner in gerontological nursing. An MSN is the minimum requirement for faculty in a Diploma or ADN and some BSN programs, while a DPN is the minimum requirement for faculty in most BSN and all MSN or DPN programs.

CERTIFICATION, LICENSURE, AND CONTINUING EDUCATION REQUIREMENTS

A current active and unrestricted professional RN license issued by the state or jurisdiction in which the practice occurs is required to practice nursing in the United States. As noted, ANCC certifies gerontological nurses, nurse specialists and nurse practitioners. Eligibility criteria vary for these certificates, but all require RN licensure, specified level(s) of nursing education and amounts of clinical practice, and successful completion of the appropriate certification examination. Recertification every 5 years is granted upon completion of professional development requirements and evidence of practice in the specialty or retesting.

CORE COMPETENCIES AND SKILLS NEEDED

Core competencies and skills are specified by each type of nursing degree and each level of gerontological nursing certification. Other necessary characteristics include:

- Commitment to patient-centered care and evidence-based practice
- Good communication skills (oral, written, listening)
- Good observational skills
- Good interpersonal skills
- Good organizational skills

COMPENSATION

This varies by one's education, licensure, experience, level of certification, type of position, employment setting, and the geographical location.

WORKPLACE(S)

These include ambulatory care settings (e.g., primary care practices, assisted living facilities, retirement communities, hospice); hospitals and long-term care facilities; settings specific to administration, leadership, and public policy (e.g., directors of nursing and vice presidents for nursing in managed care companies, automated medical records companies, state and federal departments, agencies, or organizations); schools of nursing and clinical supervision settings for nursing students; and research centers and institutes.

EMPLOYMENT OUTLOOK

Excellent, as demand continues to be greater than supply for all levels of gerontological nurses, including gerontological nurse educators.

RELATED PROFESSIONAL ORGANIZATIONS AND WEBSITES

- American Nurses Association (ANA): www.nursingworld.org
- National Gerontological Nursing Association (NGNA): www.ngna.org

- American Academy of Nursing (AAN): www.aannet.org
- American Nurses Credentialing Center (ANCC): www.nursecredentialing.org
- GeroNurseOnline.org: www.geronurseonline.org
- National Hartford Centers of Gerontological Nursing Excellence (NHCGNE; formerly known as BAGNC): www.geriatricnursing.org
- Interest Group on Nursing Care of Older Adults, Gerontological Society of America (GSA): www.geron.org

GLOBAL AGING: AN EMERGING FIELD

GLOBAL AGING SPECIALIST

BASIC DESCRIPTION

Although opportunities have become more prevalent for study abroad programs, service-learning programs, and summer field schools specific to aging, professional opportunities specific to global aging seem to reside only in a few limited sectors, including research, mission-driven nonprofits, nongovernmental organizations (NGOs), and organizations with geriatric health care initiatives.

EDUCATION AND EXPERIENCE REQUIREMENTS

Research: doctoral-level education in relevant fields. Nonprofit organizations: minimum of a bachelor's degree in an appropriate professional field (e.g., community health, community development, communications). NGOs: minimum of a master's degree in an appropriate field (e.g., public administration, public policy, gerontology, community health). Geriatric health care: minimum of a master's degree in public health, health administration, or a direct practice field (e.g., social work, nursing, occupational or physical therapy) or a doctorate in clinical medicine. At least some coursework or a degree component in gerontology is recommended.

CERTIFICATION, LICENSURE, AND CONTINUING EDUCATION REQUIREMENTS

None yet specified, except for health care/medicine professionals who would need to meet licensure requirements in the state(s) and, perhaps, in the country(ies) where practice occurs.

CORE COMPETENCES AND SKILLS NEEDED

- Knowledge of health and social services systems in development cultures appropriate to country or region where practice will occur
- Able to communicate orally and in written form in primary language(s) of native peoples in the locale where services are to be provided
- Ability to organize and supervise volunteer and paid staff
- Awareness of local customs and calendar of significant community-, regional-, and country-specific traditions and events
- Project and program management experience
- Comfort with and understanding of the complexity of travel requirements, including the coordination of group travel

COMPENSATION

Research: Compensation varies considerably and is commonly based on grant funding for a specific research study or project. Researchers involved with international research projects are more likely to receive compensation that is in addition to their base salaries as a research center staff member or professor at their primary institutions, and additional compensation to cover expenses (e.g., travel to research site, local transportation, lodging, meals, other amenities related to the project). NGOs: Compensation for global NGOs focused on aging varies, depending on experience, but covers salary and travel expenses. Health, social service and nonprofit charitable organizations: Many operate on limited funding from foundations, governmental response programs, and charitable donations, with heavy reliance on volunteers who receive minimal coverage or reimbursement of some expenses (e.g., transportation, lodging, meals).

WORKPLACE(S)

These include research centers, foundations, colleges/universities, disaster relief organizations, refugee health organizations, NGOs, government agencies, multilateral agencies, nonprofit organizations, and charitable or religious organizations.

EMPLOYMENT OUTLOOK

Hopeful and potential, but still limited.

RELATED PROFESSIONAL ORGANIZATIONS AND WEBSITES

- Global Aging Research Network (GARN): www.garn-network.org

- International Association of Gerontology and Geriatrics (IAGG): www.iagg.info
- International Federation on Ageing (IFA): www-ifa.fiv.org
- World Health Organization (WHO): www.who.int/topics/ageing/en
- Help Age International: www.helpage.org
- AARP International: www.aarpinternational.org
- National Association for the Practice of Anthropology (NAPA), a section of the American Anthropological Association (AAA), NAPA-OT Field School in Antigua, Guatemala: www.napaotguatemala.org
- Jessie F. Richard Foundation (JFRF), Global Aging Partners (GAP), and University-based Service Learning: www.jfrfoundation.org
- Portland State University, Global Aging and Health Program: www.pdx.edu/ioa/profile/global-aging-and-health-program
- Association for Gerontology in Higher Education (AGHE), Global Aging Committee (GAC): www.aghe.org
- Gerontological Society of America (GSA) Interest Groups: Aging in Asia, Chinese Gerontology Studies, and International Aging and Migration: www.geron.org

An Interview With ALAN DeLaTORRE

Foundation Director of Operations and Urban Gerontologist

Postsecondary educational background, including formal credentials and other education/training in gerontology/geriatrics:

BA, Sociology

PhD, Urban Studies, with field areas: Urban Planning and Gerontology

Graduate Certificate in Gerontology

Summer internship with State AARP: Focus on learning about aging in place and livable communities for older adults; coauthored report (summary of research findings on city's age friendliness) for local and international use

How and when did you first become interested in gerontology/geriatrics? My interest in gerontology originated when I was 18, during my first year of undergraduate studies. A professor in my Introduction to Sociology course frequently observed me with my skateboard. She challenged me to think about the built environment and why it was created (she assured me it was not for skateboarding). I started to realize that the obstacles used for skating (e.g., benches, rails, stairs) could be considered prosthetics for those with varying abilities. I also began to recognize that aging has important implications for communities. My professor explained that this was important as professionals would be needed to address arising issues and gerontologists would have an opportunity to affect positive change in communities. During that same term, a life-changing event happened to my family. My sister was in an accident and had a traumatic brain injury; after emerging from a coma, her life changed forever and our family learned firsthand the importance of rehabilitation and supportive environments.

Briefly describe your gerontology/geriatrics-related career path. Influenced by my professor's observations and my family's growing understanding of supportive environments, I chose to major in sociology. A course in social gerontology piqued my interest and inspired my decision about graduate school. I knew I was interested in gerontology as a career field, but I was not sure what I would study within the field. As I browsed a guide of graduate programs in gerontology, I discovered a university that offered a degree in urban studies with a field area in gerontology. I was excited about the program

(*continued*)

An Interview With ALAN DeLaTORRE *(continued)*

and the other available field areas, in particular urban planning and community development. I applied for the doctoral program in urban studies because it was the only program that would allow me to combine two field areas. I chose urban planning as a primary field area, with gerontology as my secondary area, so I could concurrently enroll in the Graduate Certificate in Gerontology program. In my graduate studies, I began focusing on the intersection between sustainable community development and aging. I was able to apply what I was learning from my coursework into two programs: a service-learning program on aging and health in Nicaragua and a project in collaboration with WHO that focused on making cities friendly to people of all ages and abilities. I was fortunate to evolve, through both programs, from graduate assistant to part-time program coordinator and, eventually, to full-time program manager of these programs. Since completing my doctorate, I continue to work professionally with both programs.

Briefly describe your current professional position:

Position title: Director of Operations for a locally based foundation

Primary role tasks/responsibilities: Day-to-day operations and management, coordination of university-based service-learning programs, grant development and management, international logistics and communications, research.

Type of employment setting: Small nonprofit foundation engaged with higher education and community partners locally, in Appalachia, and in Nicaragua.

Length of time in this position: 1-1/2 years

How did you first become interested in this position? My interest in the position initially emerged from participating in a study abroad program to Nicaragua. After experiencing the initial trip as a graduate student, I was given responsibilities as a team leader, then as a program coordinator, and, finally, as program faculty. Since the university and foundation were

(continued)

An Interview With ALAN DeLaTORRE (*continued*)

program partners, I became interested in the position at the foundation because it allowed me to work with additional universities on programs to Nicaragua and with international partners on research, education, and community development programs.

Describe a typical workday in your current professional position. My typical workday varies, depending on whether I am in the office or the field. In the office (a much more frequent occurrence), I communicate with the Foundation's President on a daily basis to coordinate community outreach, program management, and the development of grants and partnerships. A lot of time in the office is spent on a computer, researching new and ongoing opportunities, e-mailing partners, and making international calls. In the field, I work with university faculty, students, and community partners in the local area and in Nicaragua (4 to 5 times per year for approximately 2 weeks each trip). The time in Nicaragua is most unique, as I coordinate logistics for the group, supervise students, and communicate with our partners at long-term care facilities for older adults or other public, private, and for-profit agencies. I also meet with professionals in Nicaragua who are employed by the Foundation and/or are leaders in furthering education, training, and partnerships among U.S. students, faculty, professionals and Nicaraguan partners.

What is the time commitment required of your current professional position? My current position requires approximately 40 hours of work each week; however, there are times when I work more than that, in particular when project deadlines for reports or grant proposals are in sight. When I am traveling to Nicaragua to coordinate service-learning projects (e.g., training, clinical work), there is additional supervision needed after the scheduled activities end. Some of this is evenings and weekends, although that is often simply accompanying people to restaurants and tourist activities, such as hiking or souvenir shopping.

How do you stay up-to-date in your profession?

Professional organization memberships and/or activities?
Gerontological Society of America (GSA), Member; Social Research, Policy and Practice Section Member; present papers and posters;

(*continued*)

An Interview With ALAN DELATORRE (*continued*)

organize symposia and, recently, a pre-conference workshop that convened international scholars around the efforts to create age-friendly and livable communities.

American Society on Aging (ASA), Member, present papers and workshops.

State Gerontological Association, Member; Board Member.

World Health Organization (WHO), involved with Age-Friendly Cities Project that evolved into the Global Network of Age-Friendly Cities and Communities.

Subscribe to and/or read professional journals and/or newsletters?

The Gerontologist and *The Journals of Gerontology: Psychological Sciences and Social Sciences: Series B* (GSA, subscriptions are member benefit)

Generations (ASA; subscription is member benefit)

As a researcher I commonly read and reference journals that focus on housing for older adults, urban planning, urban studies, urban design, global aging, aging and social policy, and public health.

Attend professional conferences and/or participate in education/training programs? Regularly attend GSA's Annual Scientific Research Meeting, and the State Gerontological Society's annual conference; occasionally attend conferences/meetings of ASA, Association for Gerontology in Higher Education (AGHE), American Planning Association (APA), the State's Health and Science University's Healthy Aging Alliance, WHO and the International Federation on Ageing.

Other?

Training to learn how to use geographic information systems and spatial analyses in research, plus research training offered at my university.

Study Spanish to improve my ability to work in Nicaragua.

Training to learn more about working with the disability community, which began when I became a charter member of the city's Commission on Disability.

What are the most rewarding aspects of your current career position? The most rewarding aspect is working with students to prepare them to travel and serve the needs of older adults in Nicaragua. This unique experience

(*continued*)

An Interview With ALAN DeLaTORRE (*continued*)

is transformative to many of the participating students and allows them to see the needs and appreciate the assets that exist in communities that are different from most of their life experiences so far. The ability to travel internationally is also an amazing and unique opportunity that is not afforded to most professionals. Also, working for a nonprofit organization is rewarding based on the social goals (rather than profit-driven goals) we strive to achieve.

What are the most rewarding aspects of your gerontology/geriatrics-related career path? I would consider the most rewarding aspect to be the opportunity to improve the quality of life and well-being of older people who are and should be valued by communities. Since my youth, I have always seen older people as presenting tremendous value to me, personally, and to society, in general. In some ways, I think that my career in gerontology is a testament to my paternal and maternal grandparents and a great-grandmother, who all had profound effects on my personal and professional development.

What are the most challenging aspects of your current career position? The most challenging aspects include the need to be a "jack of all trades," the lack of opportunities for promotions and raises, and the need to travel, which is difficult for maintaining a healthy work–life balance. The latter issue (international travel) is both a perk and a drawback; overall, I appreciate the opportunity to experience different cultures, but international travel can be tiring and the distance between me and my family and friends can be difficult at times. With respect to the need for breadth of skills and limitations with wages and career advancement, this is the case with many careers in the nonprofit sector. Although rewarding, it is important to understand that nonprofit organizations offer a living wage and wonderful opportunities for furthering important social issues; however, they are not as lucrative and demand hard work and commitment to "the cause."

What are the most challenging aspects of your gerontology/geriatrics-related career path? I view a career in gerontology as challenging at this moment in time for one main reason—the field is still emerging and, although there is burgeoning need for gerontologists, the clear career options have yet to be established for many. On one hand, academic and

(*continued*)

An Interview With ALAN DeLaTORRE (*continued*)

research careers provide fairly secure career paths, yet these options are not easily found (e.g., tenured-track faculty positions) or retained (e.g., research and project management positions). On the other hand, the career paths in long-term care and service provision are growing, but do not provide well-paid careers that match with graduate degrees completed.

How do you balance career and other aspects of your life? Balancing my career and other aspects of life can be difficult at times, but there are a few things that I find important. First, it is important to set aside time for friends and family and to stick to those commitments. Second, it is critical to take care of my own health, both physical and mental. Exercise, a balanced diet, and moderating things that are bad for my health are important priorities. Finally, it is critical to disconnect from time-to-time, which means not setting the alarm on Saturday mornings, not always worrying about deadlines or the needs and problems of the world, and getting away for a walk or trip.

What advice do you have for someone contemplating a career in the field of aging? Consider the tools that are needed to accomplish your professional aspirations. For instance, I found that urban planning offered a set of tools that were useful in influencing city-related policy issues. Also, developing research skills has allowed me to ask good questions, design research projects, and translate findings into policy and action. If you are interested in gerontology, consider what your ideal career might look like and what type of skills (e.g., management, health impact assessment, program evaluation, grant development, marketing, communications) it will require and then figure out a way to acquire those skills. Also, understand that advanced degrees will lead to different opportunities. In order to ascertain the right level of education, talk to or ask for an informational interview with professionals in careers that you are considering.

What advice do you have for someone considering a professional position similar to your current position? For someone interested in a career in the nonprofit sector, specifically with an organization working with older adults, it is critically important that you are attuned to the direction of

(*continued*)

An Interview With ALAN DeLaTORRE *(continued)*

the organization. Ask yourself: Do I believe in its mission? Are the job responsibilities aligned with my skill set and interests? Would the salary and benefits meet the needs of me and my dependents? If you are able to answer affirmatively to those questions, a career in the nonprofit sector can be rewarding and fulfilling, especially with organizations that focus on improving the lives of older adults.

GRANT WRITER

BASIC DESCRIPTION

Grant writers in gerontology-specific and related settings work with grants for research studies, program development and evaluation, basic program operation, staffing and staff development, and special projects. They write grants for both pilot projects and for the continuation and expansion of existing projects. For each type of grant, however, they essentially carry out the same tasks and are involved in the total process from start to finish. They identify and do research on government, foundation, corporate, and other sources of funding; work with program/agency staff to determine the goals and objectives of funding needs; alert staff members of requests for proposals (RFPs) that are relevant to the program or agency's funding needs; write and edit grant proposals and grant-related reports; maintain a calendar for submission and report deadlines; coordinate the preparation and assembly of completed proposals; facilitate delivery of proposals; track the status of proposal documents; and keep program/agency administrators and other staff apprised of the grant preparation and funding process.

EDUCATION AND EXPERIENCE REQUIREMENTS

A bachelor's degree or higher (master's degree preferred) in a field directly related to the nature and mission of the employing agency, organization, or facility is a bonus, but not required. Coursework and/or training workshops in grantsmanship and grant writing are strongly recommended and may be required. Gerontology coursework or a degree component is strongly recommended. Two or more years of professional practice in a related field and evidence of successful grant writing is preferred.

CERTIFICATION, LICENSURE, AND CONTINUING EDUCATION REQUIREMENTS

Grant writers must meet the requirements of the employing agency, organization, or facility.

CORE COMPETENCIES AND SKILLS NEEDED

- Thorough understanding of the grantsmanship process
- Strong communication skills (written and oral)
- Detail oriented
- Ability to follow directions
- Ability to meet deadlines
- Strong organizational skills
- Ability to multitask
- Knowledge of computer software and relevant databases
- Must enjoy a creative and fast-paced environment
- Ability to work with others from diverse backgrounds

COMPENSATION

This varies by one's education, experience, level of responsibility, and the nature of the employment setting. Some positions may be part time or on a contractual fee-for-service basis.

WORKPLACE(S)

These include community-based organizations and agencies that serve older adults (e.g., senior centers, adult day programs, assisted living and long-term care facilities); aging network agencies (e.g., county commissions, departments, divisions, bureaus on aging; Area Agencies on Aging; retired senior volunteer programs); adult education, and older learner programs.

EMPLOYMENT OUTLOOK

Very good, especially for experienced grant writers who have demonstrated success at securing funding from a variety of fund-granting sources. An improvement in employment outlook is anticipated for grant writers as more organizations, agencies, and facilities look for funding from new sources to meet the interests and needs of the expanding older adult population.

RELATED PROFESSIONAL ORGANIZATIONS AND WEBSITES

- Grantmakers in Aging (GIA): www.giaging.org
- The Grantsmanship Center: www.tgci.com
- Association for Fundraising Professionals (AFP): www.afpnet.org

HEALTH SYSTEM SPECIALIST

BASIC DESCRIPTION

Health system specialists provide management services to ensure that the system for which they work complies with national programs, initiatives, regulations, and mandates specific to their type of system; support system missions, goals, objectives, and programs; and ensure up-to-date medical care and services that meet the needs of the system's patients. They also consult with and offer comprehensive support to the system's senior leaders as those leaders implement and maintain the programs and initiatives for which they are each responsible (e.g., strategic planning; analysis of relevant clinical/nonclinical research, programs, and client services; administrative management of staff and/or facilities; day-to-day system operations).

EDUCATION AND EXPERIENCE REQUIREMENTS

There are no mandatory requirements; however, a graduate degree with a health care administration or management focus is recommended. A minimum amount of time in a previous system position is required in some health care systems (e.g., Veterans Affairs and other federal government health care systems). Continuing education and specialized training that is specific to the specialist's position and role definition are often necessary to keep up with changing standards and regulations. Coursework specific to aging/gerontology/geriatrics is a bonus, but is rarely required in systems that serve aging/older adult clients. Individuals interested in potential employment are encouraged to seek internship and practicum experiences in health care systems of interest and be willing to enter the system in a lower level position and then work their way up the system's career ladder.

CORE COMPETENCIES AND SKILLS NEEDED

Although some competencies and skills are specific to each type of systems specialists, the following are key requirements to be fully functional in these positions:

- Knowledge of the missions, organizations and structures, programs and services, and requirements of health care delivery systems, both in general and in the United States
- Knowledge of the unique characteristics of the specific system in which one is employed, including facility resources, programs and services; partners and other affiliations; and community demographics, resources, and relationships

- Knowledge of the role and organization of professional societies and volunteer groups
- Familiarity with regulations and standards of regulatory and credentialing bodies and ability to reconcile disparate requirements in preparing staff and coordinating clinical, administrative, and patient services
- Familiarity with governmental (local, state, and federal) agency and facility requirements related to budget, personnel, and procurement
- Awareness of the variation in functions and motivations of all employee groups and ability to communicate effectively with each group for the purposes of information gathering, presenting recommendations for group operations and personnel, and coordinating services among groups
- Ability to analyze concerns, issues, and problems, and effectively communicate, orally and in written formats, about them in ways that fully consider the array of factors and requirements involved and support positive management of this specific health care delivery system

COMPENSATION

This varies by level of position within the system, type of system (federal, state, or local; public or private), educational background and prior relevant experience, geographical location, and specific responsibilities assigned to the position.

WORKPLACE(S)

These include hospitals, long-term care facilities, large physical and/or mental health facilities, Veterans Affairs health care facilities, and medical practice groups.

EMPLOYMENT OUTLOOK

Good, but influenced strongly by legislative and budgetary constraints at the federal and/or state level for some systems and by fluctuations in the economy.

RELATED PROFESSIONAL ORGANIZATIONS AND WEBSITES

- American College of Healthcare Executives (ACHE): www.ache.org
- American Academy of Medical Administration (AAMA): www.aameda.org

- American Hospital Association (AHA): www.aha.org
- Healthcare Financial Management Association (HFMA): www.hfma.org
- National Association of Health Services Executives (NAHSE): www.careers.nahse.org/jobs
- National Center for Healthcare Leadership: www.nchl.org
- American College of Physician Executives: www.acpe.org
- Medical Group Management Association; www.mgma.com
- USA Jobs (federal government jobs site): https://www.usajobs.gov
- Department of Veterans Affairs: www.va.gov

An Interview With TRINA SAUCEDA

Health System Specialist, Veterans Affairs

Postsecondary educational background, including formal credentials and other education/training in gerontology/geriatrics:
MA, Bioethics and Health Policy
MS, Gerontology
BA, Social Ecology
BA, Fine Arts
Credentialed Professional Gerontologist (CPG), National Association of Professional Gerontologists
Certified Aging-in-Place Specialist (CAPS), National Association of Home Builders
Internships with Veterans Affairs and State Commission on Aging

How and when did you first become interested in gerontology/geriatrics? As a licensed general contractor, I often conduct expert witness investigations related to defective construction. These investigations could be associated with structural/architectural issues or even personal injury allegations as they may relate to residential or commercial buildings. A master architect suggested it would be wise to consider an advanced degree in the field of aging to strengthen my credentials when conducting investigations related to bio-organic growth.

Briefly describe your gerontology/geriatrics-related career path. After my company provided technical support/forensic expert witness services to various entities for a number of years, I noticed more often that more cases were related to the presence of bio-organic growth (mold) requiring remediation. Mold can dramatically affect components of a building structure, regardless of whether it's steel or wood frame, commercial or residential. There appeared to be a more frequent incidence of mold in the homes of older persons and it was hypothesized it might to be due to poor air flow. Older adults seemed less likely to open windows and doors for fresh air/air circulation despite living in a southern climate. Black mold would often be found on window sills accompanied by the presence of moisture on the interior window glass. When I mentioned this to one of the state's leading custom home architects, he suggested learning more about older adults and the aging process. As a result of this particular conversation and legal cases we were involved in at the time, I decided

(*continued*)

An Interview With TRINA SAUCEDA (*continued*)

to pursue an MS in gerontology. This was followed by an internship in the Veterans Affairs Healthcare System. My new education combined with the internship experience strengthened my ability to articulate the cause and effect for human factor and construction issues related to aging. Understanding the importance of evidence-based research and acquiring expertise in the academic and professional arena supported my new knowledge. Membership in the National Association of Professional Gerontologists (NAPG) further strengthened my credentials.

Briefly describe your current professional position:

Position title: Health System Specialist

Primary role tasks/responsibilities: As a health systems specialist in a Veterans Affairs Healthcare System, I am responsible for oversight of various construction projects related to direct patient care throughout the medical center and the nursing home facilities. This includes implementation of the Safe Patient Handling Program, a national program designed to reduce work comp–type injuries related to the lifting and repositioning of patients. The goal of this program is to create a safer work environment for our aging direct-care providers through the use of equipment and hands-on training.

Type of employment setting: Veterans Affairs Healthcare System Medical Center

Length of time in this position: 5+ years

How did you first become interested in this position? An internship was required by the Master's in Gerontology program, so I sought one through the Hispanic Association of Colleges and Universities (HACU). After completing the time commitment for this paid internship, I was extended for several additional weeks and, the following year, I was invited to submit an application for employment.

Describe a typical workday in your current professional position. It varies greatly, that's why I enjoy it so much. The following are a few tasks I may be involved in daily: Oversee program-related construction projects; investigate accidents and injuries—collect facts and compile supporting documentation; collect ergonomic evaluation data; meet with vendors; contract

(*continued*)

An Interview With TRINA SAUCEDA *(continued)*

for equipment purchase or oversight for $5+ million budget; attend trade shows and conferences to ensure Safe Patient Handling (SPH) Program remains state-of-the art; provide instruction for various ANCC Courses (e.g., Environment of Care and Emergency Management, SPH training for New Nurse Orientation); participate in "Special Projects" (e.g., creation of a Bereavement Room); serve as liaison with national leadership (e.g., with federal/system administrators, Risk Management inspections); serve as committee member for Supply, Purchasing, Distribution Inspection, Emergency Management, Nursing Equipment, Facilities' Construction Review, Environment of Care); finalize Standard Operating Procedures for Reusable Medical Equipment; write grants; implement studies/findings; and write preliminary or final reports and recommendations.

What is the time commitment required of your current professional position? Regularly 40 hours a week (4 days, 10 hours per day) for the Veterans Affairs Healthcare System, but often another 20+ hours for private sector expert work on weekends.

How do you stay up-to-date in your profession?

Professional organization memberships and/or activities? As co-founder of a national professional organization/business consortium for gerontology/aging professionals, I co-chair monthly meetings, attend numerous professional conferences, and serve on several national committees. I write and speak on a variety of topics (e.g., mold, aging, grab bars, safe patient handling and safe patient movement, caregiver issues). Most of my articles are in publications for the general public.

Subscribe to and/or read professional journals and/or newsletters? The only professional journal subscription I have is for the *American Journal of Safe Patient Handling & Movement*.

Attend professional conferences and/or participate in education/training programs? I regularly attend the following annual meetings: American Society on Aging (ASA); Gerontological Society of America (GSA), California Council on Gerontology and Geriatrics (CCGG), West and East Coast Safe Patient Handling Conferences (SPH), National Association of Professional Gerontologists (NPAG), Association of Gerontology in Higher Education (AGHE), and The Let's Group (TLG).

(continued)

An Interview With TRINA SAUCEDA (*continued*)

What are the most rewarding aspects of your current career position? I work with the absolute nicest variety of professionals (e.g., direct-care providers: RNs, LVNs, CNAs), professionals in aging, AIA architects, general contractors, and a wide range of expert witnesses who continue to provide a front seat to cutting edge opportunities and innovations.

What are the most rewarding aspects of your gerontology/geriatrics-related career path? I can be as creative or innovative as I desire—the wheels are always turning. My personal goal, however, is to pass along whatever knowledge I've gained along the way to those who are new to the field.

What are the most challenging aspects of your current career position? Challenges are opportunities for growth and change. Within the federal government, change occurs very slowly and one quickly discovers patience is an appreciated virtue.

What are the most challenging aspects of your gerontology/geriatrics-related career path? My greatest challenge is not for myself, but in regard to my belief that licensure (more than accreditation) is a critical need for direct-practice gerontological professionals because it would enhance the perception of value in the eyes of the general public.

How do you balance career and other aspects of your life? I've never understood this question. It's something I just do without giving conscious thought as to how I do it. For others, I recommend you examine your personal and professional goals and try to meet them realistically, knowing that you may not be able to accomplish everything you want to.

What advice do you have for someone contemplating a career in the field of aging? Be aware of your knowledge deficits, but do not fear them. Remember, you are considered an expert when you possess more knowledge than the average individual on the street. Understand there is strength in becoming comfortable with public speaking because it will reinforce your self-confidence. Write articles and learn how to properly submit an abstract or poster. Enter this field with passion and reason, not because you "like working with old people."

(*continued*)

An Interview With TRINA SAUCEDA *(continued)*

What advice do you have for someone considering a professional position similar to your current position? Working within the limitations of the public service environment is challenging. Positions are available throughout the national Veterans Affairs Healthcare System; salaries vary, however, health care and retirement benefits are included. There is not only opportunity, but also great flexibility despite this not being a clinical position. In this position, there may be little direct contact with elderly veterans; however, the satisfaction comes in achieving goals that have lasting impact in the area of eldercare.

HOME CARE AGENCY ADMINISTRATOR

BASIC DESCRIPTION

The administrator of a home care agency or in-home assistance program for elders is responsible for overall administration of the agency/program and oversees the day-to-day operation. Job functions include creating and upholding the organization's vision and values and leading by example; identifying key goals and objectives, then planning tangible steps for achieving them; personnel recruitment, scheduling, supervision, compensation, coaching, and evaluation; monitoring expenses, developing and monitoring the agency's budget; complying with relevant policies, regulations, and procedures; marketing and public relations; responding to inquiries about agency services; networking with relevant community resources and organizations; assessing client needs and ensuring quality care for clients; and dealing with worker compensation, insurance, bonding, and union negotiations.

EDUCATION AND EXPERIENCE REQUIREMENTS

Administrators require a master's degree in gerontological studies, health care administration, social work, nursing, or a closely related field, with gerontology coursework or a degree component if at least one degree is not in gerontology. Prior experience in working with older adults is strongly recommended and often required.

CERTIFICATION, LICENSURE, AND CONTINUING EDUCATION REQUIREMENTS

Administrators must meet licensure and other requirements mandated by the state in which their professional practice occurs and by the employing agency. Recommended licenses/certificates for this profession include nursing home administrator licensure, home care manager certification, social worker licensure, and registered nurse or licensed visiting nurse designation. Yearly continuing education is strongly recommended and may be mandated by the licensing authorities and employing agency. Certifications and licensures typically require renewal every 1 to 3 years.

CORE COMPETENCIES AND SKILLS NEEDED

- Updated knowledge of local, state, and federal aging issues and legislation
- Working knowledge of policies and regulations that govern delivery of services for older adults and home care agencies
- Strong communication and interpersonal skills; excellent listener
- Agency and staff management and leadership skills
- Good marketing, public relations, and outreach skills
- Ability to multitask
- Ability to stay calm, patient, and understanding in difficult situations
- Ability to handle difficult and challenging situations

COMPENSATION

This varies by one's education, experience, the nature of the employment setting, and the geographical location.

WORKPLACE(S)

These are usually community-based home care agencies.

EMPLOYMENT OUTLOOK

Very good, especially due to the increasing number of elders living in the community rather than in care facilities and to the anticipated growth of the older adult population over the next few decades.

RELATED PROFESSIONAL ORGANIZATIONS AND WEBSITES

- American Association for Home Care and Hospice (NAHC): www.nahc.org
- American Association for Homecare (AAHomecare): www.aahomecare.org
- Home Care Association of America (HCAOA): www.homecareoa.org
- Private Duty Homecare Association (PDHCA): www.pdhca.org

An Interview With QIU (CHO), QUANHONG

Executive Director, Home Care Company

Postsecondary educational background, including formal credentials and other education/training in gerontology/geriatrics:
BA, English and International Studies
MS, Management Science and Engineering
MGS, Gerontological Studies
Home Care Manager Certificate (State Association for Health Services at Home)
Licensed Nursing Home Administrator (one state)

How and when did you first become interested in gerontology/geriatrics? I have liked and respected older people since my childhood. I have enjoyed talking with them and learned a lot from them. The death of my father was a wake-up call for me. I couldn't do anything for my dad, but I wanted to do something that could help other old people. I'd like to make some positive impact to improve the quality of life for them.

Briefly describe your gerontology/geriatrics-related career path. I started by interning as an administer-in-training at an Asian community nursing home. After finishing my MGS degree, I helped to start a home care agency from scratch. I've been active in educating, through a variety of venues (including radio interviews), community residents regarding the issues related with aging, cultural diversity in health care, home care, caregiving, and end-of-life care. Nine years ago, I came up with the idea of having a Community Health Fair and we have co-sponsored the successful Health Festival since then.

Briefly describe your current professional position:

Position title: Executive Director

Primary role tasks/responsibilities: Some of my primary responsibilities are to create proper mission; provide compassionate and high quality services; earn and maintain the best reputation; build high performance, and a loyal and dedicated team; ensure smooth operation; solve problems; build excellent rapport; work collaboratively with all interested parties; keep a positive cash flow and a strategic steady growth; work out

(*continued*)

An Interview With QIU (CHO), QUANHONG *(continued)*

strategies to address our ever-changing market; and comply with new rules and regulations.

Type of employment setting: Home care company

Length of time in this position: 12 years

How did you first become interested in this position? After working in a nursing home during my internship, I realized that I needed to work in a different area of senior care. I felt that home care would be a better career path for me because the work was more rewarding. I was hired as the executive director to build this company from scratch. This puts me in a great position to do the right thing and provide the best possible home care for our clients, which I would never be able to do in a nursing home environment.

Describe a typical workday in your current professional position. My days often are unpredictable, so I prepare to expect the unexpected and need to be good at multitasking. In a typical work day, I might communicate and or address issues from all interested parties; attend meetings and or events; create plans and strategies to improve effectiveness and efficiency, ensure quality services, and encourage growth; and participate in rotation of being on call and be available for help whenever it is needed.

What is the time commitment required of your current professional position? My work hours are supposed to be 9:00 a.m. to 5:30 p.m., Monday through Friday, but my work doesn't end when I leave the office and I often work later. I also cover on call once a week after the office hours, and more often, as needed. I attend some evening and occasional weekend professional meetings and or events.

How do you stay up-to-date in your profession?

Professional organization memberships and/or activities?
American Society on Aging (ASA), Member
Home Care Association of America (HCAOA), Member
Case Management Society of America (CMSA), Member/Board Member
Coalition of Agencies Serving the Elderly (CASE), Member
End-of-Life Network, Member
Senior Action Network, Member

(continued)

An Interview With QIU (CHO), QUANHONG *(continued)*

Subscribe to and/or read professional journals and/or newsletters?
ASA newsletters
CMSA magazine
HCAOA listserv and newsletters—most helpful to read industry updates and ideas or suggestions from colleagues

Attend professional conferences and/or participate in education/training programs? I continually seek further education/training opportunities on a wide variety of topics, including dementia updates and strategies (including translating research into practice), strengths-based approaches, medication and substance use/abuse, spirituality in case management and home care, decision-making capacity, caring for older adults with different diseases and health conditions, technologies for home- and community-based services, depression and suicide among older adults, pain management, end-of-life care, cultural diversity and competency, trends and services for boomers, aging in community, vision and hearing impairment; hydration and dehydration for the aged; caring for older adults with multiple sclerosis; understanding and assessing pain in the elderly; strategies that work: addressing challenging behaviors from medical and behavioral perspective; practical applications for meditation: stress reduction, depression, anxiety, and caregiving; heart to heart communicating and successful strategies in mediation; ethics in mediation and financial decision making at the end of life; and updates on and translating brain research and mental health into practice.

Other? I stay in touch with my advisor and professors from my MGS degree program.

What are the most rewarding aspects of your current career position? My current position enables me to fulfill part of my passion by striving to do the best for our clients, employees, and the community.

What are the most rewarding aspects of your gerontology/geriatrics-related career path? Knowing that I and my company staff members are helping to improve the quality of life for our clients is the most rewarding aspect of my career.

(continued)

An Interview With QIU (CHO), QUANHONG *(continued)*

What are the most challenging aspects of your current career position? The most challenging aspects of my career are the difficulty of recruiting enough good quality caregivers, retaining enough good quality caregivers during slow times for the company, and recruiting more clients who can afford our services.

What are the most challenging aspects of your gerontology/geriatrics-related career path? One of the biggest challenges for moving forward is the adjustments that would be necessary. For example, if I moved into a position with a care facility, it would require spending more time with regulations, government inspections and surveys, corporate management, and less time helping clients, which I enjoy doing more. If I move up the ladder, I'll need to spend more time focusing on these issues, which I'm not interested in doing. It can conflict with my goal to provide great care to the clients because more time is spent on paperwork and politics.

How do you balance career and other aspects of your life? I integrate spirituality into my daily life. I like meditation, dancing, hiking, and travel. Doing these activities helps to improve me, keep me calm, and allows me to work well with different people and challenging situations, be productive, and make the right decisions.

What advice do you have for someone contemplating a career in the field of aging? Ask yourself at least twice if the career you want is working with older adults. It's a career that needs someone who is patient and has a passion for working with seniors.

What advice do you have for someone considering a professional position similar to your current position? You need to be good at multitasking and responding to frequent changes. If you work for a start-up company or agency, be prepared to put in lots of time and effort. There will be ups and downs. Persistence, perseverance, positive attitude, staying calm, being flexible, prioritizing, and focusing on what's important will be helpful in this position. There could be more time, money, and effort needed than you thought it would take to provide high quality services. Ask yourself if you're willing and ready to put in all that is required of you by this industry and this position.

HORTICULTURAL THERAPIST

BASIC DESCRIPTION

Horticultural therapists are trained to use gardening as a therapeutic tool to help their clients and patients achieve treatment-specific goals. Horticultural therapy (HT) has been shown to help improve memory and other cognitive abilities, task orientation and initiation, language skills, socialization, muscle strength, coordination, balance, and endurance. Horticultural therapists involve those with whom they work in all phases of gardening, from plant selection and propagation to the final use of the garden products, as a means of providing cognitive therapy, social growth, physical rehabilitation, and/or vocational training. Horticultural therapists commonly work as members of multidisciplinary rehabilitation teams (along with doctors, psychiatrists, psychologists, social workers, counselors, occupational therapists, physical therapists, and/or medical or human service professionals).

EDUCATION AND EXPERIENCE REQUIREMENTS

HT education is available through three types of academic programs: college/university degree programs, American Horticultural Therapy Association (AHTA)–accredited certificate programs, and career training programs. To qualify for Horticultural Therapist–Registered (HTR), applicants must earn a baccalaureate degree with a concentration in horticultural therapy or a baccalaureate degree plus additional coursework in horticultural therapy and complete a supervised internship of at least 480 hours of HT practice. Gerontology coursework or a degree component is recommended for those who plan to work with elders.

CERTIFICATION, LICENSURE, AND CONTINUING EDUCATION REQUIREMENTS

Horticultural therapists must meet all certification, licensure, and/or continuing education requirements specified by their employers and/or by the state in which they practice.

CORE COMPETENCIES AND SKILLS NEEDED

- Ability to create barrier-free garden spaces to accommodate clients/patients with a wide range of abilities
- Comfortable working with clients who are physically, mentally, and/or socially disabled
- Ability to work collaboratively as a member of a rehabilitation team

- Enjoy gardening; comfortable with getting your hands dirty and working outside
- Patient
- Self-confident
- Flexible
- Resourceful
- Entrepreneurial
- Good physical health status, including body strength and stamina

COMPENSATION

This varies by one's educational background, HTR status, type of practice, the nature of the workplace, amount of experience, and the geographical location. Some positions may be part time or on a contractual fee for service basis.

WORKPLACE(S)

These include rehabilitation centers, psychiatric and mental health clinics, hospitals and medical centers, hospice, correctional facilities, long-term care and assisted living centers, senior centers, community and botanical gardens, and occupational training facilities and programs.

EMPLOYMENT OUTLOOK

Good, especially as HTR certification gains recognition as a valid professional credential; may be affected by mergers among health care systems and downsizing of programs/staff due to the economy.

RELATED PROFESSIONAL ORGANIZATIONS AND WEBSITES

- American Horticultural Therapy Association (AHTA): www.ahta.org
- American Horticultural Society (AHS): www.ahs.org
- American Society for Horticultural Science (ASHS): www.ashs.org
- American Society of Landscape Architects (ASLA), Healthcare and Therapeutic Design Professional Practice Network (PPN): www.asla.org

HORTICULTURAL THERAPIST–REGISTERED (HTR)

An Interview With KIRK W. HINES

Horticultural Therapist–Registered

Postsecondary educational background, including formal credentials and other education/training in gerontology/geriatrics:
BS, Ornamental Horticulture, with Horticultural Therapy concentration
Horticultural Therapist–Registered (HTR) through the American Horticultural Therapy Association
Training and in-services through my previous place of employment

How and when did you first become interested in gerontology/geriatrics? Growing up in the rural South, I was very fortunate to have close relationships and to live in close proximity to grandparents and great-grandparents. Many languid summer days were spent walking through the yard, garden, and woods with senior family members identifying plants and explaining their uses. These experiences created a comfort level with and affinity for older adults that continued into my schooling and professional life. During my horticultural therapy internship at a regional hospital, I served many different patient populations. A large portion were geriatric. I found working with older adults familiar and rewarding.

Briefly describe your gerontology/geriatrics-related career path. Upon the completion of my post graduate internship, my first job as a horticultural therapist was at an adolescent psychiatric unit. I was asked shortly thereafter to interview at a geriatric hospital that was part of a large, university-based health care system and I accepted a position in its rehabilitation therapy department. It was there that I founded the horticultural therapy (HT) program and provided service to a variety of geriatric patients (medical, rehab, psych, neuropsych) in the acute care setting. Each element of the HT program was funded over the years from grants, private donations, and plant sales. By the time I left this position, the horticultural therapy provided treatment for an average of 300 patient visits per month and had a significant physical presence at the hospital. The elements of the HT program consisted of two interior courtyard HT gardens, fluorescent growing stations on the units, a large exterior garden with an ambulation/balance confidence course, and two patient accessible greenhouses. Twenty years later, however, corporate

(*continued*)

An Interview With KIRK W. HINES *(continued)*

changes resulted in the closure of several programs and positions, including music and horticultural therapy. It was then I accepted my current position as horticultural therapist for a health and rehab system. I now provide horticultural therapy services for three long-term care/subacute rehab facilities. These services include group and individual therapy for geriatric residents and rehabilitation patients.

Briefly describe your current professional position:

Position title: Horticultural therapist

Primary role tasks/responsibilities: Development and delivery of horticultural therapy services to patients/residents at three long-term care and subacute rehab facilities. My primary tasks include designing, seeking funding for, and coordinating the installation of therapeutic gardens/greenhouses at three facilities; oversight of the facility's landscapes/therapeutic gardens; and community outreach, teaching, lecturing, volunteer supervision, marketing of the HT program.

Type of employment setting: Nonprofit long-term care and subacute rehab for seniors at three facilities in a metropolitan area

Length of time in this position: 3 months

How did you first become interested in this position? I first became acquainted with this system 2 years ago when I was asked to design a therapeutic courtyard garden for their Rehabilitation Services. When the HT program and my position at my prior place of employment were closed, the CEO offered me a position with his management office to design, develop, and deliver HT services to their three facilities. The position was very appealing to me because it allows the freedom and flexibility to design and direct my own program across three very unique facilities. Most importantly, I found the 104-year-old organization to be mission-driven and passionate about the care provided to older adults.

Describe a typical workday in your current professional position. The day usually begins with checking the greenhouses. As I am watering, grooming the plants, or cleaning up, I consider the location and patients that I will be working with that day. I also plan materials that will be needed for the

(continued)

An Interview With KIRK W. HINES *(continued)*

day's individual, group, or co-treatment sessions. Because my employment change is so recent, I am able to use greenhouses in my former program to support the new one. This requires me to load and transport materials between facilities. Horticultural therapy is offered at each facility approximately twice a week. After patients/residents are seen, I spend some time doing documentation, care plans, and meetings. Any time not spent in direct patient care or documentation is used for the development of the new horticultural therapy programming. Starting a program from scratch requires knowledge of the patient population, the inner workings of the new facility, its needs, and its culture. Time is also spent planning future therapeutic gardens, facilities, and funding requirements.

What is the time commitment required of your current professional position? It's a 40+ hours per week job. It is primarily weekdays, but there are special events or projects that may require weekend or evening work. Occasionally, the weather or greenhouse maintenance may require weekend work.

How do you stay up-to-date in your profession?

Professional organization memberships and/or activities? American Horticultural Therapy Association (AHTA): current member; past Board of Directors member

Subscribe to and/or read professional journals and/or newsletters?
AHTA Newsletter
Journal of Therapeutic Horticulture (AHTA)
Therapeutic Landscapes Network: online articles
Special Interest Groups: LinkedIn online articles

Attend professional conferences and/or participate in education/training programs?
American Horticultural Therapy Association (AHTA) national conferences
Two state AHTA Regional Chapter conferences
Alzheimer's Association conferences
Parkinson's Association conferences

(continued)

An Interview With KIRK W. HINES *(continued)*

Other? I provide frequent community presentations, college/university lectures, and workplace in-services. Preparing lectures, participating in research, and publishing professional articles keep me engaged with current information.

What are the most rewarding aspects of your current career position? Being employed as a full-time horticultural therapist—a career that I love—is a major reward. There are very few registered, credentialed horticultural therapists across the country and even fewer available jobs. That covers your base in the hierarchy of needs. Once that aspect is covered, the most rewarding aspect of my current position is the trust, flexibility, and freedom to design and deliver an effective service to the geriatric clients.

What are the most rewarding aspects of your gerontology/geriatrics-related career path? Being from the South, we have a strong tradition of storytelling. One of the most rewarding aspects of working with the geriatric clients is being able to hear the amazing, wonderful, heartbreaking stories of other people's lives. Hearing their experiences in life, as well as their relationship with gardening and nature, is very meaningful to me. It is very important to me that I bring healing, joy, comfort, or fulfillment, in any small way.

What are the most challenging aspects of your current career position? One of the most challenging aspects of my new position is also one of the most rewarding—being able to design (from scratch) a dynamic horticultural therapy program for a nonprofit organization's three facilities. Sheer size is a challenge. The number and functional level of those whom the program will serve is a challenge.

What are the most challenging aspects of your gerontology/geriatrics-related career path? Keeping my position and my program in the acute care setting has been a challenge. Though my last position lasted 21 years, it was a constant struggle living under a specter of fear each time insurance reimbursement cuts were made and the hospital had to tighten its belt. Funding new projects for a nonprofit or poorly reimbursed segment of the health care system population can be a challenge, especially when the medical community does not view such projects as money-making initiatives. Once a program is up and running with something to show

(continued)

An Interview With KIRK W. HINES *(continued)*

potential donors, the funding usually comes in when it is required. The actual work and service provided to older adults is the easiest aspect of the job.

How do you balance career and other aspects of your life? To me, if you enjoy your job to the extent that I do, the career doesn't seem like work as much as an identity. Most of my hobbies and outside enjoyment revolve around horticulture. Career and personal life have always blended well and found their own natural equilibrium.

What advice do you have for someone contemplating a career in the field of aging? Take stock of your own personal needs. Ask yourself if this field will help you meet your basic needs. Consider which career with the geriatric population is the best fit for your interests, personality or limitations. Some enjoy direct care. Others prefer supporting the business aspects of caring for older adults. If you are fulfilled and enjoy your work, whatever it may be, then you will do your very best for those who need your very best.

What advice do you have for someone considering a professional position similar to your current position? Prepare yourself with the proper education and training. Acquire the proper credentials (HTR) and then gain experience with the client population that is the best fit for you. The field of horticultural therapy is replete with well-meaning volunteers and amateur gardeners. Many facilities either do not know of professional horticultural therapists or understand the need. Horticultural therapists work with frail, critically ill, or injured clients. The untrained can and will do harm. Proper education and training will bring credibility and success to a horticultural therapy program. It will also strengthen the field by putting strong therapists and strong programs into the health care arena.

IN-HOME SERVICES PROGRAM DIRECTOR, COUNTY COMMISSION ON AGING

BASIC DESCRIPTION

The in-home services program director for a county commission on aging (COA) administers the day-to-day operation of in-home services, such as case management, homemaking, personal care, respite care, caregiver training, prescription drug assistance and emergency need, chore services, and related supplemental programs for persons 60 years of age and older who reside within the COA service area and need in-home services to maintain independence. The director is responsible for the preparation of program grant proposals; oversight of grant-funded program delivery; evaluation of grant project effectiveness; development of program budgets and maintenance of budget-related records; recruitment, training, supervision, evaluation and discipline of in-home services' full-time staff members, part-time contract workers, and volunteers; preparation of monthly financial reports and quarterly program reports; annual program reviews; networking with local, regional, and state agencies within the aging network; speaking publicly on behalf of the commission; liaison with and membership on boards and committees of local and state organizations, including institutions of higher education in the COA service area; and, when applicable, supervision of social work interns from local colleges/universities. In a smaller COA, the director of in-home services may also serve, formally or informally, as associate or assistant director of the agency.

EDUCATION AND EXPERIENCE REQUIREMENTS

A bachelor's (BSW) or master's (MSW) degree in social work from a program accredited by the Council of Social Work Education (CWSE) is required (MSW is preferred). At least 5 or more years of professional experience in aging services, including at least 1 to 2 years of both administrative and supervisory experience, is expected. Gerontology coursework or a degree component is strongly recommended or required.

CERTIFICATION, LICENSURE, AND CONTINUING EDUCATION REQUIREMENTS

Directors must meet the requirements for licensure and licensure renewal in the state where the professional practice occurs and continuing education requirements of the employing agency.

CORE COMPETENCIES AND SKILLS NEEDED

- Good working knowledge of aging processes and aging issues
- Strong personnel supervision and administration skills
- Strong interpersonal skills
- Strong communication skills (oral, written, and listening)
- Commitment to client-centered professional practice
- Good working knowledge of needs assessment tools and processes
- Public speaking skills

- Good working knowledge of board/committee processes
- Good organizational skills
- Good financial and personnel record-keeping skills

COMPENSATION

This varies by one's education, experience, size, and coverage area of the employing agency, and the geographical location.

WORKPLACE(S)

COAs are usually located in the largest community in the county, which is usually located in the county seat. If the COA covers two or more counties, the headquarters office is usually in the largest county seat and may have satellite offices in the other county(ies).

EMPLOYMENT OUTLOOK

Good, but may be affected by budgetary issues or by longevity in position, especially in more rural areas.

RELATED PROFESSIONAL ORGANIZATIONS AND WEBSITES

- Association of Social Workers (NASW): www.socialworkers.org
- State Offices or Departments on Aging

INTERGENERATIONAL SPECIALIST

BASIC DESCRIPTION

Intergenerational specialists develop, administer, and evaluate programs and services that link older adults and young people in ways that are interactive and mutually beneficial to both age groups.

EDUCATION AND EXPERIENCE REQUIREMENTS

Intergenerational specialists require a minimum of a bachelor's degree in education, human development, or a related field. Having a background in both child or adolescent and adult development or gerontology is strongly recommended.

CERTIFICATION, LICENSURE, AND CONTINUING EDUCATION REQUIREMENTS

These may be required by the employing agency, organization, or facility and may vary by state.

CORE COMPETENCIES AND SKILLS NEEDED

Six standards for intergenerational practice have been proposed:

1 Possess adequate knowledge of human development across the life span to support planning and implementation of intergenerational programs of mutual benefit to both older adult and youth program participants
2 Understand the need for and use effective communication skills appropriate to development intergenerational relationships
3 Demonstrate commitment to collaboration and partnership in program planning, administration, and evaluation
4 Integrate knowledge from a variety of disciplines and fields of study in the development of intergenerational programming
5 Employ appropriate evaluation strategies and techniques, adapted from fields such as education and the social sciences, to inform program development for diverse age groups and settings
6 Be self-reflective, caring, and true to the intended purpose of intergenerational programming

Additional competencies and skills include:

- Familiarity with curriculum development and program planning skills
- Grantsmanship and fundraising skills
- Effective oral and written communication skills
- Ability to think creatively and be innovative

COMPENSATION

This varies by the nature of the employing agency, organization, or facility. Compensation may be based on part-time positions paid by wage rather than salary. Some positions may exist only as part of time-limited grant projects.

WORKPLACE(S)

These include preschools and K-12 schools, Head Start programs, after-school programs, child care centers, senior centers, intergenerational day-care centers, community education or recreation programs/departments, community arts and theater programs, libraries, chronic disease-focused organizations, medical centers, long-term care facilities, retirement communities, senior living and grandfamilies housing, foster grandparent programs, multigenerational center, faith-based institutions, and human service agencies that serve both older adults and youth.

EMPLOYMENT OUTLOOK

Good, especially due to development of professional standards of practice and K-12 aging education initiatives, intergenerational housing programs (e.g., grandfamilies and co-housing), and ongoing strong leadership provided by Generations United and previously through Generations Together.

RELATED PROFESSIONAL ORGANIZATIONS AND WEBSITES

- Generations United: www.gu.org
- National Center on Intergenerational Shared Sites, Generations United: www.gu.org
- Seniors4Kids, Generations United: www.seniors4kids.org
- Center for Intergenerational Learning, Temple University: http://templecil.org
- Generations Together, University Center for Social and Urban Research, University of Pittsburgh: www.ucsur.pitt.edu/generations_together.php
- *Journal of Intergenerational Relationships*: http://jir.ucsur.pitt.edu

JOURNALISM AND AGING: AN EMERGING FIELD

JOURNALIST

MULTIMEDIA JOURNALIST

DOCUMENTARY FILMMAKER

BASIC DESCRIPTION

Journalism, with its original focus on print media, is a well-established professional field, and multimedia journalism (including radio, TV, photojournalism, documentary film, and now, social media) has expanded the ways in which journalists work. Connecting journalism and aging/gerontology, however, has been a relatively recent occurrence. Over the past 5 years, there have been at least three formalized efforts to engage journalists in the field of aging. The MetLife Foundation Journalists in Aging Fellows Program is a collaborative effort of the Gerontological Society of America (GSA) and New America Media (NAM) for journalists who cover aging issues and/or work for ethnic media outlets in U.S. communities. Funding for the Fellows program comes from the MetLife Foundation. Additionally, the John A. Hartford Foundation sponsors one John A. Hartford/MetLife Foundation Journalism in Aging and Health Fellow whose work will focus on the health and health care of older Americans. Those selected attend a special 1-day pre-conference session and at least 2 days general sessions at the GSA annual meeting and then complete a short-term story and a long-term project. Another effort to connect journalists to topics of aging was the Age Boom Academy sponsored by the Journalism School at Columbia University in 2012 and 2013. Also, the Associated Press (AP) and the NORC Center for Public Affairs Research sponsored a 12-month (March 2013 through February 2014) residential AP-NORC Journalism Fellowship for mid-career journalists employed by the AP or AP Media Editors. The focus of this program was on issues surrounding the aging workforce of the United States. These programs certainly open the door for undergraduate and graduate students in journalism to consider potential career paths in the field of aging.

EDUCATION AND EXPERIENCE REQUIREMENTS

Although some journalists enter the profession through alternate doors, a bachelor's degree in journalism, including coursework related to one's specialty within the field and at least one internship (more are encouraged), is strongly recommended.

CERTIFICATION, LICENSURE, AND CONTINUING EDUCATION REQUIREMENTS

Neither certification nor licensure is apparent. Formal continuing education may not be required, but journalists always must be avid learners in regard to the foci and processes of their work.

CORE COMPETENCIES AND SKILLS NEEDED

- Passion for truth, honesty, and integrity
- Courage to go out and get the story and willingness to get at the truth behind the story
- Unbiased attitude and ability to be objective
- High ethical standards
- Inquiring mind
- Passionate about knowledge and learning
- Ability to write well
- Good written, verbal, and interpersonal communication skills

- Willingness to start small
- Well-honed technical skills
- Good base knowledge of physical, mental, and social processes of aging
- Good working knowledge of formal and informal aging networks

COMPENSATION

Varies widely, from per-word fee to full salaried positions; many work on a per-job contractual basis and as freelancers.

WORKPLACE(S)

Varies widely, depending on the nature of one's work and employment setting or situation.

EMPLOYMENT OUTLOOK

Varies considerably. While there may be fewer opportunities in traditional print media, options in multimedia journalism appear to be expanding.

RELATED PROFESSIONAL ORGANIZATIONS AND WEBSITES

- MetLife Foundation Journalists in Aging program, Gerontological Society of America: www.geron.org
- New America Media: www.newamericamedia.org
- American Society of Journalists and Authors (ASJA): www.asja.org
- Society of Professional Journalists (SPJ): www.spj.org

An Interview With SHALEECE HAAS

Filmmaker and Multimedia Journalist

Postsecondary educational background, including formal credentials and other education/training in gerontology/geriatrics:
BA, Art History
MJ, Journalism: Documentary Film
Fellow, 2010 MetLife Foundation Journalists in Aging Fellowship

How and when did you first become interested in gerontology/geriatrics? I have always had elders in my life. I have often sought out the company and friendship of "old people" and I am very close to my own grandparents. My 101-year-old grandfather and 99-year-old grandmother are my connection to my family's history. They are my friends and my role models. It was through these personal connections to elders—both within and outside my family—that I became interested in reporting on issues of aging and telling elders' stories through film.

Briefly describe your gerontology/geriatrics-related career path. I am a documentary filmmaker and multimedia journalist who specializes in stories on aging. My first project related to aging was a short documentary on suicide among elders that I directed and produced while in graduate school. Later, I worked as a reporter and on-air host for a public radio station in Sitka, Alaska. I reported several stories on aging for the statewide radio network, APRN, including one about the gap in care for seniors with mental health issues. In 2010, I directed and produced *Old People Driving,* an award-winning short documentary about two men in their late 90s reaching the end of their driving years. Later that year, I was selected as a MetLife Foundation Journalist in Aging Fellow, with a project entitled "Caring for Elders in Rural Alaska," a radio story about Alaska Native elders who must leave their villages to access long-term care. In 2013, I co-produced *The Genius of Marian,* a documentary film that explores the heartbreak of Alzheimer's disease, the power of art, and the meaning of family. The film premiered at the Tribeca Film festival and was broadcast on public television (POV) in 2014.

(*continued*)

An Interview With SHALEECE HAAS *(continued)*

Briefly describe your current professional position:

Position title: Independent Documentary Filmmaker and Multimedia Journalist.

Primary roles/responsibilities: I produce, direct, and shoot documentary films and I report and produce stories for radio.

Type of employment setting: Freelance

Length of time in this position? 10 years

How did you first become interested in this position? I have always loved listening to people's stories and I enjoy the craft of weaving personal stories and reporting together for an audience. Before I came to documentary film, I told stories through still photography and, before that, through live theater.

Describe a typical workday in your current professional position. No two days are alike and no two projects are alike. Because I wear many hats, the work varies greatly. During the course of any single project, I may be reporter, producer, cinematographer, director, writer, interviewer, editor, and/or fundraiser. Sometimes, I am in the field filming or interviewing people. These are often long days (typically 10 hours). Field production is among my favorite parts of the job. As part of my work, I have had the opportunity to travel across the country and across the world to hear people's stories. Most of my time, however, is spent in the office coordinating the logistics of the project I am working on. Being a freelance filmmaker and journalist means that I am essentially running my own small business.

What is the time commitment required of your current professional position? Because I am a freelancer, I keep irregular work hours. Sometimes, I work 6 days a week for 10+ hours each day. Sometimes, there is little to no work and I have lots of time for myself. In my work, there is never a guarantee of having nights and weekends free.

(continued)

An Interview With SHALEECE HAAS *(continued)*

How do you stay up-to-date in your profession?

Attend professional conferences and/or participate in education/training programs? I do not generally attend professional conferences because they are cost prohibitive. I have, however, presented my films at several conferences, including those of the American Society on Aging (ASA), the Gerontological Society of America (GSA), and the Professional Fiduciary Association of California (PFAC).

Other? I stay up-to-date in my profession by consulting online journals, blogs, and other resources about both the craft (e.g., cinematography, documentary filmmaking) and the content of my work (e.g., aging, caregiving).

What are the most rewarding aspects of your current career position? I have the opportunity to delve deeply into people's lives through their stories. I meet extraordinary people and have the privilege to tell these stories for a living.

What are the most rewarding aspects of your gerontology/geriatrics-related career path? The more time I spend with elders, the more perspective I have on my own life and on the world around me. If we live long enough, we will all be old. I am gratified by the opportunity to think about the important issues of aging, both concrete and philosophical, as a part of my work.

What are the most challenging aspects of your current career position? I do not have a salaried position or benefits and, when one project ends, I am never sure what's coming next.

What are the most challenging aspects of your gerontology/geriatrics-related career path? As a storyteller, I regularly grapple with questions of representation. My worldview is influenced by my gender, race, class, age, and ability—and I bring this perspective to my stories. In my work,

(continued)

An Interview With SHALEECE HAAS *(continued)*

I am challenged to continually check my assumptions, preconceptions, and biases so I can better serve both audiences and the people whose stories I tell.

How do you balance career and other aspects of your life? Work–life balance is a constant struggle, as I imagine it is for most people. The flipside of having a freelance job without a predictable salary and benefits is that my schedule is often quite flexible. I have found that if I take the opportunity during the slow periods in my work to attend to the other aspects of my life (e.g., friendships, partner, exercise, chores), then I am able to achieve a kind of balance.

What advice do you have for someone contemplating a career in the field of aging? Make storytelling a part of your work, even if you don't want to be a journalist or filmmaker. Individual stories hold power and help people connect. So, whether you're interested in social work or medicine or advocacy, there is a place for storytelling (and story gathering). Ask elders to tell their stories. Share your own stories with others.

What advice do you have for someone considering a professional position similar to your current position? The world needs more thoughtful, nuanced, and complex stories about aging. If you love storytelling, media, and our elders, find a medium you enjoy and start learning about the craft. Unfortunately, there's no direct career pathway to this kind of work. There are few, if any, job postings for this type of work; opportunities come through word-of-mouth. I recommend networking and finding opportunities to apprentice with people whose work you admire.

MARRIAGE AND FAMILY THERAPIST (MFT)

BASIC DESCRIPTION

Marriage and family therapists (MFTs) are social and mental health professionals who use a holistic, psychotherapeutic, and family-systems approach in their professional practice. The family, rather than an individual, is the unit of practice, and this often means inclusion of family members from two or more generations of a family. Marriage and family therapy is intentionally short-term, problem-centered, and solution-focused. The intent of therapy is to move the family unit as effectively, efficiently, and quickly as possible toward solution of the problem(s) on which the therapy is focused. Problems addressed by MFTs include marital distress; child or adolescent behaviors; inter- and multigenerational conflicts; problems related to eating disorders, alcoholism, and drug abuse; chronic conditions (e.g., depression, schizophrenia, autism, affective [mood] disorders, other mental health conditions); chronic physical illnesses; family violence; and sexual abuse. Less visible, but emerging, is marriage and family therapy practice with older adults and their families in which the focus is on problems centered around or more related to the family elders. This includes concerns, issues, and problems related to custodial grandparenting and kinship care, grandparent visitation rights, widowhood, divorce of older couples, remarriage in later life, adult stepfamilies, caregiving for family elders, death of elderly parents, and inheritance. MFTs with doctoral degrees may become college/university faculty members or administrators in college and university departments of counseling and guidance, family studies/family science, or marriage and family therapy.

EDUCATION AND EXPERIENCE REQUIREMENTS

A master's or doctoral degree in marriage and family therapy from a program accredited by the Commission on Accreditation for Marriage and Family Therapy Education (COAMFTE) or a master's or doctoral degree in a related mental health field (e.g., psychiatry, clinical psychology, clinical social work, counseling, education), followed by a postgraduate COAMFTE-accredited clinical training program in marriage and family therapy is required. Gerontology coursework or a degree component is strongly recommended for those who plan to treat family system problems of elders and their families. A doctorate that includes research training and experience is required for college/university teaching, research, and administrative positions.

CERTIFICATION, LICENSURE, AND CONTINUING EDUCATION REQUIREMENTS

Licensure or certification is required to practice in most states. Eligibility for licensure includes completion of an extensive (approximately 2 years) postgraduate supervised clinical experience and sitting for a state licensing examination and/or the national Examination in Marriage and Family Therapy that is conducted by the Association of Marriage and Family Therapy Regulatory Boards (AMFTRB).

CORE COMPETENCIES AND SKILLS NEEDED

- Excellent interpersonal skills; demonstrated success in working with individuals/groups
- Emotional maturity
- Excellent verbal communication skills
- Attentive listening skills and keen observational skills
- Patience
- Committed to a client-centered (rather than therapist-centered) approach to practice
- Creativity and resourcefulness

COMPENSATION

This varies by one's education, experience, type of practice, and the nature of the employment setting.

WORKPLACE(S)

These include private practices, in-patient physical and mental health facilities, courts and prisons, community health centers, social service agencies, community-based agencies and organizations that serve elders, shelters for homeless persons or victims of domestic violence, and college/university-based academic departments, counseling centers, and research institutes.

EMPLOYMENT OUTLOOK

Excellent, especially with growth in the elderly population, the expanding scope of marriage and family therapy practice, and an aging population that is more comfortable engaging in therapeutic processes.

RELATED PROFESSIONAL ORGANIZATIONS AND WEBSITES

- American Association of Marriage and Family Therapy (AAMFT): www.aamft.org
- Association of Marriage and Family Therapy Regulatory Boards (AMFTRB): www.amftrb.org
- National Council on Family Relations (NCFR): www.ncfr.org

MEDIATOR

FAMILY MEDIATOR

ELDER CARE MEDIATOR

BASIC DESCRIPTION

Alternative dispute resolution (ADR) grew out of the need for identifying ways to resolve conflicts other than by taking a dispute into the courts or resorting to violence. ADR is also known by the more common terms of conflict resolution and mediation. In part, the popularity of mediation is due to the fact that it is a confidential and voluntary process in which a neutral third-party mediator facilitates civil discussion of the problems at issue and works with the disputing parties as they negotiate an equitable resolution. Mediation, negotiation, and arbitration are the most common forms of ADR. Mediation is the type of conflict resolution service most frequently requested in family dispute situations. Other forms of dispute/conflict resolution include combined mediation–arbitration, early neutral evaluation, community conferencing, collaborative law, negotiated rulemaking, and peer mediation. Mediators who work with family conflict resolution are known as family mediators. They deal with a wide variety of family conflict issues, including prenuptial agreements, divorce, custody issues, adoption, parent–child and sibling–sibling relationship problems, family business concerns, property division, inheritance, and conflicts with neighbors or among friends. Divorce mediation originally created the need for family mediation services and remains the most frequently used form for family disputes. Recently, however, the use of mediation has increased considerably for conflicts related to the care of elders and kinship care (when grandparents or other relatives provide primary care for related children/grandchildren under the age of 18 years). Mediation is also a productive process for use in situations related to employment and retirement for older adults, the housing of elders, and provision of in-home or institutional care for elders.

EDUCATION AND EXPERIENCE REQUIREMENTS

Requirements for mediator education, training, and credentialing is handled at the state level. Some states license, register, or certify mediators. Mediation training usually involves 40 hours of basic training, plus 20 hours of advanced training. Some mediators seek further education through a conflict resolution degree or certificate program at institutions of higher education. For family mediators, an undergraduate or graduate degree in family studies or marriage and family therapy is strongly encouraged. For mediators who work with elders, gerontology coursework or a degree component is recommended. Professionals in counseling and guidance, social work, law, and clinical psychology who work with families and/or elders should find mediation training to be an excellent addition to their professional "toolkit."

CERTIFICATION, LICENSURE, AND CONTINUING EDUCATION REQUIREMENTS

Mediators must meet licensure, certification, or registration requirements of the state in which the mediation practice occurs. Continuing education is required by some states for license or registration renewal or recertification.

CORE COMPETENCIES AND SKILLS NEEDED

- Working knowledge of different models of conflict resolution
- Working knowledge of the process and stages of collaborative problem solving
- Understanding of the sources of power in negotiation
- Ability to handle issues related to diversity
- Ability to diffuse emotionally charged disputes
- Ability to mediate and negotiate multiparty disputes
- Ability to draft durable agreements
- Effective communication skills
- Active listening skills and keep observational skills

COMPENSATION

This varies by education; type and amount of mediation training and experience; state licensure, registration, or certification; the nature of the employment setting; and the geographic location. The range of compensation may include volunteer services, pro bono work, part-time wages, and part-time or full-time salary or fee for service.

WORKPLACE(S)

These include community mediation and conflict resolution centers, courts, human service agencies, law firms, state and federal governmental agencies, long-term care and assisted living centers, senior centers, and other community-based settings that serve older adults and private practices or consultancies.

EMPLOYMENT OUTLOOK

Good, with the likelihood of improving as more elders turn to conflict resolution, including mediation, to resolve family disputes and other conflicts.

RELATED PROFESSIONAL ORGANIZATIONS AND WEBSITES

- Association for Conflict Resolution (ACR): www.acrnet.org
- National Council on Family Relations (NCFR): www.ncfr.org
- American Association of Marriage and Family Therapists (AAMFT): www.aamft.org

An Interview With SUSAN J. BUTTERWICK

Mediator, Mediator Trainer, and Attorney

Postsecondary educational background, including formal credentials and other education/ training in gerontology/geriatrics:
BA, Art and Art History
JD, Law

How and when did you first become interested in gerontology/geriatrics? As a trained mediator, I took an advanced training in adult guardianship mediation. This led to additional research and study on working with older adults through an elder advocacy organization, where I worked on a three-state pilot project in adult guardianship and caregiver mediation, and through additional training in mediation.

Briefly describe your gerontology/geriatrics-related career path. After additional training in mediation, I worked with a few organizations (elder advocacy and dispute resolution centers) in program development for mediation services on probate and caregiving cases where there is conflict in families over the care of an older person. I still provide advanced training for mediators around the country and teach university courses about adult guardianship and elder mediation.

Briefly describe your current professional position:

Position title: Director of Peacemaking Court Program, County Trial Court

Primary role tasks/responsibilities: I direct a new pilot court program in peacemaking, based on tribal peacemaking traditions, for family cases, as a better way for families to resolve disputes and heal relationships that have been damaged through conflict and, subsequently, the adversarial court process. Among the cases that we handle are probate adult guardianship and estate cases. I also have the opportunity to learn from our tribal peacemaking courts. Tribal elders and grandparents are some of the most highly respected members of their communities and I enjoy learning from them and thinking about what our communities could be like if this were true in Anglo-American society. In addition, I train mediators in basic civil and advanced adult guardianship mediation.

(*continued*)

An Interview With SUSAN J. BUTTERWICK *(continued)*

Type of employment setting: Court and various training venues

Length of time in this position: Court program: 13 months; training/teaching: 15 years.

How did you first become interested in this position? Court program: This is one of the most innovative and exciting projects I've worked on and, as soon as I heard about it, I was interested in the possibility of a court actually wanting to find an alternative to help families heal instead of the polarization that happens to families in the traditional justice system. Training: I've been a mediation trainer for about 15 years. After helping to write a basic civil mediation curriculum for the local dispute resolution center, I became interested in elder mediation training and taking an advanced training in this area helped me realize that elder and family mediation is a badly needed service for older adults and their families. I became interested in the fact that elder mediation draws on additional and advanced skills and knowledge beyond the basic mediation skills training, such as the fact that a mediator needs to learn about specific issues around aging (e.g., working with disabilities and diminished capacity) and on working with multiple parties who have a history of conflict with one another. These are critical issues for a mediator to understand and they make the subject matter interesting to teach.

Describe a typical workday in your current professional position. Court: Every day is different, but I work with cases that are referred to me; meet with the attorneys, families, and other parties in advance to learn more about their concerns; schedule the peacemaking sessions; and work with the families to help them find a solution that all family members can agree on and that also will help to heal and repair relationships that have become damaged through the conflict. I am responsible for training and all aspects of the program.

Training: I usually travel to another city with a co-trainer and provide a 2-1/2-day elder mediation training. I enjoy meeting new people and training mediators to do this important work.

(continued)

An Interview With SUSAN J. BUTTERWICK *(continued)*

What is the time commitment required of your current professional position? I work 30 to 40 hours per week at the court. When I teach at a local university in the spring and fall, I teach in the evenings or on weekends. When I travel out of town to give an elder training, it involves about 4 days out-of-town.

How do you stay up-to-date in your profession?

Professional organization memberships and/or activities?
State bar association, member

Local county bar association, member

Association for Conflict Resolution, member

Elder Decision Making and Mediation Making Section, member

Subscribe to and/or read professional journals and/or newsletters?
Mediation and conflict resolution publications, such as those from the Association for Conflict Resolution (ACR) and the American Bar Association (ABA) Dispute Resolution

State and local bar association magazines

Alternative Dispute Resolutions (ADR) newsletters

Attend professional conferences and/or participate in education/training programs? For mediation and conflict resolution only: I periodically attend ACR, ABA, and the Association of Family and Conciliation Courts (AFCC) conferences. My co-trainer and I also do presentations on elder mediation at various state and national gerontology and elder service provider conferences.

Other? We have gerontologists or social workers who specialize in gerontology, as well as elder law attorneys, present portions of our elder mediation trainings and I am always learning from them. I also work with a couple of national committees, one of which has developed and published training guidelines for elder mediation and another is working on criteria for developing a court program for coordination of elderly

(continued)

An Interview With SUSAN J. BUTTERWICK (*continued*)

services. I have authored and co-authored articles for professional journals and magazines. I present workshops on elder mediation at various mediation conferences and provide presentations to elder service provider organizations and groups.

What are the most rewarding aspects of your current career position? Working with families to heal conflict and pain.

What are the most rewarding aspects of your gerontology/geriatrics-related career path? Training mediators to do this work.

What are the most challenging aspects of your current career position? Individuals who don't want to end the conflict. These are very few and far between, but it does happen occasionally.

What are the most challenging aspects of your gerontology/geriatrics-related career path? One of the more challenging aspects of presenting to professionals in the gerontology, geriatric, or social work fields is to help them understand that mediation is not the same as what they do in their work and that it takes a specific set of skills that are most effectively delivered by neutral outsiders who have no stake in the outcome. We are not there to replace what they do and we are not qualified to do that; we are simply a tool that can be used to make their jobs easier. In addition, it is challenging working with longstanding family dynamics and relationships that may have been involved in conflict for many years before these issues rose to the surface.

How do you balance career and other aspects of your life? Finding time and balance is always a challenge, but I manage. Caring for older parents and spending time with younger people in my family is important and I make time for this. I don't want to retire any time soon, so these challenges will be around for a while!

What advice do you have for someone contemplating a career in the field of aging? Your skills and dedication are badly needed. Whether it is a career that is deeply involved with caring for older people, or one that interfaces with older people, like mine, it's important work.

(*continued*)

An Interview With SUSAN J. BUTTERWICK *(continued)*

What advice do you have for someone considering a professional position similar to your current position? It's hard to break into mediation as a full-time career. This area (elder mediation) is a niche in the conflict resolution field that can be good to specialize in, but it will take time to build a profession out of this. If you have another degree such as law, geriatric social work, or gerontology, stay with your day job and use this as a secondary job until you can establish yourself as an expert mediator or practitioner in ADR and can earn a living that you are satisfied with. There are many places to provide mediation services for older adults, such as working with service providers in your community, courts, ADR organizations, or in private practice. Explore all of these first and think carefully about how you want to build this career before jumping in with both feet! It takes time.

MUSIC THERAPIST

MUSIC THERAPIST–BOARD CERTIFIED (MT-BC)

BASIC DESCRIPTION

Music therapists are musicians who are specially trained to use music as a therapeutic tool in addressing the physical, psychological (emotional and cognitive), and social needs of their clients. After assessing the specific strengths, abilities, and needs of a client, the music therapist devises a treatment plan that might include creating and/or performing vocal or instrumental music, moving to music, and/or listening to music. Outcomes of music therapy for clients include facilitation of movement and overall physical rehabilitation; motivation to enter and endure treatment/rehabilitation that is physically or mentally difficult; provision of a calming and emotional supportive environment for clients, their families, and caregivers; and provision of a means of communication and expression of feelings for clients who have difficulty with direct verbal expression. Although music therapists work most frequently as members of interdisciplinary health care teams, they also work as individual practitioners.

EDUCATION AND EXPERIENCE REQUIREMENTS

Music therapists must have a bachelor's or master's degree in music therapy from an American Music Therapy Association (AMTA)-approved academic training program and internship. Gerontology coursework or a degree component is strongly recommended for those who intend to practice primarily with older adults.

CERTIFICATION, LICENSURE, AND CONTINUING EDUCATION REQUIREMENTS

Graduates of AMTA-approved degree programs at the bachelor's or master's degree level are eligible to take the certification examination administered by the Certification Board for Music Therapists (CBMT) to earn Music Therapist–Board Certified (MT-BC) credentials.

CORE COMPETENCIES AND SKILLS NEEDED

- Genuine interest in people
- Desire to facilitate the empowerment of others
- Ability to establish a caring and professional relationship with clients from diverse backgrounds
- Empathy
- Patience
- Creative, imaginative, and open to new ideas
- Understanding of oneself
- Background in and love of music; competent on several instruments and musical styles

COMPENSATION

This varies by one's education, experience, CB-MT credentials, type of professional practice, and the nature of the employment setting. Some positions may be part time, paid by wage, or on a contractual fee-for-service basis.

WORKPLACE(S)

These include general and psychiatric hospitals, community mental health agencies, rehabilitation centers, daycare facilities and adult day programs, skilled and intermediate care facilities, adult foster care homes, dementia care and memory loss units and organizations, hospice, oncology treatment centers, pain/stress management clinics, senior centers, retirement communities, in-home care agencies, other agencies and organizations that serve older adults, correctional settings, private practices, and consulting contractual services.

EMPLOYMENT OUTLOOK

Good, with potential for improvement due to the expansion of the older adult population, the increase in elders' comfort level with therapeutic treatment/intervention, and the addition of and variation in the type of venues in which music therapy can be practiced with older adults.

RELATED PROFESSIONAL ORGANIZATIONS AND WEBSITES

- American Music Therapy Association (AMTA): www.musictherapy.org
- The Certification Board for Music Therapists (CBMT): www.cbmt.org
- National Coalition of Creative Arts Therapies Associations (NCCATA): www.nccata.org

An Interview With JENNIFER D. GEIGER

Music Therapist–Board Certified

Postsecondary educational background, including formal credentials and other education/training in gerontology/geriatrics:

Bachelor of Music, Music Therapy
Master of Arts, Music Therapy
Board Certified Music Therapist (MT-BC)
Training programs at the American Music Therapy Association national and regional conferences; recent trainings include "Aging Institute" and "Evidence-Based Medical Music Therapy"
Allied Team Training for Parkinson's (ATTP) from the National Parkinson's Foundation

How and when did you first become interested in gerontology/geriatrics? In order to complete my education and be eligible to sit for the Board Certification Exam for Music Therapists, I spent my 6-month internship working in a large psychiatric hospital at which children, teens, adults, and older adults were treated. It was there that I recognized my love for work with elderly persons.

Briefly describe your gerontology/geriatrics-related career path. Upon completing my internship, I returned home and did some per-diem work in a psychiatric hospital. Eventually, I landed my first full-time job as an activities director in a skilled nursing facility (SNF) that included an Alzheimer's/dementia care unit. Beginning as a department manager fresh out of college was a challenge. I was in charge of completing multiple forms of documentation for each resident, including admission, completion of the Minimum Data Set (MDS), daily activity attendance, and quarterly progress notes. While I did not have the opportunity to co-treat with physical, occupational, or speech therapists, I did consult with them on how music could benefit individual patients. During this time, I also supervised local music therapy practicum students and mentored them as they completed their education. This prompted me to return to school for my master's degree so that I could eventually teach music therapy. Due to the need for flexible hours so I could attend classes, I changed my work setting to a psychiatric hospital and worked with adults of all ages. My graduate degree research, however, led me to work with

(*continued*)

An Interview With JENNIFER D. GEIGER *(continued)*

older adults in assisted living on the topic of music to assist with sleep. I completed this program on the use of music and relaxation as a sleep aid to older adults complaining of difficulty with sleep. After marriage, I moved to a new job, where I resumed the role of activities director at a transitional care unit at a major hospital. It helped that I was already familiar with the documentation procedures in this setting because the fast turn-around rate of admissions and discharges for short-term stays resulted in copious amounts of paperwork. During this time, I also developed my private practice by providing weekly or monthly group and/or individual music therapy experiences in local skilled nursing facilities, assisted living facilities, and wellness centers. Once my children arrived, I let go of full-time employment in deference to the flexibility that business ownership offered. I am able to stimulate my vocational desires, pay bills, and devote time to family.

Briefly describe your current professional position:

Position title: Music therapist, private practice

Primary role tasks/responsibilities: Provide music therapy interventions for older adults in individual or group settings

Type of employment setting: Self-employed business owner

Length of time in this position: 20 years in private practice; 14 years as business owner

How did you first become interested in this position? After working in skilled nursing and psychiatric facilities, I desired to have my own business with clientele hand-picked to provide a more flexible working opportunity.

Describe a typical workday in your current professional position. A typical workday includes packing up my vehicle with the instruments and supplies that I will need to provide the planned group and allow for flexibility based on client needs that day. Facilities are located in a 30-mile radius, so I commute on workdays. Music therapy sessions are 30 to 60 minutes

(continued)

An Interview With JENNIFER D. GEIGER (*continued*)

long, depending upon the group/individual needs. Documentation is provided at the request of the facility/client and includes the initial impression of the client/group, the interventions used, the responses to music, and any change reported at session end. Communication with staff is essential if they are not in the session to observe/record client responses.

What is the time commitment required of your current professional position? As I have the benefit of scheduling my own sessions/hours, I work part time (10–15 hours) each week. This includes approximately 5 to 6 hours in direct client contact, plus another 2 to 3 hours for administrative duties (session preparation, documentation, billing, banking and office work). When I have a practicum student, my work hours increase by 2 to 3 per week due to the additional paperwork and session plan review/preparation required. I choose not to schedule sessions on evenings or weekends.

How do you stay up-to-date in your profession?

Professional organization memberships and/or activities? American Music Therapy Association (AMTA), regional and national membership; served in a variety of board and committee positions and as an Assembly delegate. Most recently, I was Chair of the Professional Competencies Task Force, which reviewed and streamlined the current education and training requirements for music therapy students. My term as President-Elect, which means a total 6-year commitment (2 years each as President-Elect, President, and Past President), has just begun.

Subscribe to and/or read professional journals and/or newsletters? Through my AMTA membership, I receive the *Journal of Music Therapy* (quarterly) and *Music Therapy Perspectives* (semiannually).

Attend professional conferences and/or participate in education/training programs? Conference attendance is essential for me. For recertification, I am required to obtain 100 Continuing Music Therapy Education credits every 5 years. In additional to books, journal articles,

(*continued*)

An Interview With JENNIFER D. GEIGER *(continued)*

and conference sessions, I participate in online courses for professional development. Past courses have included web development and technology for music therapists and a Reintroduction to Piano Improvisation. Frequently, I also do presentations on music therapy and older adults at both music therapy and other conferences. I sometimes conduct in-service training for staff members at the facilities where I provide music therapy services.

Other? Having an online presence via my website, professional Facebook and Twitter accounts also is essential for me.

What are the most rewarding aspects of your current career position? As a private practice music therapist, I can tailor my schedule to fit the needs of my family. That is huge! I have had to learn the fine art of budgeting for sick and vacation time, but I'm also in charge of what I take on and what I decline.

What are the most rewarding aspects of your gerontology/geriatrics-related career path? Working with clients in geriatric settings is most rewarding. I feel appreciated and valued every step of the way. Some days, it's like being a rock star! I value my interactions with my clients. I have been given the opportunity to come into their living space and offer an experience to enhance their quality of life. For that, I am grateful!

What are the most challenging aspects of your current career position? Juggling the work-life balance by carving out time for administrative duties and educational experiences. Since I am the boss, I have to give myself time to get those things done so that I can be a better businesswoman and music therapist.

What are the most challenging aspects of your gerontology/geriatrics-related career path? The life and health issues of the aging can make my work more difficult. I am challenged by the residents who are highly confused, the families torn apart as a loved one is placed in hospice, and the person who has lost functioning because of a stroke—but it is a privilege for me that I can help my clients and their families through these issues and situations.

(continued)

An Interview With JENNIFER D. GEIGER (*continued*)

How do you balance career and other aspects of your life? I maintain regular health check-ups. Journaling regularly helps me maintain perspective on my life. I use 1:1 time in person, mail, e-mail, text messages, and phone calls to keep up with my loved ones. I track my work commitments while still finding time for fun. My family and I enjoy traveling and doing things together. I absolutely love to read, to catch up on movies, and keep abreast of the latest TV shows. As the bill payer and tracker of food, clothing, and shelter for my family, I use time management skills to keep these in check.

What advice do you have for someone contemplating a career in the field of aging? One must have a drive—a desire to affect positive change for this population of adults that is ever changing. Working with the aging clients involves more than reassurances and a pat on the arm. It involves knowledge, the willingness to be involved in care, compassion, respect, creativity, and commitment.

What advice do you have for someone considering a professional position similar to your current position? Be ready to look professional. Bring a sense of humor, objectivity, and respect to your interactions. Be prepared to offer choices to those with whom you work. This is very important because many who have left their long-time homes have not done so willingly, but out of necessity (and often due to an emergency). Be willing to be flexible. What you have to offer may not be what is needed at that time. Remember your compassion and creativity.

OCCUPATIONAL THERAPIST (OT)

OCCUPATIONAL THERAPY ASSISTANT (OTA)

BASIC DESCRIPTION

Occupational therapists (OTs) and occupational therapy assistants (OTAs) assist their clients and patients with physical, cognitive, and/or emotional limitations in ways that allow them to stay active in occupations, accomplish activities of daily living (ADLs) and instrumental activities of daily living

(IADLs), participate socially, engage in productive activity (such as employment or volunteering), and be involved in other activities that provide quality of life (such as hobbies and avocations) for older adults. Licensed OTs work independently with clients/patients or as members of multidisciplinary health care or social services teams. OTAs work under the direction and supervision of licensed OTs. They are trained to assess the client's ability to accomplish a desired task or activity, then offer recommendations for changes in the related physical environment(s) and assist clients in adapting or learning new behaviors and routines. OTs and OTAs work with issues of sensory loss (e.g., hearing loss, visual impairment), dysphagia (eating or swallowing disorders), fall prevention, mobility limitations, and role transitions (e.g., retirement, widowhood). In going through a Centennial Vision process, the American Occupational Therapy Association (AOTA) identified four "emerging niches in productive aging": Aging in Place and Home Modifications, Alzheimer's Disease and Dementia, Community Mobility, and Older Drivers and Low Vision. The profession also continues a focus on Falls Prevention. Gerontology is one of four AOTA Board Certification areas. Another Centennial Vision outcome for AOTA has been a renewed commitment to science-driven and evidence-based practice. As part of turning this commitment into action, AOTA has partnered with the American Occupational Therapy Foundation (AOTF) and other funding partners to develop a variety of research training options, including an array of pre- and post-doctoral fellowships and the Rehabilitation Research Career Development (RRCD) program for rehabilitation scholars who are OTs and physical therapists (PTs).

EDUCATION AND EXPERIENCE REQUIREMENTS

A master's or doctoral degree, including a supervised internship, in occupational therapy is required for entry into full professional practice. A doctoral degree is required for teaching in higher education. OTAs require an associate's degree or bachelor's degree in occupational therapy, including a supervised clinical internship, and then practices under the supervision of an OT. Gerontology coursework or a degree component is encouraged for OTs and OTAs whose practice is primarily with older adults.

CERTIFICATION, LICENSURE, AND CONTINUING EDUCATION REQUIREMENTS

OTs and OTAs must meet licensure and/or registration requirements of AOTA and of the state in which professional practice occurs. Gerontology is one of AOTA's voluntary certification areas.

CORE COMPETENCIES AND SKILLS NEEDED

- Commitment to evidence-based and ethical practice
- Ability to instill confidence in clients and patients
- Ability to direct or instruct clients and patients with clarity, gentleness, and firmness
- Patience
- Strong interpersonal skills
- Excellent verbal and written communication skills; attentive listener and keen observer
- Attentive to detail in therapeutic practice
- Ability to maintain accurate patient and client records
- Ability to respond and adapt quickly to client and patient needs during therapy sessions
- OTs: Ability to competently support the development of and supervision of OTAs and interns
- OTAs: Open to guidance and instruction from supervising OTs; ability to follow directions as instructed

COMPENSATION

This varies by one's education, experience, certifications, the nature of the employment setting, level of responsibility, and geographical location.

WORKPLACE(S)

For OTs and OTAs, these include hospitals, rehabilitation centers, outpatient clinics, long-term care and assisted living facilities, senior centers and other community-based settings that serve older adults, patients' homes, and home care agencies. For OTs only, workplaces can also include private practices and consulting that is frequently related to one of the "emerging niches" noted previously. Some OTs practice as "traveling OTs"; they work on a contractual basis for a specified period of time (e.g., 1 to 3 months) and travel to distant sites to provide and/or supervise OT services and offer training for non-OT personnel for a specified length of time.

EMPLOYMENT OUTLOOK

Excellent, especially for OTs in private practice and consulting and OTAs in clinical practice settings where one OT can supervise several OTAs. With more emphasis on independent living goals for older adults, such as "aging in place" and age-friendly communities/neighborhoods, there may be more opportunities for OTs and OTAs to expand the venues in which they work.

RELATED PROFESSIONAL ORGANIZATIONS AND WEBSITES

- American Occupational Therapy Association (AOTA): www.aota.org
- American Occupational Therapy Foundation (AOTF): www.aotf.org
- Rehabilitation Research Career Development Program (RRCD): http://rehabsciences.utmb.edu/k12

An Interview With BRYANNE A. CHEW

Traveling Occupational Therapist

Postsecondary educational background, including formal credentials and other education/training in gerontology/geriatrics:
BS, Occupational Science
Undergraduate Certificate in Gerontology
MS, Occupational Therapy, with Minors in Psychology and Gerontology
Occupational Therapist, Registered by National Board of Occupational Therapy and Licensed (by each state) to practice in 7 states

How and when did you first become interested in gerontology/geriatrics? As a child, I was blessed with the opportunity to camp with my grandparents as we joined multiple RV rallies and campouts. Being a grandchild in this vast network of retirees, I learned quickly that not everyone moved at my pace. My grandmother showed me that sometimes individuals needed additional time to get to where they were going or to accomplish a simple task. The process of aging was more apparent with this group of retirees. It afforded me, at a young age, insight into the difficulties of aging, but grace, confidence, and pride was also conveyed. These early experiences are what set into motion my desire to work in geriatrics.

Briefly describe your gerontology/geriatrics-related career path. As I grew up, I knew that I was going to pursue a career in the health care field, but I did not have a targeted profession. A friend of the family introduced me to pediatric occupational therapy (OT), which was fun and exciting, but I was not interested in working with children. My next connection with occupational therapy (OT) was while visiting my great aunt in a nursing home after she had a stroke. Visiting her often allowed me to go to therapy with her. Seeing the occupational and physical therapists working with her fascinated me. I thought how incredible it was that even partially paralyzed, my aunt was able to learn self-care through one-handed techniques. After observing OT in the pediatric setting and watching how some techniques could also be applied to the geriatric setting, I knew this was what I wanted to do. During my last year of high school I was able to take three college courses that enabled me to take the gerontology consortium courses and get started on my geriatrics-related career. I was then accepted to

(*continued*)

An Interview With BRYANNE A. CHEW *(continued)*

a 5-year bachelor's/master's program in OT. During my first year, I met a psychology professor who also taught gerontology. Her enthusiasm for the field fed my desire to work with older adults. I was afforded the privilege of twice presenting at American Society on Aging conferences. With each new year of college, I knew I had chosen the right path. Working with elderly persons has thus far led me to work in long-term care environments.

Briefly describe your current professional position:

Position title: Traveling occupational therapist

Primary role tasks/responsibilities: As an occupational therapist, my role is to work with clients throughout their life span by using meaningful and purposeful activities that promote health through motor, cognitive, and emotional functions. My role requires me to customize treatments; create comprehensive evaluations, assessments, and treatment plans; provide recommendations; and arrange for caregiver education in order to address activities of daily living for each individual. I supervise certified occupational therapy assistants. I generate and monitor weekly treatment plans based on individual's progress. I also participate in continuing education programs to ensure up-to-date information is being applied in each of my work settings. As a traveling occupational therapist, I have to adapt to working in several different geriatric-based settings throughout the country; these include inpatient/outpatient, acute, and subacute facilities. Within these settings, I need to learn about the culture(s) of the region in which I am working and I must acclimate myself to working with the different cultural and language barriers that I encounter. This responsibility also requires me to be up-to-date on all the laws related to occupational therapy services.

Type of employment setting: Geriatric settings, including subacute and acute in-patient and out-patient facilities, skilled nursing homes, assisted living facilities, and independent living residences.

Length of time in this position: I am in my third year as a traveling occupational therapist.

(continued)

An Interview With BRYANNE A. CHEW *(continued)*

How did you first become interested in this position? When I was younger, I had the vision of traveling our country and seeing all the sights my grandparents had visited. As I got older, the realization that I could travel for work became a main focus and I began the effort of making this dream a reality. Working across the country in multiple geriatric care settings as I meet and help to enhance the lives of elders has been a dream come true.

Describe a typical workday in your current professional position. My day usually begins with working on an individual's self-care. Rarely is a typical day only 8 hours. My responsibilities require a vast set of skills in order to assess and assist patients in their foremost goal of returning home. Usually patients are seen back-to-back and rarely at the same time. While seeing the patient, I complete written assessments and a plan of care is discussed with the patient or patient's family. Due to the demand for 90% productivity, my lunchtime is usually used to complete additional paperwork. Afternoons consist of treating remaining residents on caseload and evaluating new patients.

What is the time commitment required of your current professional position? The amount of time commitment per week varies according to the contract I sign with each facility. Demands and hours can vary. In my 2-plus years of traveling, I usually work 40 hours but this can vary with the work load. Other facilities have asked me to work Tuesday through Saturday, work more than 40 hours (my longest week was 54 hours), stay late one night a week for incoming admissions, and/or be on-call on weekends from 7 a.m. to 7 p.m. Saturday and Sunday or four 10-hour days. Between contracts, I can have up to 2 weeks off without losing my health insurance. Personal vacation time during the assignments can be specified and usually is accepted by the facilities. Vacation time is often spent visiting family, completing continuing education courses, and traveling to the new assignment.

How do you stay up-to-date in your profession?

Professional organization memberships and/or activities?

American Occupational Therapy Association (AOTA), member

National Board of Occupational Therapy (NBCOT), member

(continued)

An Interview With BRYANNE A. CHEW (*continued*)

Subscribe to and/or read professional journals and/or newsletters? As an AOTA member benefit, I receive *OT Practice* and *The American Journal of Occupational Therapy (AJOT).* These, plus *The Australian Occupational Therapy Journal* (all published in both print and online), have been the most beneficial for me to stay current on relevant information and evidence-based research. I also subscribe to other online evidence-based journals that are convenient when traveling.

What are the most rewarding aspects of your current career position? The most rewarding aspect is watching my patient's progress with OT. Seeing my patients on a daily basis affords me the ability to get to know them and adjust their treatment plans accordingly. My reward is the trust earned, the viable progress, and the ability to make an impact in so many individual lives. For me, increased independence is the most gratifying part of my job.

What are the most rewarding aspects of your gerontology/geriatrics-related career path? The most rewarding aspect is the ability to sit and listen to the life experiences of those I treat. Through my patients' personal histories, I have learned how to work with different personalities and cultural differences. Through these experiences, I have been able to provide education to the staff working with these individuals and ensure individualized treatments. To me, this individualized connection is the most gratifying part of my gerontology/geriatrics career path.

What are the most challenging aspects of your current career position? The biggest personal challenge of my current career position is working with a patient who has become a daily inspiration and leaving them to travel to a new position. It is reassuring, though, to know that I have set the individual up for success prior to my departure. Another challenge as a traveling therapist is productivity expectations and ethical dilemmas. I have maintained the belief that I work for the patient not the corporation. My job is to help heal, adapt, and encourage the patients to be as independent as possible—not just provide an income to the facility.

What are the most challenging aspects of your gerontology/geriatrics-related career path? The hardest and most challenging aspect of my career in geriatrics is losing a patient.

(*continued*)

An Interview With BRYANNE A. CHEW *(continued)*

How do you balance career and other aspects of your life? When I'm at work, my focus is on my job. When I'm at home, I try to balance between physical, social, and spiritual activities. Although work is not a primary focus at home, I always am planning a treatment and looking for items to increase the success of independence for my patients. Being a traveler requires me to be flexible with both my career and personal life.

What advice do you have for someone contemplating a career in the field of aging? This is a challenging but rewarding field that requires an appreciation of being and working with geriatric clients. One should have exposure to this population prior to starting a career in the field. Exposure is necessary to diminish misconceptions.

What advice do you have for someone considering a professional position similar to your current position? Like many careers, it requires patience, understanding, love, and empathy. Unlike many careers, death is an inevitable part of this field. You must know yourself, know your ethics, and be able to stand up for yourself and your patients. You need a foundation before beginning as a traveler. As a traveler, your life changes every 3 to 6 months. You have to be willing to pack everything up at a moment's notice, challenge your contract to ensure you are getting your needs met, and understand that any time you could be given a 30-day end-of-contract notice with no prospect of a new job placement. Flexibility is a must. This is a fast-paced, individual career choice. It can be isolating and lonely at times, but when it all comes together—the people, the environment, and the job—it is the most incredible opportunity of a lifetime.

PROFESSIONAL GEROPSYCHOLOGIST

GERIATRIC PSYCHIATRIST

BASIC DESCRIPTION

Within the discipline of psychology, two primary career paths specific to aging—professional geropsychology and geriatric psychiatry—have emerged. *Professional Geropsychologist:* Clinical geropsychology was first recognized as a proficiency by the American Psychological Association (APA) in 1998 (recognition renewal was scheduled for 2008). In 2010, however, APA upgraded the status by declaring it a Specialty in Professional Geropsychology with a "scientist-practitioner" approach that has been adopted for graduate programs in geropsychology at several universities. Professional geropsychologists address multiple biopsychosocial problems (e.g., depression, anxiety, dementia, and related behavioral/lifestyle changes, coping with and managing chronic illness, grief and loss, family caregiving strains, adjustment to age-related stresses such as marital/family conflict and changing roles, end-of-life care) for older adults and their families. Assessment, intervention, and consultation are the primary processes used by professional geropsychologists in their practice with and/or on behalf of their aging and elderly clients. *Geriatric Psychiatrist:* Geriatric psychiatry is a specialty in the field of medicine. Geriatric psychiatrists are medical or osteopathic doctors with special training in the diagnosis and treatment of mental disorders (e.g., depression, anxiety, late life addiction disorders, schizophrenia) that occur for older adults. They take a holistic approach in diagnosing psychiatric problems and developing comprehensive treatment plans for their aging clients.

EDUCATION AND EXPERIENCE REQUIREMENTS

Professional Geropsychologist: A Doctor of Philosophy (PhD) or Doctor of Psychology (PsyD) in clinical psychology, with a concentration in geropsychology (coursework in both psychology and gerontology), is required. Postdoctoral fellowships are encouraged, especially for those with research interests. *Geriatric Psychiatrist*: A Doctor of Medicine or Doctor of Osteopathy degree, plus a 4-year approved residency in general psychiatry and a 1-year specialty fellowship training in psychiatric work with older adults through an accredited residency in geriatric psychiatry, is required.

CERTIFICATION, LICENSURE, AND CONTINUING EDUCATION REQUIREMENTS

Certification in General Psychiatry and Geriatric Psychiatry: Certification may be earned (although not required for practice) by successfully passing the certification examination in general psychiatry given by the American Board of Psychiatry and Neurology (ABPN). Further examination is then available for ABPN certification in the subspecialty of geriatric psychiatry. To maintain certification, general and geriatric psychiatrists must meet standards of APBN's Maintenance of Certification Program (MOC). Licensure: Both geropsychologists and geriatric psychiatrists must meet licensure requirements in the state where their professional practice occurs. Continuing Education: May be required for license renewal or by an employing agency, but also is vital to staying updated in their specializations.

CORE COMPETENCIES AND SKILLS NEEDED

Although there are differences in the focus and practice of professional geropsychologists and geriatric psychiatrists, there are strong similarities in the required core competencies and skills they need for successful practice with aging clients.

- Good knowledge base on adult development and aging in regard to normal aging; biological, psychological, and social changes; and relevant sociocultural factors (e.g., gender, ethnicity)
- Thorough working knowledge of behavioral and mental health in later life
- Thorough working knowledge of mental health assessment theory, research, and practice
- Thorough working knowledge of mental health intervention and consultation processes and practice
- Commitment to patient-centered practice
- Commitment to ethical professional practice
- Good listener and observer
- Good interpersonal and communication skills
- Good problem-solving skills
- Patience and calm demeanor
- Willing and comfortable with working collaboratively as a team member when appropriate

COMPENSATION

This varies by specialization, education, experience, specific type of practice, and nature of the employing agency, organization, or facility.

WORKPLACE(S)

These include research centers, medical centers, in-patient medical or psychiatric hospital units, geropsychology clinics and institutes, long-term care facilities, health care management corporations, community mental health agencies, community substance abuse programs and agencies, organizations specific to mental health disorders (e.g., Alzheimer's disease, depression, Parkinson's disease), independent or group private practice, outpatient settings, daycare programs and home care agencies, elder law clinics, and hospice.

EMPLOYMENT OUTLOOK

Very good, especially due to an increase in percentage of older persons with mental health issues or disorders (expected to double by 2030); currently a shortage of professionals with geriatric expertise and a shortage of faculty members to educate/train new geropsychologists and geriatric psychiatrists.

RELATED PROFESSIONAL ORGANIZATIONS AND WEBSITES

- American Psychological Association (APA): www.apa.org [See APA Division 20: Adult Development & Aging]
- American Geriatrics Society (AGS): www.americangeriatrics.org
- American Association for Geriatric Psychiatry (AAGP): www.aagponline.org
- Geriatric Mental Health Foundation (GMHF): www.gmhfonline.org
- American Board of Psychiatry and Neurology (ABPN): www.abpn.com
- Interest Group on Mental Health Practice and Aging, Gerontological Society of America (GSA): www.geron.org
- Interest Group on Emotion and Aging, Gerontological Society of America (GSA): www.geron.org
- Mental Health and Aging Network (MHAN), American Society on Aging (ASA): www.asaging.org/mhan

REGISTERED FINANCIAL GERONTOLOGIST (RFG)

BASIC DESCRIPTION

Registered financial gerontologists (RFGs) are professionals from an array of finance-related fields (e.g., accounting, banking, insurance, financial/retirement planning, development and fundraising, estate planning, social work) who assist elders and their families in developing and maintaining appropriate financial strategies that allow them to achieve their changing financial needs and goals across the lifespan.

EDUCATION AND EXPERIENCE REQUIREMENTS

RFGs must complete the American Institute of Financial Gerontology (AIFG) training program, which includes required courses on wealth-span planning, basic processes of aging, serving older clients, and financial longevity, plus elective courses on subjects such as families and aging, aging network and long-term care delivery systems, long-term care solutions, financial preparedness for later life, and successful marketing to midlife and older consumers. Becoming a RFG also requires completing the AIFG-approved service learning activity, passing a comprehensive exam, and agreeing to an ethical practice pledge.

CERTIFICATION, LICENSURE, AND CONTINUING EDUCATION REQUIREMENTS

Admission to a RFG training program requires the verification of one's existing financial background (in the form of a license, degree, or verifiable professional experience). The annual renewal of an active RFG designation requires additional continuing education coursework, a service learning activity, renewal of the RFG pledge, and payment of a membership fee.

CORE COMPETENCIES AND SKILLS NEEDED

- Excellent financial status assessment skills
- Updated knowledge of current legal/regulatory mandates related to financial planning
- Commitment to client-centered professional practice
- Good mathematical skills
- Excellent interpersonal communication skills
- Ability to maintain confidentiality about client information
- Comfortable working with two or more generations of the client's family
- Adherence to legal and ethical professional practice

COMPENSATION

This varies by type of professional practice, one's education, experience, the nature of the employment setting, level of position, and the geographical location.

WORKPLACE(S)

These include accounting firms, banks, law firms, insurance agencies, private consulting firms, investment firms, wealth management firms, and mortgage agencies.

EMPLOYMENT OUTLOOK

Excellent, especially due to the rapid growth in the older adult population, stronger interest in planning for financial security, and an emerging focus on wealth management that encompasses all aspects of life.

RELATED PROFESSIONAL ORGANIZATIONS AND WEBSITES:

- American Institute of Financial Gerontology (AIFG): www.aifg.org

An Interview With ROSANNE ROGÉ

Registered Financial Gerontologist, Certified Financial Planner, and Certified Senior Advisor

Postsecondary educational background, including formal credentials and other education/training in gerontology/geriatrics:

AAS, Secretarial Studies
BA, Human Relations
Certified Financial Planner (CFP) Education Designation Course
Certified Financial Planner (CFP) Designation, CFP Board of Standards
Certified Senior Advisor (CSA) Designation Course, Society of Certified Senior Advisors
Registered Financial Gerontologist (RFG) Designation, American Institute of Financial Gerontology (AIFG)
Ongoing continuing education is required for my Certified and Registered designations.

How and when did you first become interested in gerontology/geriatrics? I became interested in gerontology/geriatrics after caring for my elderly mom in my home for 10 years. During this time, services that are now offered for elders and their caregivers were basically nonexistent.

Briefly describe your gerontology/geriatrics-related career path. When I began working at my current place of employment, I noticed that the client base was older and "aging." Having taken care of my mom, I felt very close to this "situation." In my professional world of financial planning, I found my interests were in insurance, retirement, and estate planning. These areas, in addition to my personal experiences with Mom, led me to pursue the CSA and RFG designations related to gerontology. My interest in geriatrics was further developed when my husband's parents moved to a continuing care retirement center (CCRC) near where I live and I have been involved in this community ever since. I have helped clients transition from independent living in their own homes to a new life at the CCRC and I also serve as an Associate Trustee for the CCRC's Foundation. I am a contributor to the AgingCare.com website and write informative articles to help caregivers of elderly parents find answers on a variety of senior issues, such as housing, home care, caregiver support, and senior financial

(*continued*)

An Interview With ROSANNE ROGÉ *(continued)*

and legal information. My passion is to continuing to work with the "aging" population of our clients and their children. I have helped a number of our clients and their families transition to the next phase of their lives.

Briefly describe your current professional position:

Position title: Managing Director, Client Services

Primary role tasks/responsibilities: I oversee all phases of prospect/client activities from initial prospect meetings, onboarding of new clients, financial planning preparation and delivery, implementation and monitoring of their plan to ensure the client's goals are met. Financial geriatrics is part of my primary responsibility.

Type of employment setting: Family-owned wealth management firm

Length of time in position: 16 years in this position; 19 years with the company

How did you first become interested in this position? I was initially hired as a registered paraplanner (the first employee of the firm) and then eventually worked my way to my current position.

Describe a typical workday in your current professional position. There are no "typical" workdays in our office. Every day is different, which is what makes my position unique.

What is the time commitment required of your current professional position? Our regular work week is Monday through Friday, 9 a.m. to 5 p.m., but in this position, I usually am checking e-mail during the evening and on weekends. As a recent survivor of breast cancer, I am trying to pare down my work time to four days a week so I can enjoy other activities outside of the office. For example, I would like to get more involved in the Successful Aging Project that is being run at the CCRC.

(continued)

An Interview With ROSANNE ROGÉ (*continued*)

How do you stay up-to-date in your profession?

Professional organization memberships and/or activities?
National Association of Personal Financial Planners (NAPFA), Financial Services Affiliate
Financial Planning Association (FPA), member
American Society on Aging (ASA), member
Gerontological Society of America (GSA), member

Subscribe to and/or read professional journals and/or newsletters? I particularly like to read ASA's journal, *Generations,* and the *CSA Journal* published by the Society of Senior Advisors. I also subscribe to two magazines—*Financial Planning Magazine* and *Investment Advisor.*

Attend professional conferences and/or participate in education/training programs? I attend the NAPFA National or Regional Conferences, TD Ameritrade Annual conference, and CSA conferences. I also participate in various teleconferences that are sponsored by Charles Schwab and by the Society of Certified Senior Advisors. To keep up-to-date and to maintain my designations, I participate in conference calls, attend conventions/seminars, and do research for articles that I write for our website and other publications for which I may be requested to write on a topic dealing with financial geriatrics. I particularly enjoy the live CSA Designation classes because they afford me the opportunity to meet with a variety of individuals in the field of gerontology (outside of the financial planning field) and provide a great networking opportunity.

What are the most rewarding aspects of your current career position? Being with the same company for the past 18 years, I have been very fortunate to see financial plans come to fruition and join in the celebration as clients achieve their goals and have been very grateful to be part of a very special process. I have also had the privilege of meeting multigenerations of family members who truly appreciate what we do for them and share in their accomplishments.

(*continued*)

An Interview With ROSANNE ROGÉ (*continued*)

What are the most rewarding aspects of your gerontology/geriatrics-related career path? I am so grateful to have had the opportunity to meet so many people in the geriatric field who are so willing to share their knowledge and help another colleague work through issues on aging that may not be our expertise.

What are the most challenging aspects of your current career position? The financial world is changing every day and keeping up with these changes to be well-versed for our clients can be somewhat challenging.

What are the most challenging aspects of your gerontology/geriatrics-related career path? Through the financial plans that we prepare for our clients, we try to ensure that they are more than 100% funded, if possible. This way, both the client and we are comfortable that they are able to fund any type of health need (e.g., related to aging in place or moving to a facility) and their retirement goals (e.g., philanthropy). We try to address anything that relates to a "quality of life." This is not always easy to do when a client is more focused on how long they will live; however, we prepare our financial plans with a life expectancy to age 100. Many clients laugh at this, but when you talk about medical advances and how we are all going to live longer, they realize this is a possibility. We also ask them about longevity in their family and, all of a sudden, they recall a relative who lived into their 90s long before our advances in medicine.

This brings a true sense of reality to their plan and they often become more focused on saving and planning.

How do you balance career and other aspects of your life? Fortunately, I work with my spouse and we "counter balance" one another. We are great partners in the business and in life, so he is truly my balance. I am a recent breast cancer survivor and this has definitely helped us put things in perspective. I practice yoga and Pilates, kayak, hike, walk ... I'm an "outdoors" person and this definitely helps me in my life.

(*continued*)

An Interview With ROSANNE ROGÉ *(continued)*

What advice do you have for someone contemplating a career in the field of aging? I think it is a fabulous career path to pursue. There are so many aspects to the field of aging and many opportunities to consider as you search for the option that is right for you. Explore a wide array of possibilities. There are so many outlets to help you define the "niche" where you would enjoy sharing your passion. You need to find your passion and follow it through. Attend conferences, networking events and study groups. You'll meet individuals who may already be experienced in your field of interest and provide you with a "track to run on."

What advice do you have for someone considering a professional position similar to your current position? Attaining the level at the firm came through experience and my relationships with the clients. It really is a matter of tenure and experience. Follow through and empathy are important characteristics for a managing director. When I started at the firm 19 years ago, we had roughly 50 clients. Over the years, we've reached approximately 260 clients, each with their own planning goals and issues. Since all of our clients have different needs and goals, it was challenging to do research for them on different issues, meet with their families and explain our planning process in detail, and deliver both good news (and see a plan come to fruition) or also the bad news (when more work needs to be done to achieve their goals). I've also been part of transitioning clients through retirement, "right-sizing" (moving from a large home to a smaller, more manageable space), and death of a spouse and/or child. Having been through all these phases with a variety of clients is critical to the development of those who wish to become managers and managing directors in a wealth management firm such as ours. Taking your time, listening and learning from your clients, and then integrating what you learned with your management and financial planning knowledge and skills will benefit you, your clients, and your firm.

RESEARCHER

RESEARCH ASSOCIATE

RESEARCH ASSISTANT

BASIC DESCRIPTION

Researchers are the primary investigators for qualitative and quantitative studies that are conducted to add to the base of gerontological knowledge; describe the elderly population; understand change across time for individuals and age cohorts as they move into and through later life; determine patterns of stability and change with age; identify, test and evaluate interventions and treatments; evaluate programs and services; and learn about other aspects of aging and the elderly population. Researchers are responsible for the overall design of the study, including determination of the theoretical base for the study, hypotheses to be tested and/or research questions to be asked, study subjects and the processes through which they will be involved in the study, and the procedures or strategies to be used for data gathering and analysis. When the study is completed, they will disseminate the findings through written products (e.g., research reports, books or book chapters, professional journal articles) and in-person presentations to study stakeholders and professional conferences. Gerontological researchers come from a wide variety of academic disciplines and professions; most hold doctorates in their disciplines or professional fields. Research associates work alongside researchers to assist in the design, implementation, and analysis phases of the research project; serve as project managers; coordinate project team activity; maintain communication with institutional, funding, and national/international project partners; and assist with the preparation of reports and dissemination of information about the study and its results. Research associates also have diverse backgrounds but most frequently have master's degrees or are doctoral students in the field(s) directly related to the research project on which they are working. Research assistants commonly are students in master's and doctoral degree programs in the fields relevant to a specific research project; as such, they are often considered to be "researchers-in-training." They primarily assist with the design, conduct data analysis phases of the research project, and may be involved in the reporting and dissemination of data. In a growing number of situations, rather than designing and conducting their own studies, some researchers are employed as data and business analysts who review, analyze, and synthesize results from the studies conducted by others and then report on the implications of those results for the organization or agency where they are employed.

EDUCATION AND EXPERIENCE REQUIREMENTS

A doctorate is required for researchers in academic and federal governmental agencies. Other researcher positions require at least a master's degree in a field relevant to the work to be done. Successful research experience with research of the type being conducted is expected. Research associates require a minimum of a master's degree or higher in gerontology or a closely related discipline or professional field; experience with research of the type being conducted is strongly recommended. Research assistants require the minimum of a bachelor's degree in gerontology or a closely related discipline or professional field, plus the successful completion of research design/methodology and statistics coursework.

CERTIFICATION, LICENSURE, AND CONTINUING EDUCATION REQUIREMENTS

Researchers must meet the requirements of the employing center, institute, department or agency, and/or funding agency. Requirements may be more stringent for governmental or private research centers and institutes, especially for those who work in medical, biological, and health-related research.

CORE COMPETENCIES AND SKILLS NEEDED

- Demonstrated competence in research design and methodology
- Excellent analytical skills
- Demonstrated competence in the use of a broad range of statistical processes
- Excellent foundation of knowledge related to topic of research project/study
- Ability to concentrate and stay focused
- Very good written and oral communication skills
- Ability to work both independently and collaboratively
- Ability to supervise or be supervised

COMPENSATION

This varies by level of position, one's education, experience, the nature of the employment setting, and funding resources for a specific research project/study/career position. Compensation is also determined by whether the research role is part of another position (e.g., faculty member, graduate or teaching assistant) or if the individual is hired independently as a researcher, research associate, or research assistant. Some positions may be part time and/or combined with other positions, and some may wage based or paid by contractual fee for service.

WORKPLACE(S)

These include independent or governmental research institutes, centers, or groups; academic departments; academic or independent gerontology institutes and centers; corporations and other businesses that develop products, programs, and services for older persons; and private or public agencies or organizations that serve older adults. Opportunities for consulting work also exist for researchers with doctoral degrees. More recently, positions are opening up for researchers who are primarily data analysts for business or agency purposes.

EMPLOYMENT OUTLOOK

Good, but also quite dependent on funding by government, institutions, foundations, and other funding sources.

RELATED PROFESSIONAL ORGANIZATIONS AND WEBSITES

- Intramural Research Program, National Institute on Aging (NIA): www.grc.nia.nih.gov
- Gerontological Society of America (GSA): www.geron.org
- American Statistical Association: www.amstat.org
- American Psychological Association (APA): www.apa.org
- American Sociological Association (ASA): www.asanet.org

An Interview With ABBE LACKMEYER

Business Intelligence Analyst

Postsecondary educational background, including formal credentials and other education/training in gerontology/geriatrics:
BA, Sociology, with minor in Management
Master of Gerontological Studies (MGS)

How and when did you first become interested in gerontology/geriatrics? As a child, I was always drawn to older persons. You would often find me chatting with a friend's grandparent as opposed to playing with children my own age. I would think, however, that my first true interest in working in the field of gerontology came after an internship my senior year of high school. I interned with an occupational therapist at a local nursing facility. Following this internship, I made the decision to go to school to study occupational therapy, with the idea that I would be working with an older clientele.

Briefly describe your gerontology/geriatrics-related career path. I started out in undergrad as a biology major with the goal of eventually completing a degree in occupational therapy. During my first 2 years of school, while fulfilling other general requirements, I took a number of sociology- and management-related courses. It was then that I decided my path toward working with older adults would be more on the social side rather than the medical side. Following a year off from school, I applied and was accepted into the MGS program. While in the MGS program, my interests took a more applied approach and I was drawn to internships and a critical inquiry that focused on policy and programming involving older adults. I took an internship at the National Council on Aging (NCOA) in Washington, D.C., where I looked at the low-income subsidy of the Medicare Prescription Drug program. Upon returning for my last year of grad school, I reached out to the community and educated groups of older adults about the Prescription Drug benefit and what to expect when enrollment occurred. Following graduation, I took a position at a senior housing facility as a service coordinator, where I assisted in the coordination of services and programs for the residents of the facility. I then accepted a position as a research associate in a university's gerontology center. I worked as a project manager on a multi

(*continued*)

An Interview With ABBE LACKMEYER *(continued)*

faceted, federally funded grant for which I surveyed all Area Agencies on Aging across the nation, analyzed data, created reports, presented data, and coordinated learning opportunities across the network.

Briefly describe your current professional position:

Position title: Business Intelligence Analyst

Primary role tasks/responsibilities: Design and build reports, measure agency performance and outcomes, develop and implement surveys, conduct data analyses, present data, work with customers to understand data and analysis needs, train users on analysis and data related tools and reports, and help drive decision making across the agency that aligns with the agency's business objectives.

Type of employment setting: Area Agency on Aging (AAA)

Length of time in this position: 3+ years

How did you first become interested in this position? I was very interested in the work of the Area Agency on Aging in my community. Not many Area Agencies on Aging have business analysts on staff, so I was interested in taking my prior data analysis and evaluation work into this sector.

Describe a typical workday in your current professional position. The tasks vary from day-to-day, which is a part of this position that I enjoy. Every day will undoubtedly involve checking e-mails, responding to and keeping customers updated. Some days I will spend time in meetings, whether it is to conduct an intake for a particular deliverable or project, or act as a consultant or subject matter expert for an upcoming project (e.g., identifying what we are or are not able to do with the data we have access to). I also spend time using statistical software to analyze data and build reports. In addition, I spend time educating users about

(continued)

An Interview With ABBE LACKMEYER *(continued)*

reports and how to use the data in ways that will impact performance and outcomes.

What is the time commitment required of your current professional position? At present, I am considered a part-time employee because I have one full day off a week (this was my decision to have an extra day with my small children). I work every weekday except on Thursdays. Our agency has a flexible work schedule, so while the operating hours are 8:00 a.m. to 4:30 p.m., we can determine our start and finish time each day. I can also work from home. There are no expected evening or weekend hours, but if something needs to be completed, that can run into the evening or weekend time.

How do you stay up-to-date in your profession?

Professional organization memberships and/or activities? Association of Professionals in Aging (APA), a local organization, in the recent past.

Subscribe to and/or read professional journals and/or newsletters? I keep in contact with the gerontology center where I used to work and read their newsletter, which keeps me informed of new research projects.

Attend professional conferences and/or participate in education/training programs? I attend local conferences/programs, my state's Association of Area Agencies on Aging conferences, and the National Association of Area Agencies on Aging conferences. I also attend SAS conferences and trainings to keep up on the technical skills required for my position.

Other? I am an active member on numerous statewide committees that focus on outcomes across the AAA network.

What are the most rewarding aspects of your current career position? I like that I know I am having an impact on the lives of older adults in my community. I may not have the direct, one-on-one contact with the

(continued)

An Interview With ABBE LACKMEYER *(continued)*

clients we serve, but I know that the analysis and work that I do contributes to improving the services we provide to our clients, ensuring that we are performing at our best and we are reaching our outcomes as an agency.

What are the most rewarding aspects of your gerontology/geriatrics-related career path? That I know I am contributing in a positive way to the lives of older adults. I believe we have this amazing opportunity to use our skills and expertise in this field to directly impact the quality of life of older adults and ensure we have created systems that support the aging process.

What are the most challenging aspects of your current career position? I would say that the most challenging aspects of my job are very much related to the data-related aspects. Data analysis can sometimes be a messy job and can present unexpected challenges. This can have a direct impact on my ability to get everything to come together to report the correct information in the right format.

What are the most challenging aspects of your gerontology/geriatrics-related career path? I cannot really identify anything specific at this time. I think, in general, there has yet to be a shift in employers seeking out individuals with a gerontology-related degree as a requirement for a position. In speaking to individuals just out of a gerontology program, I think there is a perception that we need to be able to "sell" what we do and what we can offer as a professional in gerontology.

How do you balance career and other aspects of your life? I make a conscious effort to separate the two. Unless I am wrapping up a project to meet a deadline, I will not access my e-mail or log on to my computer while I am home. I decided about a year and a half ago that I would like to drop hours in order to spend more time with my children while they are at young ages. I anticipate this changing as my children get older, but having an extra day each week has really worked to allow me to devote time to my career and my personal life in a healthy and productive way.

(continued)

An Interview With ABBE LACKMEYER *(continued)*

What advice do you have for someone contemplating a career in the field of aging? Take time to research educational programs focused on gerontology so that you know what is offered in these programs. Scan the positions in your area that either require or prefer a background in aging so that you know what is available in the workforce. Be open-minded regarding what you can do and the impact you can make. Gerontology spans many areas—including health care, policy, academia, finance, and programming—so keeping an open mind about where you fit in will allow you more opportunities. When I first entered the master's degree program, I initially thought that I would be an administrator in a nursing facility; after a few courses, however, my interests changed. It took knowing my options to decide which path to take.

What advice do you have for someone considering a professional position similar to your current position? This position requires someone who is very detailed and data driven and who is interested in translating data into a usable format that will inform decision making. At the same time, this position also requires someone who can see the big picture and apply that to analysis and deliverables. Finally, this position requires a component of being customer-focused to work with them and develop deliverables that will make an impact on the goals of and outcomes for customers.

SOCIAL WORKER

SOCIAL WORKER IN GERONTOLOGY (SW-G)

CLINICAL SOCIAL WORKER IN GERONTOLOGY (CSW-G)

ADVANCED SOCIAL WORKER IN GERONTOLOGY (ASW-G)

BASIC DESCRIPTION

According to the National Association of Social Workers (NASW) and the Council on Social Work Education (CSWE), a "professional social worker" is a graduate of a CWSE-accredited social work program at the bachelor's (BSW), master's (MSW), or doctoral (DSW) level. Social workers with BSW and MSW degrees assess the needs of older adults, their families, caregivers, and social support network; provide information about and referrals to programs and services to meet these needs; and evaluate the outcomes of the services provided. At times the social workers provide the services needed (e.g., care and case management, counseling, education). The primary goals of social workers in direct practice with older adults include maintaining independence and self-determination, ensuring adequate financial resources through income assistance programs, promoting and maintaining the well-being of elders and their families, and improving the quality of life for their elderly clients. While the majority of social workers are in direct practice roles and positions, some work on behalf of elders through advocacy, policy development, and policy enactment. In 2006, the National Association for Social Workers (NASW) established credentials for Social Worker in Gerontology (SW-G), Clinical Social Worker in Gerontology (CSW-G), and Advanced Social Worker in Gerontology (ASW-G). These credentials certify that the social worker holds the appropriate degree from an accredited university; meets the national standards of knowledge, skills, and experience in the social work field of gerontology; and agrees to abide by NASW's code of ethics, standards for providing social work services in long-term care facilities, and standards for continuing professional education. To meet the demand for social workers and the social work faculty members to prepare them, the Geriatric Social Work Initiative (GSWI), funded predominantly by the John A. Hartford Foundation, is designed to cultivate faculty leaders in gerontology education and research through the Faculty Scholars Program, the Doctoral Fellows Program, and the Doctoral Fellows Pre-Dissertation Awards Program; to develop excellent training opportunities in real-world settings through the Hartford Partnership Program for Aging Education; and to infuse gerontological competencies into social work curricula and teaching through the National Center for Gerontological Social Work (Gero-Ed Center).

EDUCATION AND EXPERIENCE REQUIREMENTS

A BSW degree is required for entry-level direct service positions in human service agencies. A MSW degree is preferred for many entry-level positions and is required for clinical social work and most positions involving supervisory, administrative, planning, and policy responsibilities. A DSW degree is required for most academic teaching and research positions.

CERTIFICATION, LICENSURE, AND CONTINUING EDUCATION REQUIREMENTS

The NASW certification program outlines specific requirements for each level of certification. SW-G requires a bachelor's degree from an accredited university, at least 3 years (4,500 hours) of experience working under social work supervision with older adults and appropriate license, examination, experience, and/or continuing education. CSW-G requires a master's degree in social work from a CSWE-accredited program; 30 contact hours of post-degree continuing education on bio-psychosocial issues, interventions, or the dynamics of working with elders and their families or other caregivers; and a current state clinical social work license. ASW-G requires a master's degree in social work from an accredited university, 20 contact hours of professional education relevant to work with older adults, documentation of at least 2 years (3,000 hours) of experience working with elderly persons, and a current state MSW-level license or an ASWB MSW-level exam passing score. Licensure is required in the state where the professional practice occurs and may require passing an additional examination. Some states and/or employing agencies may have their own continuing education requirements for licensure and renewal of licenses.

CORE COMPETENCIES AND SKILLS NEEDED

- Commitment to culturally sensitive professional practice
- Good communication (oral, written, and listening) skills
- Good interpersonal skills
- Patience, persistence, perseverance
- Good organizational skills
- Good working knowledge of the aging process and the physical, social, and mental health issues that older adults face
- Good working knowledge of programs, services and facilities for older adults
- Ability to assess needs and functional capacity of older persons
- Good working knowledge of legislation, policies, and regulations related to provision of services to older adults

COMPENSATION

This varies by education, experience, licensure, certification level, type of position, nature of employment setting, and geographical location.

WORKPLACE(S)

These include adult daycare centers and programs, public social service agencies, adult protective services, county units on aging (e.g., commissions, departments, bureaus), Area Agencies on Aging (AAAs), information and referral agencies, alcohol and substance abuse services, hospitals and medical centers, outpatient primary care settings (e.g., group medical and dental practices), assisted living facilities, long-term care facilities, rehabilitation centers, hospice and bereavement service programs, respite programs, elder abuse and neglect centers/programs, faith-based organizations, home health care agencies, family services agencies, life care communities, mental health agencies/centers, ombudsperson and advocacy programs, senior centers, senior housing centers and retirement communities, research centers/institutes, veterans' services, corporate eldercare programs and firms, courts and legal/paralegal services and firms, managed care organizations, Social Security Administration offices (Medicare, Medicaid, and SSI), federal and state offices and programs for older adults (e.g., Senior Health Counseling and Assistance Program, Senior Companion, Foster Grandparent, RSVP), banks and investment firms, and insurance companies.

EMPLOYMENT OUTLOOK

Excellent, with demand currently exceeding supply; recent projections indicate the need for 70,000 new social workers.

RELATED PROFESSIONAL ORGANIZATIONS AND WEBSITES

- National Association of Social Workers (NASW): www.socialworkers.org
- National Association of Social Workers Foundation: www.naswfoundation.org
- Council on Social Work Education (CSWE): www.cswe.org
- The National Center for Gerontological Social Work (Gero-Ed Center): www.cswe.org/CentersInitiatives/GeroEdcenter.aspx
- CWSE Career Center: careers.cswe.org
- Geriatric Social Work Initiative: www.gswi.org
- Geriatric Social Work Initiative Careers: www.gswi.org/careers

An Interview With JENNIFER KHUONG

Director of Social Services

Postsecondary educational background, including formal credentials and other education/training in gerontology/geriatrics:

BS, Psychology, with Minor in Gerontology
MSW, Social Work
Minor in Gerontology (undergraduate)
Geriatric Fellowship (graduate)
Specialist in Aging Certificate (graduate)
Licensed Master Social Worker (LMSW) (state licensure)

How and when did you first become interested in gerontology/geriatrics? I first became interested in gerontology while working in a nursing home the summer before I went to college. I had started out working in a day-care setting with the thought of becoming a teacher; however, I did not enjoy the experience. I then applied for a job as a hospitality aide at a nursing home. I made beds, visited with residents, and refilled beverages. I found that I had patience and compassion for the elderly residents and enjoyed interacting with them. I also observed situations (such as agitated residents, frustrated staff, and a sometimes depressing living environment) that I did not think were right and wanted to change. In addition to this experience, I had a positive view of older adults growing up as my grandmother was a licensed practical nurse (LPN) and had opened her home as an adult foster care home to six ladies. At a young age, I would visit with them frequently. My great-grandmother also lived with my family for a short time while I was growing up. I think my passion for older adults developed at a young age and influenced my future career interests.

Briefly describe your gerontology/geriatrics-related career path. During my sophomore year of college, I decided to minor in gerontology and found that the courses further piqued my interest in aging. After earning my degree in psychology, I tried to determine a way to use my degree to work with older adults. I debated about a PhD in psychology with a focus on teaching and research with older adults or a social work degree that would allow me to work directly with older adults. I chose to apply for Master of Social Work programs. I was fortunate to be chosen to

(*continued*)

An Interview With JENNIFER KHUONG *(continued)*

participate in the Geriatric Fellowship, which was a 16-month program for individuals focused on working with the elders at various levels. My area of study was Aging and Families in Society at the Interpersonal level. I was offered a variety of internship opportunities that included working with a state health insurance program to provide health insurance counseling and community education to a small nonprofit in a low-income urban area that provided day services and home visits to enhance well-being and independence. I also earned my Specialist in Aging Certificate. After graduating, I applied for jobs throughout the United States that would involve working with older adults on some level. I found my "perfect job" working at an Agency on Aging where I was able to use my knowledge and interest in health insurance and interpersonal skills to assist older adults and their families. I also obtained Licensed Master of Social Work (LMSW) licensure. I worked at the Agency on Aging for 3 years before leaving to work at a large hospital as a social work care manager. I learned a great deal about the health care setting that prepared me for my current administrative position in an 81-bed skilled nursing/rehabilitation and nursing home.

Briefly describe your current professional position:

Position title: Director of Social Services

Primary role tasks/responsibilities: Twice a week, I coordinate family meetings, called interdisciplinary team (IDT) meetings, in which the team (i.e., nurse manager, dietary director, therapist, admissions) reviews a resident's care plan with that individual (as appropriate) and/or his or her family. We generally hold four to six IDT meetings each day. Another staple of my week is utilization review (UR) in which the team only reviews each resident admitted at a skilled level of care for nursing and therapy needs, payment, and discharge planning. We also review any long-term care residents receiving therapies. As a result of UR, I then follow-up on tasks related to discharge planning for residents who will be discharged; this includes communicating anticipated discharge plans to residents and families, setting up home care, discussing plans for transitions to long-term care, assistance with financial applications,

(continued)

An Interview With JENNIFER KHUONG *(continued)*

ordering appropriate state assessments, and providing timely denial notices. Some conversations with families can be time-consuming and emotional and I do my best to notify families early on about what to expect. On the other end of the spectrum, when residents are admitted to our home, either for a short-term rehab stay or long-term care, I meet with the residents and their families, complete admission paperwork, collect verifications, and set up an IDT meeting. All of the above tasks require documentation which takes time. I am also responsible for completing daily assessments called the Minimum Data Set (MDS) or Resident Assessment Instrument (RAI). This involves completing resident mood interviews (PHQ-9), resident quality assessments, and identifying areas for social services to care plan. Additionally, I attend monthly department head meetings, quality meetings, and participate in our employee recognition committee, which plans various activities to show staff appreciation.

Type of employment setting: Skilled nursing/rehabilitation facility and nursing home

Length of time in this position: 3 years

How did you first become interested in this position? I first became interested in my current position after working in the hospital and wanting more interaction with older adults on a personal level. I considered a nursing home setting because it tended to involve my population of interest. A former coworker informed me of the position and I was pleased to interview and be offered the position.

Describe a typical workday in your current professional position. In my current position, I keep a "to do" list with me all the time to keep track of what I can squeeze in when I have 10 minutes between a meeting or what I need to prioritize. There are days, however, when something comes up that needs attention and everything else gets put on the back burner and, frustratingly, remains on the list. Despite this, there are some general tasks I described earlier that occur each week in my current position.

(continued)

An Interview With JENNIFER KHUONG (*continued*)

What is the time commitment required of your current professional position? Social work job responsibilities in a nursing home setting can vary depending on the particular facility where you work; however, my current scheduled hours are 8 a.m. to 4:30 p.m. Monday through Friday. I am fortunate to not work on the weekend, yet I rarely work only 40 hours per week. I would estimate that I average closer to 45 hours per week; some weeks are closer to 50 hours. The time I spend outside of regular working hours usually involves catching up on documentation (with fewer interruptions) and meeting with families who may not be available during regular business hours due to their own work schedules.

How do you stay up-to-date in your profession?

Attend professional conferences and/or participate in education/training programs? While I am not currently a member of any professional social work organizations, I do attend educational sessions of the state Health Care Association (HCA). There are a variety of topics offered (e.g., ethics, death, dying and bereavement, defensive documentation, Alzheimer's care) that I have found most applicable to my profession.

What are the most rewarding aspects of your current career position? Some of the most rewarding aspects of my current position involve advocating for residents and seeing a positive outcome, whether it involves a short-term rehab resident going home or working to obtain a benefit for a long-term care resident or even a successful roommate match. It also feels good to receive a thank you note from a family. It can be rewarding to help a family and their loved one navigate the often complex health care setting and provide genuine comfort. I also find humor an enjoyable part of my position.

What are the most rewarding aspects of your gerontology/geriatrics-related career path? I feel fortunate and glad to say that I would not change the population that I have chosen to work with. I find working with older adults rewarding because oftentimes these individuals are

(*continued*)

An Interview With JENNIFER KHUONG (*continued*)

forgotten or viewed negatively and I have opportunities daily to provide friendly support or dispel a negative stereotype. We are all aging and will likely know someone who is aging and it is rewarding and exciting to contribute to something that affects society on an individual and larger scale basis.

What are the most challenging aspects of your current career position? Some of the most challenging aspects of my current position are related to systems problems, such as insurance company restrictions and state regulations that prevent access to benefits or do not allow processes to be efficient. On a smaller scale, time management is a challenging aspect of my current position due to competing demands. Burnout is another challenge due to working with people at an interpersonal level who are often in stressful situations that can become overwhelming. At times, I need to remind myself that it is not my role to "fix" everyone's problems. Instead, I should discuss options and provide resources for informed decisions.

What are the most challenging aspects of your gerontology/geriatrics-related career path? One of the challenges I faced when looking for employment was finding jobs specifically focused on working with older adults. For example, prior to my current position, I worked in a hospital as a social work care manager. I certainly encountered many older adults in the hospital, yet I worked with many other populations that I knew were not a good fit for me. While I gained experience in a health care setting and working with these other populations, the experience further verified my interest in geriatrics. Another challenge I encountered initially was finding positions that offered competitive pay. After finishing graduate school, I was grateful for any type of paycheck; however, it took some time to find positions of interest that I could support myself. I do not think I am unique to this difficulty, but it is something to be mindful of in choosing social work. A final challenge that I face is providing compassionate care to a group that is often overlooked. I have observed health care professionals not taking the time to listen to older adults or their families or assume that because someone is old,

(*continued*)

An Interview With JENNIFER KHUONG (*continued*)

we should not use resources to help him or her. For example, during my weekly UR meetings, it is a challenging balance to meet the needs of our residents in a timely manner yet still respect their wishes and provide quality customer service.

How do you balance career and other aspects of your life? At times, it has been difficult for me to "leave work at work" when I come home. To be honest, this is an area that I struggle with on a regular basis. I have found it most helpful to have distractions, such as reading a good book, running, and spending time with family and friends right after work and on the weekends. If I can engage in something non-work related, it usually helps me to relax enough to not think about work constantly. During the weekend, I try to spend at least some time, even if only a half hour, doing something relaxing. I also try to put my relationships and health in perspective and evaluate where these fall in relation to my job and why these, too, need to be priorities.

What advice do you have for someone contemplating a career in the field of aging? I encourage you to explore all career opportunities, not just traditional career choices, to find a good fit. I also recommend spending time with older adults to see if you enjoy this population. Read about various topics related to the field of aging; some of these might include culture change, intergenerational programming, elderhostel, caregiver support, improving dementia care, adult day programming, hospice and home health care, state health insurance programs, and many more! There are also professional organizations (locally and nationally) that can provide education and current resources in the field of aging. In many states, there are state-based gerontological societies that have wonderful websites with relevant information and resources.

What advice do you have for someone considering a professional position similar to your current position? To be a social worker in a skilled nursing and rehab and/or long-term care facility, it is necessary to be self-motivated, patient, and genuinely caring about older adults. I am

(*continued*)

An Interview With JENNIFER KHUONG (*continued*)

fortunate to have a supportive supervisor who allows me to work independently. It can take a great deal of patience to work with individuals who are vulnerable. In order to remain patient and motivated, one must be intrinsically committed or rewarded by working with older adults. Communication with coworkers, residents, and families is also a vital component of my position.

STRATEGIC POLICY ADVISOR

STRATEGIC POLICY ANALYST

BASIC DESCRIPTION

Strategic policy advisors and analysts identify emerging policy issues, propose and advocate for policy legislation and regulations that fit organizational mission and goals, monitor relevant proposed legislation, and keep organizational peers and constituents apprised of relevant policy actions. They serve as resource persons for professional peers within the organization and represent the organization in external interactive or collaborative policy efforts with legislative/regulatory bodies and other organizations/agencies. They may conduct or oversee original research related to policy issues of concern; prepare, review, and/or provide oversight for reports and organizational publications; and make presentations at press conferences and professional meetings or for boards, technical/advisory panels and commissions.

EDUCATION AND EXPERIENCE REQUIREMENTS

This profession requires a master's or doctoral degree in public policy, political science, social sciences, law, or a closely related field, with the doctorate preferred. Gerontology coursework or a degree component is strongly recommended, and 5 or more years of directly relevant policy experience usually is required.

CERTIFICATION, LICENSURE, AND CONTINUING EDUCATION REQUIREMENTS

No certification or licensure (except for lobbyists) is required. Continuing education is a constant process required of this type of work.

CORE COMPETENCIES AND SKILLS NEEDED

- Excellent working knowledge of the processes of advocacy and policy development/enactment
- Technical knowledge of federal and state legislative processes related to older adult needs, issues, and concerns
- Specific knowledge related to the focus of the employing agency or specific agency program (e.g., health, financial security, housing, long-term care, grandparent caregiving, or visitation)
- Knowledge of research methodologies related to the identified focus for a specific career position
- Excellent written and oral communication skills
- Excellent interpersonal skills
- Excellent presentation skills; capable of presenting subject matter information to various types of audiences
- Ability to persuade peers of the merits of proposed policy and relevance to organizational goals
- Ability to objectively analyze and critique proposed legislation and regulations of relevance

COMPENSATION

This varies by one's education, experience, level of responsibility, the nature of the employment setting, and the geographical location. Some may work on a contractual fee-for-service basis.

WORKPLACE(S)

These include national advocacy organizations, legislative staff positions (including campaign staffs), lobbying organizations, and professional organizations.

EMPLOYMENT OUTLOOK

Good potential, but may be limited due to budget restrictions and lack of broader recognition of the need for and value of policy professionals with gerontology expertise.

RELATED PROFESSIONAL ORGANIZATIONS AND WEBSITES

- American Political Science Association (APSA): www.apsanet.org
- National Academy on an Aging Society (NAAS): www.agingsociety.org
- Center for Policy Research on Aging, UCLA Luskin School of Public Affairs: luskin.ucla.edu/content/center-policy-research-aging
- Health and Aging Policy Fellows: www.healthandagingpolicy.org
- National Council on Aging (NCOA): www.ncoa.org

URBAN GERONTOLOGY: AN EMERGING FIELD

URBAN GERONTOLOGIST

BASIC DESCRIPTION

One of the newer subspecializations in the field of aging is urban gerontology, where professionals work at the intersection of environmental gerontology, urban design/planning, and systems science. It appears that early emerging career positions are most frequently related to housing, transportation, and growing interest in age-friendly neighborhoods, communities, and cities.

EDUCATION AND EXPERIENCE REQUIREMENTS

Minimum of a master's degree in urban studies/planning, community development, social work, public administration and policy, or a related field, plus a certificate, minor, cognate, or specialization in gerontology. Employers may prefer candidates who have at least 2 to 3 years of direct service in the assessment, planning, and delivery of programs and services to older adults.

CORE COMPETENCIES AND SKILLS NEEDED

- Basic understanding of aging and age-related changes as they relate to design of housing, transportation, and community design in urban and suburban settings
- Able to assess needs and think creatively about how to meet those needs, including fostering opportunities for engagement of older adults and intergenerational interaction
- Understanding of concepts of community development, advocacy efforts, and policy

- Research design and data analysis skills related to needs assessment, community-based participatory research, program evaluation, and both quantitative and qualitative methods
- Understanding of urban politics and sociology
- Training to lead mediation, public engagement processes, and conflict resolution training
- Excellent verbal and written communication skills
- Active listener and keen observer

COMPENSATION

Research and program management: compensation varies widely based on experience, supporting organization(s), and funding and commitments from universities, public, and/or private organizations.

WORKPLACE(S)

Universities, nonprofit organizations, and governmental agencies.

EMPLOYMENT OUTLOOK

Positive potential, but not yet measurable. Interest in the area is growing globally, although funded positions are still limited.

RELATED PROFESSIONAL ORGANIZATIONS AND WEBSITES

- DC Office of Aging: dcoa.dc.gov/page/age-friendly-dc-initiative
- Age Friendly Portland: agefriendlyportland.org
- Age-Friendly NYC: www.nyam.org/agefriendlynyc
- AARP Livable Communities/Age-Friendly Program: www.aarp.org/livable-communities

---

VOLUNTEER PROGRAM DIRECTOR

VOLUNTEER PROGRAM COORDINATOR

BASIC DESCRIPTION

Volunteer program coordinators and directors recruit, train, supervise, and evaluate individuals who provide volunteer services to or on behalf of their organization, agency, or facility. They solicit volunteer worksites, serve as the liaison with staff members and clients at the volunteer site, match volunteers with worksites, keep records of volunteer schedules and hours, provide ongoing support for their volunteers, organize award ceremonies to honor outstanding volunteers, and keep their own supervisors and colleagues apprised of volunteer activity. This position may require considerable travel time to potential and actual volunteer worksites and offsite locations where work-related meetings, training sessions, and events are held.

EDUCATION AND EXPERIENCE REQUIREMENTS

This position requires a minimum of an associate's or bachelor's degree in a relevant field. Prior experience as a volunteer and with volunteer programs is strongly recommended, as is gerontology coursework or a degree component and prior experience working with older adults. Coursework, seminars, and/or training sessions on volunteer management, interpersonal communication skills, time management, and working with diverse populations are encouraged.

CERTIFICATION, LICENSURE, AND CONTINUING EDUCATION REQUIREMENTS

The Certification in Volunteer Administration (CVA), sponsored by The Council for Certification in Volunteer Administration (CVAA), is available for practitioners in volunteer resource management. This credential is an increasing preference of employers. To earn CVA designation, the applicant must have at least 3 years of full-time (or the equivalent) experience related to volunteer resource management experience and at least 30% of their current professional role must be related to volunteer resource management. Participation in organizations and conferences for volunteer managers is encouraged.

CORE COMPETENCIES AND SKILLS NEEDED

- Follows ethical professional practice
- Able to design and implement policies, processes and structures to support a match between volunteer involvement and the organizations mission and goals
- Good time-management skills
- Good organizational skills and the ability to stay organized
- Able to successfully recruit, train, and supervise volunteers
- Good interpersonal communication skills
- Good people-management skills
- Computer and technology proficiency
- Working knowledge of volunteer management

- Need to stay current with volunteerism issues and trends
- Knowledge of new initiative on Civic Engagement in an Older America
- Ability to work with diverse groups of people
- Patience
- Able to and comfortable with work-related travel requirements

COMPENSATION

This varies by one's education, experience, the nature of the employing agency, level of position, and the geographical location. The position may be part time or combined with responsibility for another program or service.

WORKPLACE(S)

These include governmental agencies or organizations that serve elders (e.g., Area Agencies on Aging, county departments/commissions on aging), organizations that offer programs and services for older persons, medical and long-term care centers, and arts and humanities organizations that rely on older volunteers (e.g., community art, music, and theater organizations; museums).

EMPLOYMENT OUTLOOK

Excellent, especially due to the trend toward civic engagement of older persons.

RELATED PROFESSIONAL ORGANIZATIONS AND WEBSITES

- Association of Leaders in Volunteer Engagement: www.volunteeralive.org
- Council for Certification in Volunteer Administration (CCVA): www.cvacert.org
- State and regional volunteer managers and administrators organizations

An Interview With GRETCHEN JORDAN

Coordinator of Volunteers

Postsecondary educational background, including formal credentials and other education/training in gerontology/geriatrics:
AA, General Studies
BS, Community and Human Services

How and when did you first become interested in gerontology/geriatrics? My early career positions included management in the service industry, government, and nonprofit sectors in youth and family services. Often this work would intersect working with elders and I experienced many positive opportunities to work with and for older generations. Nearly 15 years ago, I realized there would be many more work opportunities within this field in many different areas that interested me—human services, volunteerism, advocacy, and education. As my family members aged, I felt I could learn so much personally and professionally by becoming involved in a gerontology path.

Briefly describe your gerontology/geriatrics-related career path. After working in the youth and family sector for more than 20 years, I turned my job search to positions related to advocacy, education, and service in gerontology. I realized that the population demographics of America were changing and, with my prior career focus on youth and families, I could see at times where issues for elders didn't have the same priority. The media embraced the stereotype of the "little old lady" or "cranky old man" and how they were not taken seriously. I wanted to work in a field where working with elders could bring more awareness to everyone about what it was like to be aging well. At this point in my career, I also began connecting with a mentor who helped me to realize that working with elders was going to be an emerging field that would become more and more relevant as boomers need to deal with their aging parents and the boomers themselves begin to age into whatever their vision of aging is. In 2000, I was hired by a national elder advocacy nonprofit organization and that is where my gerontology career path began. Also, I personally faced dealing with aging parents as my in-laws went through the process of no longer being able to stay in their own home and the entire family becoming embroiled in the constant

(*continued*)

An Interview With GRETCHEN JORDAN (*continued*)

struggle and dilemma of "what to do about Mom." After 5 years in the national and statewide advocacy field, my next job continued the advocacy work, but on a more personal level, with a state agency tasked with protecting the rights and dignity of elders in long-term care facilities. For both of these positions, I have not done direct service work with the clients; instead, I have managed the volunteer programs and outreach programs.

Briefly describe your current professional position:

Position title: Coordinator of Volunteers

Primary role tasks/responsibilities: I recruit volunteers for the program, work with volunteers tasked with additional recruitment and screening activities, provide outreach and information to the public about the program, and coach, educate, and collaborate with staff who work with volunteers.

Type of employment setting: Office of State Long-Term Care Ombudsman (state government)

Length of time in this position: 4-1/2 years

How did you first become interested in this position? I really enjoyed my advocacy and education work and wanted to continue on this level. I learned of this position from networking with my colleagues.

Describe a typical workday in your current professional position. My daily tasks most often include answering e-mail and phone messages; conferring with staff about volunteer issues, such as performance, screening, or training; planning for an outreach event and quarterly local and statewide all-volunteer training; communicating with volunteers about upcoming trainings; processing incoming applications; and completing administrative tasks, such as composing letters, preparing expense reports, and volunteer mailings.

(*continued*)

An Interview With GRETCHEN JORDAN *(continued)*

What is the time commitment required of your current professional position? I am on a 40-hour work week and the hours are generally 8 a.m. to 5 p.m., but I will work an extended day when on travel or to meet with a volunteer. Weeknight work usually is necessary two to three times a month and weekend events happen about once a quarter. I can work a flexible schedule to accommodate my 40 hour schedule. About 30% of my work is in the office and 70% is for frequent in-state travel for outreach, meeting with volunteers and community partners, and field work.

How do you stay up-to-date in your profession?

Professional organization memberships and/or activities?

Association of Leaders in Volunteer Engagement (ALIVE!), member; involved with Member Engagement Committee and lead quarterly national networking calls with my peers.

Mid-Valley Volunteer Managers Association (MVVMA), member; involved with education and networking on a local and face-to-face level; networking with those who work with volunteers in other state agencies; present on volunteer management issues once a year.

Society of Government Meeting Professionals (SGMP), member; involved with education about event and meeting planning on the small and large level; networking with other state agency staff and the suppliers (hoteliers) who also plan meetings and events.

Subscribe to and/or read professional journals and/or newsletters?

Susan Ellis's website: especially her e-volunteerism journal, online library, listing of state and local professional volunteer manager associations, and monthly newsletter.

VolunteerMatch: Our state agency is a community member; we receive a monthly email and newsletter. This is a national resource for Webinars on volunteer management issues (recruiting, recognition, and retention) and recruiting volunteers.

The Aging Network's Volunteer Collaborative: weekly emails with resources, webinars, and information about volunteer management, specifically in programs that serve elders.

(continued)

An Interview With GRETCHEN JORDAN (*continued*)

Attend professional conferences and/or participate in education/training programs?

MVVMA, monthly local meetings with networking and a professional development topic.

Quarterly and annual local trainings or day conferences on volunteer and event management issues.

Monthly webinars from Volunteer Match and Aging Network's Volunteer Collaborative.

Points of Light Foundation national conference on volunteering and service.

Other? The local and national professional groups I belong to are very helpful because of the networking. I can reach out to colleagues nationally and locally about a specific question or challenge and others reach out to me. In most cases, the volunteer manager is the only person with that role in an agency, so being able to talk to someone who understands my role is very helpful.

What are the most rewarding aspects of your current career position? I really enjoy being able to connect folks who are searching for a meaningful volunteer role with the right volunteer opportunity. Most of our volunteers are retired professionals and they enjoy the skill set used, the flexible schedule and the high degree of autonomy. I also appreciate the ability to work a flexible schedule, when needed, and having the tools I need to complete my tasks. It is rewarding to let the public know about our agency and the good work we do on behalf of the residents.

What are the most rewarding aspects of your gerontology/geriatrics-related career path? As I am aging, I've learned a lot about planning for my personal aging path and I embrace the changes in myself, personally and professionally. I see so many who inspire me every day who are making the most of their time and abilities in all aspects of their life, including what they are doing at home, supporting friends or family, or in the community. I am not afraid of aging and I am so much more comfortable living in the moment.

(*continued*)

An Interview With GRETCHEN JORDAN (*continued*)

What are the most challenging aspects of your current career position? Although I have the tools I need to do my job, there is always a lack of time. In our smaller agency, I have several roles that include doing press releases, event management, social media, and website management. With my responsibility for outreach and volunteer recruitment statewide, it does take a lot of travel time to get to rural areas where the need for volunteers is even greater. As volunteers leave the program (which is a natural event in any volunteer program), I must always recruit and train more to provide a basic level of service for the residents.

What are the most challenging aspects of your gerontology/geriatrics-related career path? I would like to keep up more on age-related disease research, but there isn't enough time for in-depth learning. I rely upon colleagues to share relevant information.

How do you balance career and other aspects of your life? I really enjoy being part of the local and national professional associations, as the networking and mentoring are rewarding and important for my professional development (and, at times, my sanity!). As I am still dealing with a parent who is aging well and an in-law who is not, I make sure to spend time for myself and with my husband, truly listening to the caregiving advice of taking time for yourself. We are trying to plan ahead and be prepared for our personal aging issues and make sure our friends and family understand our wishes. Travel, hobbies, and grandchildren are always wonderful and necessary distractions.

What advice do you have for someone contemplating a career in the field of aging? Consider volunteering in the field and in a variety of service programs. You will get a real feel for the needs of elders, what kinds of services are provided, and the resources available. These will all vary on a national, state, or local level. Understanding about the aging process and the challenges that go along with them will be valuable. Talk to those already in the field. Getting a mentor who can answer questions and give advice may prevent you from having to find out about something the "hard way."

(*continued*)

An Interview With GRETCHEN JORDAN (*continued*)

What advice do you have for someone considering a professional position similar to your current position? Many times, especially if you are managing a volunteer program in a small- to medium-sized agency, you may wear many hats and will be working with all facets of an agency. Managing volunteers will involve human resources skills, marketing, fundraising, communications, community organizing, event planning, and risk management. You will often work directly with the population your agency serves, the board of directors, program staff, and the general public. It is a role that often manages multiple projects with changing priorities. Expect to advocate for your volunteers to ensure they have a rewarding experience. Work with fellow staff members to help them utilize the volunteer's skills for the most positive impact to the agency. Do not overlook the importance and impact of technology as it is used at every level of work in this field. Technology is a major tool, especially for communication and training, and it is often the primary way for those you serve to communicate with you and your agency and for you to communication with the broader community.

3 ■ . . . AND MORE

An increasing number of job postings related to aging and work with or on behalf of older adults seek applicants with a background that includes gerontology education and work experience. More college graduates, at all levels, have completed at least some gerontology coursework and many have formal credentials in the form of minors, majors, cognates, specializations, certificates, and degrees. More disciplines and professional fields are adding gerontology to programs of study for their undergraduate and graduate students. More college graduates have had an intergenerational service learning experience or have completed an internship, practicum, or fieldwork that is gerontology/geriatrics-related. As a result, there is an expanding menu of gerontology options for you to consider as you select undergraduate majors and minors, pursue graduate study, or make decisions about a mid-career transition. In addition to the career options already addressed, here are more possibilities for you to consider.

ACCOUNTING

Although gerontology is not part of the academic education of accountants, many do have older adult clients and some handle quite complex accounting situations with their elderly clients. Certificate and registry programs for business and financial professionals, however, are opening the door for accountants to focus their practice more visibly on accounting and financial planning services for elders. Possible professional positions for persons with a combined accounting and gerontology background include:

- Tax advisor for older clients
- Certified Senior Advisor (CSA)
- Certified Financial Planner (CFP)
- Registered Financial Gerontology (RFG)

RELATED PROFESSIONAL ORGANIZATIONS AND WEBSITES

- American Institute of Certified Public Accountants (AICPA): www.aicpa.org
- American Institute of Financial Gerontology (AIFG): www.aifg.org
- Certified Financial Planner Board (CFP Board): www.cfp.net
- Society of Certified Senior Advisors (SCSA): www.csa.us

ADVERTISING

With the growing population of elders and a wider array of products and services being designed to meet their needs, there is a parallel need for advertising professionals to portray more accurate images in the advertising they create. Possible positions for persons who combine advertising and gerontology include:

- Account executive for products for older adults
- Ad writer
- Director of advertising for a publication aimed at older adults

RELATED PROFESSIONAL ORGANIZATIONS AND WEBSITES

- American Advertising Federation (AAF): www.aaf.org
- Ad Council: www.adcouncil.org
- American Association of Advertising Agencies (4As): www.aaaa.org

ANTHROPOLOGY

There is a relatively small but steady group of academic researchers and educators, especially in the subfields of cultural and medical anthropology, whose teaching and research focus on aging. Recently, there also appears to be some movement toward the creation of applied or clinical practice opportunities for persons with bachelor's and master's degrees in anthropology who are interested in aging. Possible professional positions for those who combine anthropology and gerontology/geriatrics include:

- Ethnographer
- Consultant on aging for community-based cultural affairs programs
- Trainer on culturally competent professional practice with older adults, their families, and caregivers
- Global aging specialist

RELATED PROFESSIONAL ORGANIZATIONS AND WEBSITES

- American Anthropological Association (AAA): www.aanet.org
- Association for Anthropology and Gerontology (AAGE): anthropologyandgerontology.com
- The Society for Applied Anthropology (SfAA): www.sfaa.net
- Network of Multicultural Aging (NOMA), American Society on Aging (NOMA): www.asaging.org/noma
- International Aging and Migration Interest Group, Gerontological Society of America (GSA): www.geron.org

BANKING

Changes in banking processes and in the aging population jointly create new opportunities for banking officials to devise new and appropriate ways to market their services to older persons and to educate their elderly clients about new banking products and processes. Possible professional positions for persons who combine banking and gerontology backgrounds include:

- Older adult customer service representative
- Trust officer
- Reverse mortgage specialist
- Educational consultant to train bankers about aging and older adult service needs
- Consultant on aging to marketing division of a banking corporation

RELATED PROFESSIONAL ORGANIZATIONS AND WEBSITES

- American Bankers Association (ABA): www.aba.com

CLOTHING AND TEXTILES

Except for some attention to the need for adaptive clothing for persons of all ages who are physically disabled, the clothing and textiles industry has been slow to respond to the desire of older consumers for clothing, household textiles, and textile-based furnishings that are attractive, stylish, and also accommodate normal physical changes with age in human bodies. It also seems necessary to develop education/training about aging for clothing designers, buyers, and sales/store personnel. Possible professional positions for individuals who combine the study of clothing and textiles with gerontology include:

- Custom clothiers
- Designer of clothing to meet the diverse needs and interests of older adults along the functional continuum from active and well to frail and disabled
- Trainer on aging for retail clothing sales personnel
- Freelance personal shopper for older clients
- Gerontology consultant to designers and buyers
- In-store consumer representative for older clients
- Clothing and textiles instructor
- Buyer of textiles products for older adult residences or long-term care facilities
- Consultant on aging for a fabric manufacturer
- Costume designer for a senior theater company

RELATED PROFESSIONAL ORGANIZATIONS AND WEBSITES

- Association of Sewing and Design Professionals (ASDP): www.paccprofessionals.org
- American Association of Family and Consumer Sciences (AAFCS): www.aafcs.org
- International Textile and Apparel Association (ITAA): www.itaaonline.org
- American Association of Textile Chemists and Colorists (AATCC): www.aatcc.org

CREATIVE WRITING

While a career as a creative writer does not require a college degree, there seems to be an explosion of creative writing programs, especially master's in fine arts (MFA) degrees. It is unlikely that any of these degree programs have linkages with the gerontology programs on their campuses, but such a linkage could be very fruitful for persons interested in writing about aging in any genre. Possibilities for persons who combine creative writing and gerontology include:

- Screenwriter
- Playwright
- Essayist
- Novel and/or short story author
- Creative nonfiction writer
- Memoirist
- Biographer or autobiographer

- Greeting card writer
- Freelance writer for magazines
- Acquisitions editor for books on aging for a publisher
- Copyeditor for writings on aging
- Consultant on aging for writers, writing programs, and writer's retreats

RELATED PROFESSIONAL ORGANIZATIONS AND WEBSITES

- Association of Writers and Writing Programs (AWP): www.awpwriter.org
- Modern Language Association (MLA): www.mla.org
- Poets & Writers: www.pw.org/mfa

EDUCATIONAL GERONTOLOGY

In addition to the career position profiles for and interviews with educational gerontologists in higher education, many other career paths are open to those who combine education and gerontology, including:

- K-12 teachers and curriculum specialists who design learning experiences about aging for elementary and secondary school students
- Administrators, teachers, curriculum developers, and program coordinators with Road Scholar (formerly known as Elderhostel), its Road Scholar Institute Network (RSIN) of Lifelong Learning institutes, and other participative learning experiences for older persons
- Curriculum developer on aging for corporate and industry professionals
- Coordinator of an older learner program for a senior center
- College/university professor of adult education or educational gerontology
- Coordinator of a campus-based initiative, program, or center to involve older adults in campus life (as students, mentors, and in other roles)
- Curriculum designer of training seminars and workshops for Alzheimer's Association or similar organizations

RELATED PROFESSIONAL ORGANIZATIONS AND WEBSITES

- Road Scholar (formerly known as Elderhostel): www.roadscholar.org
- Road Scholar Institute Network (RSIN): www.roadscholar.org/n/institute-network-lifelong-learning

- Lifetime Education and Renewal Network (LEARN), American Society on Aging (ASA): www.asaging.org/learn
- Association for Gerontology in Higher Education (AGHE): www.aghe.org

ELDER ABUSE, NEGLECT, AND EXPLOITATION

Attention to the various forms of elder abuse has been gained through media coverage, the development of interagency coalitions to raise awareness about and decrease the incidence of elder abuse, and governmental funding at state and federal levels for initiatives to prevent elder abuse, neglect, and exploitation. Professionals from many professions (e.g., family studies, marriage and family therapy, social gerontology, sociology/applied sociology, law, law enforcement, social work, geriatric medicine, gerontological nursing) are involved in these efforts. Possible professional positions related to one or more aspects of elder abuse include:

- Adult/older adult protective services caseworker
- Consumer fraud prevention educator for elders
- Support program coordinator for older adult victims of abuse, neglect, or exploitation
- Law enforcement officer who specializes in elder abuse, neglect, and/or exploitation
- Team leader for a collaborative community consortium to prevent elder abuse, neglect, and exploitation
- Counselor/therapist for family and caregiving abusers of elders
- Domestic violence counselor or therapist in family practice with elders and their families
- Consultant on sexual abuse of elders

RELATED PROFESSIONAL ORGANIZATIONS AND WEBSITES

- National Center on Elder Abuse (NCEA): www.ncea.aoa.gov
- Interest Group on Abuse, Neglect and Exploitation of Elderly People, Gerontological Society of America (GSA): www.geron.org

EMERGENCY MEDICAL SERVICES (EMS)

Standards for national emergency medical services are established through the National Highway Traffic Safety Administration (NHTSA). Although the current National EMS Core Content domain of practice is for all patients, without separately addressing special patient populations (e.g., children, elders, cardiac, trauma), the *EMS Education Agenda for the Future: A Systems Approach* must ensure preparation of EMS professionals to care for the uniqueness of each of these patient populations. According to the 2006 National EMS Scope of Practice Model, there are four levels of direct EMS practice: emergency medical responder, emergency medical technician (EMT), advanced emergency medical technician (AEMT), and paramedic. Two other professional roles are EMS management and EMS educator. Into this schema of EMS practice, management, and education, there are potential career position roles for gerontology specialists and gerontologists to be:

- Curriculum consultants
- Adjunct educators
- Professional mentors and advisors for local EMS services

RELATED PROFESSIONAL ORGANIZATIONS AND WEBSITES

- National Association of Emergency Medical Technicians (NAEMT): www.naemt.org
- National Highway Traffic Safety Administration (NHTSA), Office of National Emergency Medical Services: www.ems.gov
- National Association of State EMS Officials (NASEMSO): www.nasemso.org
- National Association of EMS Educators (NAEMSE): www.naemse.org

EXERCISE, FITNESS, AND WELLNESS

Research findings indicate that older adults are increasing their involvement (voluntarily and through prescription) in exercise, fitness, and wellness activities via sport programs (such as Senior Olympics), fitness centers operated by medical centers or available in their retirement communities, and privately owned fitness programs, wellness centers, and spas. Possible professional positions for persons who combine exercise physiology, physical education, therapeutic recreation, or related fields and gerontology include:

- Personal trainer for older adults
- Training coordinator for Senior Olympics
- Exercise consultant for in-home care agency
- Fitness specialist for a continuing care retirement community
- Lifestyle director for an active-adult facility

- Wellness director for a retirement community's wellness center
- Program coordinator for health club and spa that caters to elders

RELATED PROFESSIONAL ORGANIZATIONS AND WEBSITES

- American Alliance for Health, Physical Education, Recreation and Dance (AAHPERD): www.aahperd.org
- International Council on Active Aging (ICAA): www.icaa.cc
- National Senior Games Association (NSGA): www.nsga.com
- American Association of Physical Therapy (APTA): www.apta.org
- American Society of Exercise Physiologists (ASEP): www.asep.org

FAMILY GERONTOLOGY

Family gerontology is a newly emerging subfield of both gerontology and family studies (also known as family ecology, family relations, and family science). If this recent attention is a good indicator, it appears that the academic attention to family gerontology is beginning to open more doors for direct practice opportunities for family gerontological specialists. Professional positions that are or should be open to persons with a family gerontology background include:

- Coordinator of a Kinship Care project program or research project
- Family life educator for elders and their families
- Gerontological family specialist for hospice programs and facilities
- Marriage and family therapist specializing in older adult relationships and concerns
- Family mediator specializing in elder care and kin care
- Adult Care Services vocational education instructor at the secondary school or community/junior college level
- Coordinator of family services, including support groups, for disease/chronic condition-specific organizations (e.g., Alzheimer's disease, Parkinson's disease, arthritis, type 2 diabetes)

RELATED PROFESSIONAL ORGANIZATIONS AND WEBSITES

- National Council on Family Relations (NCFR): www.ncfr.org
- American Association of Marriage and Family Therapy (AAMFT): www.aamft.org
- American Association of Family and Consumer Sciences (AAFCS): www.aafcs.org

FILM AND TELEVISION

Films—documentary, educational, and feature length—and television programs and news reports on aging are a major educational tool for both professionals in the field of aging and the American public. Many of those involved with the production and delivery of these films, programs, and reports, however, do not have a professional background in gerontology/geriatrics. To improve the accuracy of information about aging and portrayal of aging in film and on television, there is a need for more film and TV career professionals who add gerontology coursework or degree components to their training. Possible professional positions for persons with a combined background in film/TV and gerontology include:

- Faculty member in a school of film and/or television
- Gerontological consultant as a member of the filmmaking team
- Coach on aging for actors who play aging characters
- Scriptwriters

RELATED PROFESSIONAL ORGANIZATIONS AND WEBSITES

- For further information on education about and careers in film and television, contact related college/university departments and professional school administrators and faculty.

HISTORY

History is another field in which the professionals with a gerontology background have been employed primarily in the academic ranks as history professors and/or researchers, although their numbers are quite limited. To encourage consideration of combining history and gerontology in a professional position, here are a few possible positions:

- Project director/coordinator for an oral history project related to aging/older adults
- Research writer on topics related to history of aging and field of gerontology
- History professor who specializes in history of aging and related topics

RELATED PROFESSIONAL ORGANIZATIONS AND WEBSITES

- American Historical Association (AHA): www.historians.org

HOSPITALITY SERVICES AND TOURISM

As older adults turn more frequently to the hospitality and tourism industry to help them spend their leisure time, this is an industry with considerable potential for creation of gerontology-related professional positions, including the following:

- Gerontology consultant for hotel or restaurant chain
- Hospitality director/coordinator for a retirement community
- Staff trainer for hospitality services at a retirement community
- Director of travel for older adult organizations and active "senior living" residences
- Travel and tours coordinator for a county commission/division/bureau on aging
- Coordinator for a senior center or retirement community travel program
- Gerontology consultant to a travel industry organization or business, such as a bed and breakfast innkeepers association
- Director of grandparent–grandchild travel and education programs for an organization like Road Scholar's Grandparent Travel program or for theme parks
- Owner of a travel company that specializes in tours for older adults

RELATED PROFESSIONAL ORGANIZATIONS AND WEBSITES

- Business Forum on Aging (BFA), American Society on Aging (ASA): www.asaging.org/bfa
- Interest Group on Business and Aging, Gerontological Society of America (GSA): www.geron.org
- For further information on education about and careers in hospitality services and tourism, consult related college/university departmental/ program administrators and faculty

INTIMACY AND SEXUALITY, SEXUAL ORIENTATION, AND SEXUAL HEALTH IN LATER LIFE

Yes, older adults can have sex, many do and probably quite a few others find ways to maintain or rekindle intimacy and sexuality in their lives as they age. As gerontological specialists and gerontologists, it is possible to create supportive environments, provide social and emotional support, do appropriate research, and develop education and training programs—for elders, future and current professionals, caregivers, and others—in ways that support intimacy and sexual expression and sexual health for elders, regardless of age, gender, or sexual orientation. Possible professional positions for those who focus on intimacy and sexuality in later life include:

- Academic and professional school professors who teach courses on intimacy and sexuality in later life, sexual orientation, and sexual health
- Intimacy and sexuality educators for older adult learner programs
- Program coordinator or counselor for programs serving lesbian, gay, bisexual, and transgender (LGBT) elders
- Program coordinator for organizations that serve parents/families of gay and lesbian elders
- HIV/AIDS educator or counselor for older adults
- Intimacy and sexuality counselors/therapists in medical and mental health clinics or private practice
- Sexuality and aging specialists for a country or state health department

RELATED PROFESSIONAL ORGANIZATIONS AND WEBSITES

- American Association of Sexuality Educators, Counselors and Therapists (AASECT): www.aasect.org
- Lesbian and Gay Aging Issues Network (LGAIN), American Society on Aging (ASA): www.asaging.org/lgain
- HIV, AIDS and Older Adults Interest Group, Gerontological Society of America (GSA): www.geron.org

MARKETING

With the rapid expansion of the elderly population over the next 2 decades, the field of marketing may be one of the big winners in the number and types of professional positions that will be enhanced by mixing it with gerontology. A nice feature of careers in marketing is that many entry-level positions are open to persons with bachelor's degrees and master's in business administration (MBA) degrees. Among the jobs open for professionals with a combined background in marketing and gerontology are the following:

- Market analyst on goods and services targeted at the older adult population for a corporation
- Marketing director for a retirement community, long-term care facility, or health care corporation

- Marketing coordinator for a consortium of senior centers
- Marketing director for a gerontology professional organization

RELATED PROFESSIONAL ORGANIZATIONS AND WEBSITES

- American Marketing Association (AMA): www.marketingpower.com [See Marketer Career Resources section]
- Business Forum on Aging (BFA), American Society on Aging (ASA): www.asaging.org/bfa

PHILOSOPHY

As with most disciplines, philosophy is a field of study that opens the door of employment for academic professors, theorists, and researchers. With a rising interest among current elders to find meaning in their lives through thoughtful and spiritual endeavors that are beyond or different from religion, there has been a parallel interest in philosophy. Concurrently, there also seems to be movement toward incorporating (or reincorporating) two philosophical approaches—ethics and gerotranscendence—into gerontological professional practice, especially in medical and long-term care settings. Codes of ethics are now written into the standards of practice for most professional organizations and adherence to those codes is a requirement for many professional certifications, registries, and licensures. Gerotranscendence is a way of thinking about later life that has roots in geropsychology, philosophy, life course development, and gerontology. Potential professional positions for persons who blend philosophy and gerontology include:

- Multidisciplinary health care team ethicist
- Ethics or gerotranscendence trainer for long-term care and assisted living facility staff members
- Resident ethicist for a long-term care facility
- Philosophy instructor for courses offered through Institutes for Learning in Retirement, Road Scholars, and other older learner programs

RELATED PROFESSIONAL ORGANIZATIONS AND WEBSITES

- American Philosophical Association (APA): www.apa.online
- American Philosophical Society (APS): www.amphilosoc.org
- Association for Practical and Professional Ethics (APPE): appe.indiana.edu

POLITICAL SCIENCE/POLICY AND AGING

Policy, in the form of the Social Security Act and the Older Americans Act, set the stage for gerontology, and the formal aging network was created by a marriage between policy and gerontology. Courses on policy and aging are required or strongly recommended for students completing degrees or degree components in gerontology. At least one of the newer doctoral degree programs in gerontology are specific to policy and aging. Positions are open at local (city and county), state, and federal levels for professionals, and the work of the following professionals would be enhanced greatly by adding gerontology to relevant undergraduate and graduate programs of study:

- Legislator
- Legislative aide
- Policy on aging analyst for governmental entities, national and international organizations and associations, and other organizations, agencies, and facilities whose mission is affected by policy and regulatory measures
- Policy on aging advocate for organizations/initiatives for elders
- Policy development consultant for local- or county-level boards, commissions, agencies, and facilities that do not have a regular staff position related to policy
- Lobbyist

RELATED PROFESSIONAL ORGANIZATIONS AND WEBSITES

- American Political Science Association (APSA): www.apsanet.org

RELIGIOUS/SPIRITUAL GERONTOLOGY

In the world of gerontology, religion and spirituality may be related but are not necessarily synonymous. Regardless, there is strong interest in both fields, and more gerontology-related professional positions are emerging in a variety of settings, including the following:

- Religious leader for an older adult ministry
- Coordinator of training or gerontology educational consultant/trainer for a faith-based older adult outreach program
- Director of education for a family and older adult programs in a religious center

- Director of spiritual education for a retirement community or long-term care facility
- Gerontology consultant for a spiritual retreat center
- Gerontology educator in a college/university religion department, seminary, or other religion education school or center
- Writer of articles on aging or columnist for a religion-sponsored periodical or other publications

RELATED PROFESSIONAL ORGANIZATIONS AND WEBSITES

- Forum on Religion, Spirituality and Aging (FORSA), American Society on Aging (ASA): www.asaging.org
- Formal Interest Group on Religion, Spirituality and Aging, Gerontological Society of America (GSA): www.geron.org

SUBSTANCE ABUSE AND CHEMICAL DEPENDENCY

Older adults are not excluded from the ranks of those who abuse and misuse illegal drugs, prescription and over-the-counter (OTC) drugs, and alcohol and other social drugs. While some elders initiate or become victims of substance abuse and chemical dependency in later life, many enter with poor habits and behaviors begun at earlier life stages. As the population of elders grows over the next few decades, it is anticipated that there will be an increased need for professionals to work with elders who have had access to a broader range of drugs of all types and a higher number of persons who enter later life with drug use–related histories already well established. Gerontological specialists and gerontologists with education and/or training related to substance abuse and chemical dependency will be needed in the following positions:

- Substance abuse and chemical dependency prevention educators
- Substance abuse and chemical dependency counselors and therapists
- Substance abuse and chemical dependency rehabilitation specialists
- HIV/AIDS educators and counselors for older adults
- Trainers for professionals and paraprofessionals who work directly with abusive and addicted elders

RELATED PROFESSIONAL ORGANIZATIONS AND WEBSITES

- Interest Group on Aging, Alcohol, and Addictions, Gerontological Society of America (GSA): www.geron.org

THEATER ARTS

"Senior theater" is theater for, by, and about older adults and is designed to involve older adults in theater for recreational and therapeutic purposes. Academic programs and noncredit learning experiences in playwriting, actor training, and technical theater are offered for undergraduate and graduate theater arts degree students, older adults who are studying theater arts, and practitioners currently involved with senior theater groups. Types of senior theater productions include standard drama, reader's theater, musical revues, oral history, and plays based on research about aging and older adults. Possible professional positions for persons who combine theater arts and gerontology include:

- Director of a senior theater program
- Instructor or acting coach for older adults involved with a senior theater
- Manager or producer for a senior theater
- Technical theater director and stage or lighting designer for a senior theater company
- Consultant to community theater groups interested in developing a senior theater
- College/university instructor on senior theater

RELATED PROFESSIONAL ORGANIZATIONS AND WEBSITES

- Association for Theater in Higher Education (ATHE): www.athe.org
- Senior Theater Research and Performance (STRP): www.athe.org/groups/STRP

TRANSPORTATION

One of the major issues that older adults face is in regard to transportation, especially if their ability to drive is limited or restricted due to physical disability, memory loss, medication regimens, financial limitations, or other reasons. Transportation is key to mobility for most older persons. Driving and Community Mobility is part of the American Occupational Therapy Association's Productive Aging foci. While many programs and services have focused on older drivers and improving their driving behaviors, there is a need for more effort in creating supportive alternative transportation options for those who are no longer able to drive. Potential career options for those who combine gerontology and transportation include:

- Coordinator of a door-to-door community transportation program for older adults
- Trainer or coordinator of training on aging and driving for law enforcement personnel or medical and mental health professionals
- Gerontology consultant to city, county, or state public transportation department

RELATED PROFESSIONAL ORGANIZATIONS AND WEBSITES

- Transportation Issues, Grantmakers in Aging (GIA): www.giaging.org/issues/transportation
- Driving & Community Mobility, American Occupational Therapy Association, Inc. (AOTA): www.aota.org/en/Practice/Productive-Aging/Driving.aspx
- Transportation and Aging Interest Group, Gerontological Society of America (GSA): www.geron.org

Hopefully, these potential and possible career opportunites have stimulated your thinking about the breadth of career options in the field of aging. While some of these positions actually do exist, others are waiting for someone to step into them. Perhaps you found some positions of interest to explore further as you seek to identify the niche in the field of aging that appeals to your specific interests and needs. Best wishes, and welcome to a wonderful professional world!

4 ■ GERONTOLOGY AND GERIATRICS PROFESSIONAL ORGANIZATIONS

INTERNATIONAL-LEVEL ORGANIZATION

INTERNATIONAL ASSOCIATION OF GERONTOLOGY AND GERIATRICS (IAGG): www.iagg.info

Focus: Gerontological research and training worldwide to enable a high quality of life and well-being for all people as they experience aging as individuals and in society.

Membership: Members are national gerontological organizations (societies) with national scope, multidisciplinary membership, and primary orientation toward research and teaching of gerontology; individual members of national organizations in good standing with IAGG are considered to be IAGG members.

World Congress: IAGG World Congress of Gerontology and Geriatrics is held every 4 years, usually in June, July, or August; the next World Congress will be in 2017.

INTERNATIONAL FEDERATION ON AGEING (IFA): www.ifa-fiv.org

Focus: Research, advocacy, and policy knowledge specific to the rights of older people around the world.

Membership: Full Members: Local, regional, provincial/territorial not-for-profit or nongovernmental organizations, in cluding for-profit organizations working with or representing the rights and interests of older people. Associate Members: Individuals and sectors of society interested in understanding the issues and improving the lives of older people.

Global Conference: Biannual Global Conference on Ageing; the next Global Conference will be in 2016.

Publications: *Global Ageing: Issues and Actions* (annual journal); *IFA-eNews* (monthly electronic newsletter)

NATIONAL-LEVEL ORGANIZATIONS

AMERICAN GERIATRICS SOCIETY (AGS): www.americangeriatrics.org

Focus: Health care professionals working to improve health, independence, and quality of life for older adults.

Membership: Full Members (by category: Full Members [Nurse/Nurse Practitioner, Pharmacist, Physician, Physician Assistant, Recognized, Social Worker, Physical/ Occupational Therapist, Other Health Care Professional, International]); Trainee Members (Fellow-in-Training; Resident, Post-Grad/ Pre-Doc Trainee; Student)

Member Sections: Optional networking opportunities; nine sections (Fellow-in-Training; Medical Subspecialties; Nurses; Pharmacists; Physician Assistants; Residents; Social Workers; Surgical and Related Medical Specialists; Teachers)

Special Interest Groups: Thirty-plus optional grassroots, topic-specific networking and discussion groups (e.g., acute hospital care, care transitions, disaster planning and preparedness, elder abuse and neglect, e-learning in geriatrics, ethnogeriatrics, Hospital Elder Life Program [HELP], information technology issues, international activities, Interprofessional Education and Practice [IPE/P], junior faculty research career development; medical humanities, palliative care, Veterans Health Administration, wound prevention and management)

State Affiliates: In 25 states and Metro DC

Annual Meeting: Annual Scientific Meeting, usually in May

Publications: *Journal of the American Geriatrics Society* (*JAGS*, monthly); *Annals of Long-Term Care* (*ALTZ*; published monthly in partnership with the American Association for Long-Term Care Nursing); *Clinical Geriatrics* (monthly journal)

AMERICAN SOCIETY ON AGING (ASA): www.asaging.org

Focus: Professionals (multidisciplinary) who work with older adults

Membership: Individual; Organization; Students and Emerging Professionals (STEP)

Constituent Groups: Eight optional, free-of-charge, groups: Business forum on Aging (BFA); Forum on Religion, Spirituality and Aging (FORSA); Healthcare and Aging (HAN); LGBT Aging Issues Network (LAIN); Lifetime Education and Renewal Network (LEARN); Mental Health and Aging Network (MHAN); Network on Environments, Services and Technologies for Maximizing Independence (NEST); Network on Multicultural Aging (NOMA)

Annual Meeting: Annual Aging in America (AiA) Conference, usually in March

Publications: *Generations* (quarterly journal, single topic focus for each issue); *Aging Today* (bimonthly newspaper)

GERONTOLOGICAL SOCIETY OF AMERICA (GSA): www.geron.org

Focus: Research

Membership: Regular; Emerging Scholar and Professional Organization (ESPO, Student); Transitional Student; Undergraduate Student; Spouse; Emeritus

Membership Sections: Each member affiliates with one of the following Sections: Biological Sciences (BS); Behavioral and Social Sciences (BSS); Health Sciences (HS); Social Research, Policy, and Practice (SRPP); Emerging Scholar and Professional Organization (ESPO)

Interest Groups: Forty-plus topic-specific groups (e.g., abuse, neglect, and exploitation of elderly people; business and aging; disasters and older adults; grandparents as caregivers; HIV, AIDS, and older people; research methods; older workers; reminiscence and aging; rural aging; technology and aging; transportation and aging)

Annual Meeting: Annual Scientific Meeting, usually in November

Publications: *The Gerontologist* (bimonthly); *Journals of Gerontology, Series A* (bimonthly; includes *The Journal of Gerontology: Biological Sciences* and *The Journal of Gerontology: Medical Sciences*); *Journals of Gerontology, Series B* (bimonthly; includes *The Journal of Gerontology: Psychological Sciences* and *The Journal of Gerontology: Social Sciences*); *Gerontology News* (monthly newsletter); *Public Policy & Aging Report* (*PP&AR*, quarterly report)

ASSOCIATION FOR GERONTOLOGY IN HIGHER EDUCATION (AGHE): www.aghe.org

Focus: Education on aging; educational unit of the Gerontological Society of America (GSA)

Membership: Institutional Membership: General Membership (six categories: 2-Year College, 4-Year College, Professional School, University, Educational Affiliate, International Affiliate); Other Affiliate Membership (two categories: Organizational Affiliate, Sustaining Affiliate); Student Committee (open to all gerontology and geriatrics students, but not a formal membership category)

Annual Meeting: Annual Meeting and Educational Leadership Conference, usually in late February–early March

Publications: *AGHExchange* (published three times per year—Fall, Winter, Spring/Summer); *Gerontology & Geriatrics Education* (quarterly journal selected as AGHE's official journal)

SIGMA PHI OMEGA (SPO): www.sigmaphiomega.org

Focus: National academic honor and professional society in gerontology

Membership: Student: Undergraduate or graduate students majoring or minoring in gerontology/aging studies, are in at least their second term of enrollment, and who meet grade point average requirements (undergraduate: 3.3 to 4.0; graduate: 3.5 to 4.0). Faculty, alumni, professional, and honorary memberships available

Chapters: SPO Chapters are commonly attached to an existing gerontology program at a college or university (see the SPO website for listing of currently active chapters)

REGIONAL-LEVEL ORGANIZATIONS

New England Gerontological Association (NEGA): www.negaonline.org

Southern Gerontological Society (SGS): www.southerngerontologicalsociety.org

STATE-LEVEL ORGANIZATIONS

Alabama Gerontological Society (GGS): www.agsinfo.org

Arkansas Gerontological Society (AGS): www.agsociety.org

California Council on Gerontology & Geriatrics (CCGG): www.ccgg.org

Colorado Gerontological Society (CGS): www.senioranswers.org

Florida Council on Aging (FCOA): www.fcoa.org

Georgia Gerontology Society (GGS): www.georgiagerontology society.org

Hawaii Pacific Gerontological Society (HGPS): www.hpgs.org

Gerontology Society of Iowa (GSI): www.gerontologysocietyofiowa .org

Kentucky Association for Gerontology (KAG): www.kagky.org

Maine Gerontological Society (MGS): http://mainecenteronaging .umaine.edu/MGS.php

Maryland Gerontological Association (MGA): www.mdgerontology .org

Massachusetts Gerontology Association (MGA): www.massgeron .org

Michigan Society of Gerontology (MSG): www.msginfo.org

Minnesota Gerontological Society (MGS): www.mngero.org

Mississippi Gerontological Society (MGS): http://mgsms.net

Montana Gerontology Society (MGS): http://montanagerontology.org

Ohio Association of Gerontology & Education (OAGE): www .oage.org

Oregon Gerontological Association (OGA): www.oregongero.org

State Society on Aging (SSA) of New York: http://ssany.org

Texas: Dallas Area Gerontological Society (DAGS): www.dags.org

Texas: Houston Gerontological Society (HGS): www.hgsociety.org

Texas: Tarrant Area Gerontological Society (TAGS): www .tagstarrant.org

5 GLOSSARY OF ACRONYMS

GERONTOLOGY-SPECIFIC ACRONYMS

AAA	Area Agency(ies) on Aging
AAGE	Association for Anthropology and Gerontology
AAGP	American Association for Geriatric Psychiatry
AAHID	American Academy of Healthcare Interior Designers
AAHSA	American Association of Homes and Services for the Aging
AAIA	American Association for International Aging
AARP	AARP (formerly known as American Association for Retired Persons)
ABSCD	American Board of Special Care Dentistry
AFAR	American Federation of Aging Research
AGE-SW	Association for Gerontology Education in Social Work
AGHD-HBCU	Association for Gerontology and Human Development in Historically Black Colleges and Universities
AGHE	Association for Gerontology in Higher Education
AGS	American Geriatrics Society
AIFG	American Institute of Financial Gerontology
AIM	Aging in Motion Coalition
AJAS	Association for Jewish Aging Services
ANPPM	Asociación Nacional Pro Personas Mayores (See NHCOA)
AoA	Administration on Aging

APS	Adult Protective Services
ASA	American Society on Aging
ASHA	American Seniors Housing Association
BFA	Business Forum on Aging (ASA)
CAAR	Current Awareness in Aging Report
CAPS	Certified Aging-in-Place Specialist
CASE	Coalition of Agencies Serving the Elderly
CCAL	Center for Continuing Adult Learning
CCGP	Commission for Certification of Geriatric Pharmacists
CDHA	Center for Demography of Health and Aging
CIAW	Careers in Aging Week
COA	Commission on Aging (county-level unit on aging)
CPG	Certified Geriatric Pharmacist
CREATE	Center for Research and Education on Aging and Technology Assessment
CSA	Certified Senior Advisor
EDRT	Elder Death Review Teams
ESPO	Emerging Scholar and Professional Organization (GSA)
FAST	Financial Abuse Teams
FGP	Foster Grandparent Program
FONIA	Friends of the National Institute on Aging
FORSA	Forum on Religion, Spirituality and Aging (ASA)
GEC	Geriatric Education Center
GCM	National Association of Professional Geriatric Care Managers
GIA	Global Aging Initiative
GIA	Grantmakers in Aging

GMHF	Geriatric Mental Health Foundation
GNP	Gerontological Nurse Practitioner
GSI	Geriatrics for Specialists Initiatives
GRCC	Geriatric Research, Education and Clinical Center
GSA	Gerontological Society of America
GSWI	Geriatric Social Work Initiative
GU	Generations United
HAN	Healthcare and Aging Network (ASA)
HCAOA	Home Care Association of America
IAGG	International Association of Gerontology and Geriatrics
ICAA	International Council on Active Aging
IFA	International Federation on Ageing
ILC	International Longevity Center
ILCUSA	International Longevity Center-USA
ISG	International Society of Gerontechnology
LAIN	LGBT Aging Issues Network (ASA)
LCOA	Leadership Council of Aging Organizations
LEARN	Lifetime Education and Renewal Network (ASA)
MHAN	Mental Health and Aging Network (ASA)
LGAIN	Lesbian and Gay Aging Issues Network (ASA)
MGS	Master's of Gerontological Studies
MOWAA	Meals on Wheels Association of America
MCUAAAR	Michigan Center for Urban American Aging Research
N4A	National Association of Area Agencies on Aging
NAAS	National Academy on an Aging Society
NADSA	National Adult Day Services Association

NAELA	National Academy of Elder Law Attorneys
NAFGPD	National Association of Foster Grandparent Program Directors
NAHC	National Association for Home Care and Hospice
NAHOF	National Association on HIV Over Fifty
NAIPC	National Aging in Place Council
NANASP	National Association of Nutrition and Aging Services Programs
NAPCA	National Asian Pacific Center on Aging
NAPGCM	National Association of Professional Geriatric Care Managers
NAPSA	National Adult Protective Services Association
NARSVPD	National Association of Retired and Senior Volunteer Program Directors
NASCPD	National Association of Senior Companion Project Directors
NASUA	National Association of State Units on Aging
NATLA	National Academy for Teaching and Learning about Aging
NCBA	National Caucus and Center on Black Aging
NCEA	National Center on Elder Abuse
NCMHA	National Coalition on Mental Health and Aging
NCOA	National Council on Aging
NCPSSM	National Committee for the Preservation of Social Security and Medicare
NCSGOP	National Coalition for Sleep Guidelines for Older People
NELF	National Elder Law Foundation
NEST	Network on Environments, Services and Technologies for Maximizing Independence (ASA)

NGNA	National Gerontological Nursing Association
NHCGNE	National Hartford Centers of Gerontological Nursing Excellence
NHCOA	National Hispanic Council on Aging
NIA	National Institute on Aging
NICA	National Indian Council on Aging
NOMA	Network on Multicultural Aging (ASA)
NOWCC	National Older Worker Career Center
NSCLC	National Senior Citizens Law Center
NSGA	National Senior Games Association
NSHAP	National Social Life Health and Aging Project
OAA	Older Americans Act
OWL	Older Women's League
PDHCA	Private Duty Home Care Association
PGCM	Professional Geriatric Care Manager
RFG	Registered Financial Gerontologist
RSIN	Road Scholar Institute Network
RSVP	Retired Senior Volunteer Program
SAGE	Senior Action in a Gay Environment
SAGE	Services and Advocacy for GLBT Elders and National Resource Center on LGBT Aging
SCDA	Special Care Dentistry Association
SCORE	Senior Core of Retired Executives
SCP	Senior Companion Program
SCSA	Society of Certified Senior Advisors
SCSEP	Senior Community Service Employment Program
SPO	Sigma Phi Omega

STEP	Students and Emerging Professionals (ASA)
STRP	Senior Theatre Research and Performance

GERONTOLOGY-RELATED ACRONYMS

AA	Alzheimer's Association
AAA	American Academy of Actuaries
AAA	American Academy of Advertising
AAA	American Anthropological Association
AAAA	American Association of Advertising Agencies (aka 4As)
AAACE	American Association for Adult and Continuing Education
AACC	Association of Family and Conciliation Courts
AAF	American Advertising Federation
AAFCS	American Association of Family and Consumer Science
AAHCM	American Academy of Home Care Managers
AAHPERD	American Alliance for Health, Physical Education, Recreation and Dance
AALNA	American Assisted Living Nurses Association
AAMFT	American Association of Marriage and Family Therapy
AAN	American Academy of Nursing
AAO	American Academy of Optometry
AASECT	American Association of Sexuality Educators, Counselors and Therapists
AATA	American Art Therapy Association
AATCC	American Association of Textile Chemists and Colorists
ABFM	American Board of Family Medicine
ABIM	American Board of Internal Medicine

ABPN	American Board of Psychiatry and Neurology
ACA	American Counseling Association
ACAE	Accreditation Commission for Audiology Education
ACHE	American College of Healthcare Executives
ACHCA	American College of Health Care Administrators
ACR	Association for Conflict Resolution
ACT-AD	Accelerate Cure/Treatment for Alzheimer's Disease Coalition
ADA	American Dental Association
ADA	American Dietetic Association
ADA	Americans with Disabilities Act
ADEA	American Dental Education Association
ADEA	Age Discrimination in Employment Act
ADEAR	Alzheimer's Disease Education and Referral Center
ADED	Association for Driver Rehabilitation Specialists
ADR	Alternative Dispute Resolutions
ADTA	American Dance Therapy Association
AFP	Association for Fundraising Professionals
AHA	American Historical Association
AHP	Association of Healthcare Philanthropists
AHRQ	Agency for Healthcare Research and Quality
AHS	American Horticultural Society
AHTA	American Horticultural Therapy Association
AIA	American Institute of Architects
AIAS	American Institute of Architect Students
AICPA	American Institute of Certified Public Accountants
ALA	American Library Association

ALF	Assisted Living Facilities
AMA	American Marketing Association
AMA	American Medical Association
AMFTRB	Association of Marriage and Family Regulatory Boards
AMTA	American Music Therapy Association
ANA	American Nursing Association
ANCC	American Nurses Credentialing Center
AOA	American Optometric Association
AOSA	American Optometric Students Association
AOTA	American Occupational Therapy Association
AOTF	American Occupational Therapy Foundation
APA	American Psychological Association
APHA	American Public Health Association
APPE	Association for Practical and Professional Ethics
APS	American Philosophical Society
APSA	American Political Science Association
APTA	American Physical Therapy Association
ASA	American Sociological Association
ASCP	American Society of Consultant Pharmacists
ASDP	Association of Sewing and Design Professionals
ASEP	American Society of Exercise Physiologists
ASGPP	American Society for Group Psychotherapy and Psychodrama
ASHA	American Speech-Language-Hearing Association
ASHS	American Society for Horticulture Science
ASJA	American Society of Journalists and Authors
ASLA	American Society of Landscape Architects

ASPA	American Society of Pension Actuaries
ASPPB	Association of State and Provincial Psychology Boards
ASSECT	American Association of Sexuality Educators, Counselors and Therapists
ATCB	Art Therapy Accreditation Board
ATHE	Association for Theatre in Higher Education
AWP	Association of Writers and Poets
CCA	Conference of Consulting Actuaries
CCMC	Commission for Case Manager Certification
CCRC	Continuing Care Retirement Center
CCVA	Council for Certification of Volunteer Administrators
CEAL	Center for Excellence in Assisted Living
CFP	Certified Financial Planner
CMS	Centers for Medicare and Medicaid Services
CMSA	Case Management Society of America
CNCS	Corporation for National and Community Service
CVA	Certification in Volunteer Administration
CVAA	Congress of Volunteer Administrators Association
CSWE	Council on Social Work Education
EDRA	Environmental Design Research Association
ERISA	Employee Retirement Income Security Act
FOVA	Friends of VA Medical Care and Health Research
FPA	Financial Planning Association
GARN	Global Aging Research Network
HAA	Hospice Association of America
HFES	Human Factors and Ergonomics Society
HRSA	Health Resources and Services Administration

IATO	International Art Therapy Organization
ILC	Independent Living Communities
ITAA	International Textile and Apparel Association
LEAD	Leaders Engaged on Alzheimer's Disease
LGBT	Lesbian, Gay, Bisexual, and Transgender
LMSW	Licensed Master Social Worker
LNHA	Licensed Nursing Home Administrator
LTC	Long-Term Care
MLA	Modern Language Association
NACCM	National Academy of Certified Care Managers
NADTA	North American Drama Therapy Association
NAEMSE	National Association of Emergency Medical Services Educators
NAEMT	National Association of Emergency Medical Technicians
NAFC	National Association for Continence
NAHB	National Association of Home Builders
NAHC	National Association for Home Care and Hospice
NAHSE	National Association of Health Services Executives
NAHTSA	National Highway Traffic Safety Administration
NAPEA	National Association of Personal Financial Planners
NAPT	National Association of Poetry Therapy
NASEMSO	National Association of State Emergency Medical Services Officials
NASOP	National Association of State Long-Term Care Ombudsman Programs
NASW	National Association of Social Workers
NBCOT	National Board of Occupational Therapy
NCAL	National Center for Assisted Living

NCCATA	National Coalition of Creative Arts Therapies Associations
NCDA	National Career Development Association
NCFR	National Council on Family Relations
NCHS	National Center for Health Statistics
NCSBN	National Council of State Boards of Nursing
NECA	National Employment Counseling Association
NHF	National Hospice Foundation
NHTSA	National Highway Transportation Safety Administration
NLC	Nurse Licensure Compact
NSLTCP	National Study of Long-term Care Providers
PACE	Program for Acquiring Competence in Entrepreneurship
PFM	Partnerships for the Future of Medicare
PRB	Population Reference Bureau
RRCD	Rehabilitation Research Career Development Center
SCDA	Special Care Dentistry Association
SfAA	Society for Applied Anthropology
SNF	Skilled Nursing Facility
SOA	Society of Actuaries
SPJ	Society of Professional Journalists
SSA	Social Security Administration

ALPHARETTA
Atlanta-Fulton Public Library